WHOLE LOTTA LED

WHOLE LOTTA LED
Our Flight with Led Zeppelin

RALPH HULETT
and
JERRY PROCHNICKY

CITADEL PRESS
Kensington Publishing Corp.
www.kensingtonbooks.com

CITADEL PRESS BOOKS are published by

Kensington Publishing Corp.
850 Third Avenue
New York, NY 10022

PHOTO CREDITS:

Insert 1: p.1, Michael Ochs Archives.Com; p.2, Jeffrey Mayer; p.3, Jorgen Angel—www.angel.dk; p.4, (*top*) Atlantic Records, (*bottom*) Norwood Price; p.5, Jay Good/Star File; p.6, Jim Cummins/Star File; p.7, (*top*) Chuck Boyd/Photosrock, LLC, (*bottom*) Copyright © 1969, Ron Raffaelli; p.8, Norwood Price; p.9, Robert Knight; p.10, Jeffrey Mayer; p.11, Copyright © 1969, Ron Raffaelli; p.12, Cleveland Public Library; p.13, Dave Richardson; p.14, (*top*) Chuck Boyd/Photosrock, LLC; (*bottom*) Jim Cummins/Star File; p.15, (*top*) Clyde Johnson; (*bottom*) Ralph Hulett; p.16, Lisa Law.

Insert 2: p.1, (*top*) Neil Zlozower, (*bottom*) Neil Zlozower; p.2, Copyright © 2004 by Koh Hasebe/Shinko Music; p.3, Copyright © 2004 by Koh Hasebe/Shinko Music; p.4, (*top*) Donald Meek, (*bottom*) Donald Meek; p.5, (*top*) Michael Ochs Archives.Com, (*bottom*) Michael Ochs Archives.Com; p.6, Robert Knight; p.7, (*top*) Barrie Wentzell/Star File, (*bottom*) Robert Knight/Star File; p.8, Jeffrey Mayer; p.9, Neil Zlozower; p.10, Neil Zlozower; p.11, (*top*) Neil Zlozower, (*bottom*) Neil Zlozower; p.12, Michael Ochs Archives.Com; p.13, Ralph Hulett; p.14, (*top*) Baron Wolman, (*bottom*) Baron Wolman; p.15, Rob Verhorst/Redferns; p.16, Victoria Oliver.

All Kensington titles, imprints, and distributed lines are available at special quantity discounts for bulk purchases for sales promotions, premiums, fund-raising, educational, or institutional use. Special book excerpts or customized printings can also be created to fit specific needs. For details, write or phone the office of the Kensington special sales manager: Kensington Publishing Corp., 850 Third Avenue, New York, NY 10022, attn: Special Sales Department; phone 1-800-221-2647.

First printing: September 2005

10 9 8 7 6 5 4 3 2 1

Printed in the United States of America

Library of Congress Control Number: 2005922712

ISBN 0-8065-2639-4

Dedicated to my father, Ivan Prochnickyj

—JP

Dedicated to my late father, Ralph W. Hulett,
and my mother, Shirley L. Sullivan

—RH

CONTENTS

FOREWORD

Right from the start, Led Zeppelin was never small. They cast a massive shadow, both artistically and commercially. Countless bands from Aerosmith to Guns N' Roses to U2 have tried to appropriate some of Zeppelin's aura, but none of them have been able to match the musical scope or sheer intimidating force of the original. And with over 200 million albums sold worldwide, Led Zeppelin is the biggest selling rock group in history.

In retrospect, Led Zeppelin represented an era of rock as surely as Elvis or the Beatles. From California to Kashmir, they were the personification of power and fame for the '70s. The legend of Led Zeppelin still lives on today and is an ongoing living record, rather than a moment in history frozen forever in the past.

Yet they were the most mysterious of bands. There have never been many interviews and few press conferences. Led Zeppelin was, and still is today, a law unto themselves. The music will be around long after the myth. But you can't ignore or deny the myth that Jimmy Page made a deal with the Devil to make sure his group got famous. And after Zeppelin's decade of superstardom, maybe the Devil came a callin'.

Whole Lotta Led charts their twelve-year flight from takeoff to soaring at the top to being grounded. It is the first of its kind written from a fan's perspective. Our fierce passion sets it apart from other books. It is more than just a Led Zeppelin biography—it's our story as well. Led Zeppelin provided the soundtrack to our lives through the good times and even the bad times. The musicians were our heroes to idolize and emulate, if only in our imagination. What is portrayed is the Led Zeppelin that we grew up with. Here are our recollections of growing up with the band, combined with other fan accounts, plus photographers' views from behind the camera, as well as Led Zeppelin in their own words.

Supplying the power to the text are the photographs. Not just your greatest hits compilation, but a stunning visual biography. It is our attempt to put into focus the memory of Led Zeppelin with new photos. Seeing is believing. The photos are moving not only for what they show, but for what they mean in the eyes and heart of the beholder. And the photographs lend a resonance to Zeppelin's music which continues to enthrall over three decades of rock fans with a sound, which remains as powerful and cosmic in 2005 as it was in the 70s.

Please note that when the first person narrator is used in the text, it refers to Ralph Hulett; Jerry Prochnicky is referred to in the third person. However, we want to make clear that this book is the result of a total collaboration between the two authors, and no readers should infer otherwise.

This book would not have been possible without the invaluable contributions of Lois Aguirre, Jorgen Angel, David Causer, Cameron Crowe, Pamela Des Barres, Roman Diaczenko Jr., Jessica Fairchild, Howard Fields, Craig Folkes, David Gordin, Rick Gould, Patricia Hilderbrand, Sharon Hulett, Clyde Johnson, Hugh Jones, Eulah Keith, Ron Kellerman, Robert Knight, Michael Lawryk, Dave Lewis, Jeffrey Mayer, Erica Meek, Phil O'Brien, Victoria Oliver, Norwood Price, Anna Prochnickyj, Ron Raffaelli, Sam Rapallo, Dave Richardson, Lisa Robinson, Steve Rosen, Katrina Shimasaki, Dorothy Stadnyk, Brad Tolinski, Thomas Weschler, Baron Wolman, Tom Wright, Art Zippel, and Neil Zlozower.

And a special thanks to our literary agent, Madeleine Morel of 2M Communications in New York, for landing us a publisher, and to our editor, Miles Lott at Kensington, for helping us get it all together.

And thank God for Led Zeppelin—Jimmy Page, John Paul Jones, John Bonham, Robert Plant, and Peter Grant.

CHAPTER 1

"Shapes of Things"

Before there was Led Zeppelin, there were the Yardbirds. They ushered in the dawning of the heavy metal movement, of psychedelic music, of pushing back the boundaries of rock to someplace new. If there was just one word to describe the Yardbirds, it would be *experimental*. As suggested by the futuristic sound of their hit single "Shapes of Things," this band pointed where rock music was headed. That direction was for the guitar to be the dominant instrument. In their five short years together, the Yardbirds became the training ground for three guitar legends to be: Eric Clapton, Jeff Beck, and Jimmy Page. There is also no other band that played such a pivotal role in the creation of Led Zeppelin.

Growing up with most 1960s bands meant that you followed the course of the artists' singles and saved $3 to buy the next long-playing record. Yardbirds fans were different, especially on the West Coast where the band had a cult following. We often talked about how this band's music sounded uniquely electric, nearly out of this world, and like no other British invasion group out there. We put Yardbirds concert posters and fliers from local music stores

1

on our walls and religiously hunted down the latest releases and played them to our select friends. And some of us got really lucky and got to see the group live. But what made this band so different? They had no large mainstream following, like the Beatles or the Rolling Stones. The attraction of the Yardbirds was largely due to the free-form playing, with an emphasis on an unbridled, raw, and intense volume.

Because of the largely innovative nature of their material, they were ahead of their time, so they were unable to muster enough commercial appeal to regularly place themselves in the top 40 set. And underground FM rock radio hadn't come into play yet. Plus, to their great misfortune the Yardbirds suffered from internal problems that perhaps kept the band from ever reaching its true potential. But there were still many exciting moments on their records, and at its height the music produced was on the cutting edge.

In the late 1950s and early 1960s, while the Beatles were listening to Elvis Presley, Buddy Holly, and Little Richard, the Yardbirds were searching record stores for rare sides by exotic names such as Howlin' Wolf, Elmore James, Muddy Waters, and Sonny Boy Williamson. Formed in 1963, the Yardbirds (beat slang for a railroad hobo) consisted of Keith Relf, vocals and harmonica; Chris Dreja, rhythm guitar; Paul Samwell-Smith, bass; Jim McCarty, drums; and Eric "Slowhand" Clapton, lead guitar. Clapton's ironic nickname was derived from the furious, speedy blues licks that he churned out onstage.

Looking for an opportunity to play their brand of music and to make beer money, in 1963 they auditioned and were hired at the famous Crawdaddy Club in Richmond, following the Rolling Stones' residency there. Even though the Yardbirds had rhythm and blues roots like the Stones, they also slowly built their own style. This was prominently displayed on their stunning debut LP *Five Live Yardbirds*, which was recorded in 1964. It was also the first imported Yardbirds album that I laid eyes on.

I discovered it in a small record store in Laguna Beach, California, where my family had a small summer vacation home. This store was located downtown on the ocean side, where a variety of head shops were springing up, imitating San Francisco's Haight Ashbury District. I walked along the Coast Highway to Cleo Street, where a two-story Victorian-style house had been converted into a vintage clothing store called Visions. I continued about three blocks north and stopped at a little shop at 533 Coast Highway that caught my eye. On the glass window were these red and orange letters that emanated out from a small pyramid-type design. In a psychedelic explosion of color and wild shape were the words *Sound Spectrum*.

Intrigued, I peered through the window. Nobody was inside. There were sawhorses with planks thrown across them, some paint buckets, and drop clothes. But there was something else, too: a plywood display wall with some imported records on it. I looked closer, pushing my head up against the window like any curious sixteen-year-old kid would do. My eyes scanned the display. They stopped at one in particular that had a huddled group of long-haired guys in a strange setting. The glare on the glass made it hard to see, so I shaded my eyes. Keith Relf and company stared back at me, looking like they were in jail behind an old, rusty, barred gate. Behind the group rose a high, imposing fortress-type wall. Below them was the name *Five Live Yardbirds*. I was spellbound. This was the debut Yardbirds album that I'd heard about from my friends, but I'd never seen it. Now it was staring me in the face! This little record shop would soon move half a mile south next to the Pottery Shack, but it has survived the passing years by always offering a little something or other you can't find anywhere else.

The Beatles and Rolling Stones were gigantically popular in America by the mid-1960s with their Chuck Berry– and Buddy Holly–inspired form of rock and roll. By comparison, the Yardbirds played supercharged blues. Once I bought the *Five Live Yardbirds* album, a musical world entirely different from the Beatles and Rolling Stones was opened up. I always thought blues had to be played slowly, but I soon heard differently. All the songs seethed with fast-paced, rhythmic energy—they pulsated and flowed along in an array of blues-soaked intensity.

There was the frantically paced "Too Much Monkey Business," where Clapton lived up to his nickname—notes flew out with lightning speed. Then there was "Smokestack Lightning" with its incredible interplay between Clapton's guitar and Relf's harmonica. Relf could blow a mean harp. The flow of the music rose to climaxes during "Respectable," as well as the rollicking "Here 'Tis." These both had a buildup of primitive rhythm and vocal interchanges that created images of natives in Africa, chanting and pounding their drums by jungle torchlight. The mixture of rock and blues was like nothing I'd ever heard; it was highly infectious and unbelievably exciting. There was a definite underground feel to this music. This constant improvisational rhythm that went back and forth like either gentle, rippling tides or violently crashing ocean waves came to be called the "rave up."

This music was an early form of rock jamming, building more and more on the music's inner rhythms than on a basic melody. The results were dynamic, with "Too Much Monkey Business" and "Smokestack Lightning" taking on long instrumental stretches. The harmonica and guitar moved together in geometric precision, sometimes wildly slicing the original song into segments that lasted as long as thirty minutes. For the most part, attention would be focused on the lead guitar. The first "Clapton Is God" graffiti appeared on buildings and walls all over London during his Yardbirds days.

As a lead player, Clapton would sound restrained in places and snake in notes during verses. But when a break came, all the power was forcefully unleashed. The Marquee Club audience whooped and shouted. But teenage girls didn't scream wildly, tear their dresses, and throw panties and bras at the band, like they did at

Rolling Stones shows. What shocking, crazy, and wild behavior! No, the Yardbirds' audience was much more controlled. It was a strange irony: the music sounded chaotic, yet it didn't create such wildness from the listeners. This could be because there was a basic blues framework that everything worked around, with the stabilizing force of Samwell-Smith's bass, the chain-gang strumming of Dreja's rhythm guitar, and McCarty's precise yet unrestrained drums. Above it all soared Clapton's leads, played with lighting-fast speed at times or stretched out slowly note by note. His blues playing style of bending notes and playing the guitar with an emotional feel was unheard of.

The live album was successful, but the group also wanted to break into the hit singles market and go national. Their two releases in June and October were failures, so the Yardbirds began to think seriously of changing directions. Change directions they did on their next single, "For Your Love," which went straight to the top of the singles chart in 1965. The group hit pay dirt with a harpsichord and bongos sound. The harpsichord opening sounded so gothic coming out of AM radio. This was too much for Clapton, who considered himself a strict blues guitarist. He regarded "For Your Love" as a commercial betrayal of the band's commitment to the blues. Disgusted, he packed his bags and joined John Mayall's Bluesbreakers.

The Yardbirds had been wanting to replace Clapton with the session ace Jimmy Page. He was getting well known as a guitarist, having served an apprenticeship with anything the music business could throw at him. He had been anything but a late starter. At a young age, Page was seduced by the rock and roll of the 1950s. He was an only child and a loner who taught himself to play the guitar by practicing six to eight hours a day. The guitar was his salvation and sanctuary. In 1958, when Page was just fourteen, he had appeared on the BBC's *All Your Own* program with his skiffle group, a British form that combined blues, folk, and country. Then in late 1960 Neil Christian saw Page playing in an amateur band.

"He'd been in them about a year," Christian remembered. "They started doing this Jerry Lee Lewis number and it was damn good. I knew the boy had something. . . . Jimmy lived and died by the guitar. Every time you went to see him he had a guitar around his neck." Later, he did a stint with the newly formed Neil Christian and the Crusaders. The material they did was covers of Gene Vincent, Johnny Burnette, and Chuck Berry. Page now started to develop his own style and other guitarists came to watch him.

Despite the reputation he began to earn in the Crusaders, it came with a price. The band lived out of a van, at cafés, and at girlfriends' homes. Sick with glandular fever, Page left the Crusaders in 1962 and decided to enroll in art school. He pursued painting and drawing, and became hugely influenced by the flamboyant and eccentric Spanish artist Salvador Dali. This painter created some of the most indelible visual images of the twentieth century that hold up in today's surreal world. Excited about art, Page considered painting as a possible vocation. But he found that the guitar was still his first love, so his painting ambitions were put on hold.

He still kept in touch with the music scene by jamming at the Marquee Club. It was here that Page's playing was noticed by the music arranger Mike Leander, who hired him as a session man. Page was now inducted into pop's most subterranean universe, where the talents of unknown session players were almost as important as those of the artists whose names were on the records. The work was seven days a week, with three sessions lasting three hours each on a typical day. Page learned from producers and engineers how recording equipment worked, how arrangers made songs into records, and the way musicians interacted. In short, he got valuable studio experience for his later years with Led Zeppelin. The session singer and recording artist John Carter worked with Page during this time and praised Page's ability. He noted, "Jimmy Page was a guy you could get a good performance from without trying. He was a very fast player, he knew his rock and roll and added to that. He would always get a good sound in the studio. He was very quiet and a bit of an intellectual (and interested in) all sorts of odd cult things."

By 1965, session work had been incredibly productive and profitable for Page. He had worked with the Kinks and the Who, released a solo single, and became house producer at Immediate Records. He'd even produced some blues recordings with Clapton for Immediate and later recorded more blues jams at his Epsom home. Did Page want to turn his back on all this? Not yet; session work was going so well that Page turned down the offer to join the Yardbirds. But there was also another reason Page didn't accept the position: Page and Clapton had become good friends. The two were going to dinner and sharing ideas about mutual subjects, such as art school, films, books, and music. To Page the offer may have looked too much like a cloak-and-dagger scenario. The Yardbirds' manager came up to Page and offered him the guitarist spot in the band. Page considered this offer as being made behind Clapton's back and so he turned it down.

Page recommended that Jeff Beck be offered the open position for the Yardbirds. This was no mere coincidence, because both musicians went back a long way. Both had been raised in Surrey, located just thirty miles south of London. They were the freaks— the 1 in 400 kids at school who played electric guitar. But their musical kinship brought them close together. As teenagers, they listened to and studied hard-to-get early American rock and blues albums that British teens treasured. Then they jammed and traded licks, inspiring and competing with each other.

Little did Page know that there were also three other teenage music freaks in England by the names of John Paul Jones, Robert Plant, and John Bonham. Jones first played church organ as well as piano. He wanted to be a bass player, although his dad insisted that he take up saxophone instead. But Jones had his mind made up, and the bass won over. He even had bass guitars drawn all over his schoolbooks and started playing bass at fourteen. Also, his dad's shortwave radio picked up all sorts of radio stations. Jones was often glued to it, getting an earful of music education, and learned to play bass by playing along with whatever came on the air.

Robert Plant got his schooling from clubs instead of the classroom. He watched country, blues, and jazz performers and sat in the back, where he wouldn't get noticed and thrown out for being underage. When he was fifteen, he decided to become a blues singer and learned to play harmonica. His influences ranged from Elvis Presley and Ray Charles to Muddy Waters, Howlin' Wolf, and especially Robert Johnson. For Plant, Johnson was a seductive music force whose playing weaved through both pain and anticipated pleasure. Plant started to concentrate on women and music instead of school subjects and let his hair grow long. Meanwhile, his parents wanted him to become an accountant or to go into some other profession. Their ambitions for him created too many conflicts. By the time he was sixteen, he had moved out to pursue music full time. He even went a step further and was living with his Calcutta-born girlfriend and future wife, Maureen, who he married when he was seventeen and had a baby girl, Carmen.

John Bonham always wanted to be a drummer, beating on his mom's pots and pans. Even though he never had any drum lessons, one thing he never lacked was enthusiasm. He got his first snare drum at age ten and his first full drum kit by the time he was fifteen. Influenced by early soul records, he joined his first group. As a teenager, Bonham put in stints with various bands until he eventually met up with Plant, where he played blues in the Crawlin' King Snakes. Their real schooling together, though, came with the next group, the Band of Joy. Like Plant, Bonham had married at seventeen. When Bonham wasn't pounding the drums at night, he pounded a hammer by day at construction sites.

Unlike Page, Beck didn't have any reservations about taking Clapton's place in the Yardbirds. Beck recalled, "I was playing in a very good band called the Tridents, and they were always raving about the Yardbirds. I had never really heard them, but they were always talking about Eric Clapton this, and Eric Clapton that. I can tell you, I was getting pretty tired of that adulation for someone else. I was like, 'Fuck Eric Clapton,' you know, *I'm* your guitarist."

In reality, Beck wasn't making much money from the Tridents; there were times that he could hardly afford guitar strings. By March 1965 and for the next twenty months, Beck was in the lead guitarist's chair for the Yardbirds. But whereas Clapton had kept the band firmly grounded in the blues, Beck's impact on the Yardbirds was to push the band in a much more avant-garde direction. The power of his Fender Esquire electric guitar was unleashed via unearthly sounds filled with distortion, feedback, echo, and fuzz tone pumped hard through his twin Vox AC30s.

The first American Yardbirds album, *For Your Love*, was released the summer of 1965. Some singles cut with Clapton such as "I Ain't Got You" were included, as was a Freddy King–style instrumental entitled "Got To Hurry," which showed Clapton's clear, precise, blues breaks. Beck emulated Clapton's style with the licks on "I Ain't Done Wrong," but he added some new touches here and there as well, such as the use of fuzz tone. Page had used it on various sessions like on his work with the Who. Beck employed it on "I'm Not Talking," the buzzing lead sounded like an angry wasp zooming about madly in a box, trying to escape. Beck's creative playing was now a part of the Yardbirds' sound. He would become a guitar hero, partly from his guitar work and partly from the image that he presented. The manager Giorgio Gomelsky had gotten Beck a pudding-basin haircut and flashy Carnaby Street clothes. Beck was being noticed more and more for his guitar workouts in London gigs. With his eyes closed, he used volume and striking his strings in ways that forced distortion from the amps. He'd lean his guitar against the amplifiers and get the tone droning, then wrench screams of feedback that virtually leaped out at the audience. He made playing feedback look easy. But Beck said about this gimmick that "your immediate reaction is to go over and turn it off. You think it'll hurt the instrument, but after a while you find that it can contribute something. I like using many different effects and noises. It's something very hard to control and it's hard to do in tune."

The Yardbirds left their British turf for the United States in the summer of 1965. "Heart Full of Soul" was a single then, and the group needed to generate support for it. Beck had only joined the group three months prior, and he was already leaving on his first tour. Before he left, he stopped by Page's house. He handed Page a collector's item in guitar circles: a 1958 Fender Telecaster. There had developed a musical kinship between the two that nearly surpassed friendship. As far as gifts went, Beck sure knew how to pick something for Page. This was the least he could do—after all, Page had placed Beck smack into stardom.

For a first tour, everything seemed to go well. According to Gomelsky, America was a whole new world and the group was enthusiastically received at shows. "I think people who saw those gigs will always remember them: the Yardies were possibly the most advanced group that was around then. The impact was made in those live performances. But the pressures of success can exhaust young and inexperienced people, which they all were. But no one had any experience of touring America: it was a completely new trip."

Before 1965 ended, Bo Diddley's "I'm a Man" and "Shapes of Things" both turned out to be huge hit singles in America. With Beck's and Relf's classic call-and-response between harmonica and guitar on "I'm a Man," the Yardbirds' wild rave-up rhythms pulsated for the first time ever on Top 40 radio. Beck held all six strings down on his guitar neck and stuck them at the same time, which made the sound of a chicken running madly across the road. Along with this was the pounding rhythm of Samwell-Smith's bass and McCarty's smashing drums The results were devastating: carved from the 1960s pop music was a new niche by the Yardbirds' frantic, hardhitting music. As far as "Shapes of Things" went, it was aptly named, for this song took the Yardbirds into a new musical dimension. It stood out for Beck's sonically charged guitar parts and the unique ending, where his Telecaster sounded like Ravi Shankar's sitar as it faded out. Also, the lyrics made it an ahead-of-its-time antiwar song. The lyrics asked, "Shapes of things before my eyes, just teach me to despise, will time make man more wise?" Vietnam had some American advisors, but President Lyndon B. Johnson hadn't escalated the war to the seething controversy that it would later become.

I asked my mother about Vietnam around 1966. Was it going to get worse? Would I have to go there when I was out of high school? She answered, "Don't worry, you won't be out of school for three more years. By then the whole thing will be over. The president will fix it. I wouldn't worry about it at all, Ralph." At the time, those words were pretty comforting to me, and I went back to pursuing the things that teenagers enjoy: hanging out with friends, listening to music, and playing sports like baseball and basketball. I started changing when I adopted the surfing lifestyle. There were great breaks in Laguna, like Brooks Street, which on a large swell boasted powerful waves, and also Thalia, a reef break a few blocks north that often had hollow, smaller waves. Communing with nature by riding waves truly made me into someone who respected nature's sights, sounds, and smells.

It was in 1966, the same year that I took up surfing, that Beck also started showing changes, although less positive than the changes in my life. He was becoming moody and difficult to work with. When he was fifteen or sixteen, he had suffered a concussion that may have affected him later, for he would suffer terrible headaches. Gomelsky arranged a tour in Denmark, but Beck wouldn't go. A solution had to be found.

Gomelsky thought that perhaps Beck needed a stabilizing influence like Jimmy Page around, someone to remind him of the original aims of the band and also just talk about problems. The music press started to report that Page was going to join the Yardbirds, but he dispelled the rumors. He felt that part of the band's mystique was about there being five Yardbirds, something that a sixth member could have destroyed. Besides, Page was still pretty involved with his studio work, as he had been when Clapton left. He saw no reason to walk away—it was still profitable. Plus, there were interesting ideas that he gained from studio work, such as a suggestion by a studio violinist, who was the father of David McCallum, the star of the television series *The Man from U.N.C.L.E.* He asked Page if he'd ever tried to bow the electric guitar. Page said no but was intrigued with the idea. He began to experiment, and although he could play only two strings at the same time, when he hit the others it created wild, sonic sounds. The bass strings made more moaning sounds, while the higher string shrieked. "This is something that has possibilities," Page must have thought. Working with new ideas was important, and he continued to experiment in the studio setting. Page discovered that if he put a lot of rosin on the bow, the rosin stuck to the strings and made it vibrate.

Despite Beck's shortcomings, his playing really got the attention of audiences. But it wasn't just his playing that helped the band take off in 1966. The new American record had very strong material, taken from extended play 45s released in England, which produced one of the greatest rock and roll sides ever recorded. Some people in my ninth-grade typing class spent less time on keyboard practice and more on talking about how great the new *Rave Up* album was.

I got in trouble for it, too. Here I was, minding my own business and typing an excerpt from Ernest Hemingway's *The Old Man and the Sea* when from behind me came the voice of my friend and fellow music fan, Earl Henderson. "Hey, Ralph! The Yardbirds came out with a new album. It's got 'I'm a Man' on it." My interest grabbed, I stopped typing, turned around, and asked where he saw the record and what the cover looked like. "It's at Builder's Emporium, by Thrifty's on Foothill Boulevard," he went on. He stopped typing, leaned toward me, and kept on about the Yardbirds. "And the cover's got them wearing these funny black suits. They look too normal, but the music's crazy."

"Whaddya mean? What's so crazy about it?" I asked, my curiosity growing. By now I'd totally forgotten about Hemingway. And so had many others around me, for the typing had stopped. This was rock news, important stuff to a ninth grader.

"Well, there's this one song where the harmonica starts off like a train. I'm not kidding." He cupped his hands over his mouth, "Like this, whoo—whooo!" Laughter erupted around us.

"Henderson! Hulett! See me outside in the hall now!" yelled Mr. Simmons, our teacher who had been standing behind us the entire time. Clacking typewriters furiously went into action, and we went outside feeling like two convicted criminals. We faced him, our heads looking at the ground. Mr. Simmons glared at us. "So, what's so important to talk about instead of doing your work?"

"The new Yardbirds album!" I blurted out. "These guys are far out!"

"Yeah, it's called, *Having a Rave Up*," added Henderson. "It's the best rock ever done! Better even than the Beatles, Stones, Kinks, or anybody!"

"They're all the same to me! Ridiculous!" Mr. Simmons yelled. "Forget about those Beatles-type groups and get back to work. And see me today after school for detention! You distracted everyone, and half the class is failing as it is! Don't you want to *learn* anything?"

I did not like getting yelled at, and my temper snapped. "They're not like the Beatles," I shot back. "They're way different. Something that you wouldn't know about!" That got me two detentions. But I didn't care—I only cared about the new Yardbirds album. After detention I rode my skateboard down La Crescenta Avenue to Foothill Boulevard and hurried to the record section at Builder's.

Some of the *Rave Up* albums were still there. Ignoring all the other records, I grabbed a Yardbirds and headed for the register. While in line, I looked at the cover more closely. The group was in black suits and ties, sort of looking like freaky FBI agents. Samwell-Smith had a goofy smile while playing his bass, Relf was turning around and clapping, and behind him a smirking Beck was partially hidden. Dreja and McCarty were the only ones with normal looks on their faces. But once I got the record home, tore off the plastic, and threw the disc on the turntable, nothing sounded at all normal: the music was untamed and laced with guitar distortion that painted all sorts of mental pictures. There was no doubt about it. This music was not like other British bands at all!

The sinister-sounding opening notes of "You're a Better Man Than I" blared out of my little mono record player, and I was immediately intrigued. I turned up the volume and heard Relf's words sung with sincerity that painted a scenario about human relationships. People shouldn't judge others by appearances but instead look inside; what stories they tell may mean more than how they speak or spell. I wondered about that, especially since I was supposed to be doing schoolwork right then. When the guitar break exploded with Beck's first fuzz tone notes, I spun the volume dial to the right some more. I shook my head in disbelief—these guys were rocking out, and it was only the first song! My homework was going to have to wait.

My mom pounded on my sliding door but didn't open it. "Dear, aren't you on your homework? You can get it done now— we're eating in an hour, once your father gets home. He's working late at Disney's again."

Beck's howling solo had been interrupted by my mom, so I put the needle over to the beginning of the song again. When I heard the guitar part in the middle, I found it to build in intensity, the drums banging away in the background. The guitar break ended, echoing in reverb. I found it haunting and mesmerizing—and not like anything I'd ever heard before!

There were many awesome guitar songs—"You're a Better Man Than I" and "Evil Hearted You"—but "I'm a Man" was the ultimate party song. Relf's harmonica traded solos with Beck's licks, and the song's climax with bass and drums going crazy was exciting and infectious. The next songs were totally different: "Still I'm Sad," with its slow pace and Gregorian chants for background vocals, and "Heart Full of Soul," a basic rhythm riff with two contrasting guitar parts fitting together perfectly, Beck's fuzz tone and Dreja's acoustic. Next, I was awestruck as Relf's distorted harmonica mimicking a train traded opening licks with Beck. The train song I'd heard about in my typing class burst forth. Underneath it all were the drums and that grinding rhythm-bass progression that Page would love and use so much later with Led Zeppelin. "Train Kept A-Rollin'" nearly defied description, but what I first liked about it was the double harmonicas and vocals, along with Beck's frantic solo and the heavy strumming at the end. The tune exploded at the end like a freight train smashing into a wall. I figured I'd never know the answers to all the questions that sprang to mind while listening to the lyrics, "On a train, I met a dame . . ." But no getting around it: here was an interesting story, and one hell of a rocker! Relf later claimed that most studio cuts were done in one take, with a few overdubs here and there. This first side really showed how the band's sound had jelled. The other half of the record was four of the best songs from *Five Live Yardbirds* with Clapton. The Yardbirds were definitely now getting known in America and in fact would end up more popular here than in England.

It was obvious to me that the Yardbirds were well known in America. The band was very popular in California. I noticed this in Laguna Beach after a surfing session. I'd have to carry my nine-foot Wardy surfboard from the top of Oak Street, where my parents' house was, all the way to the waves. That wasn't so bad, but going back up the hill was tiring, especially after surfing for a few hours. But the steep walls at Oak and the fast-breaking reef waves at

Thalia made it worth it. It was my way of getting away from the pressures of school and family. There were days that I'd be carrying my board on my head around the corner of the deadend drive near the house and I'd hear a live band playing. The sound floated over this huge grove of eucalyptus trees, so I couldn't see anything. I remember that warm spring day when I first heard live versions of "Over Under Sideways Down" and "Smokestack Lightning" played live by a band that never made the big time, just a local Laguna Beach band. Everywhere, teenage bands sprang up playing in garages or basements and wanting to play this kind of music. A kid could buy an electric guitar like a Sears Silvertone for $125.

Once when I was sitting on the beach enjoying the sun and watching the waves come in, I heard about a Yardbirds concert scheduled for August 23, 1966. I sometimes brought a transistor radio with me, and on that day it was tuned into a Los Angeles rock station, KFWB. The disc jockey said the Yardbirds were just pulling out of Long Beach Harbor, California, on their way to a concert at Catalina Island, twenty-two miles in the Pacific. There had been a radio contest, and the winners got to go on the boat with the band and see them play on Catalina. I wished that I could have gone. But I felt better when I saw what a sunny day it was and how great the waves were building. Nature helped me rationalize sometimes—especially if it involved surfing. *Besides,* I thought, *maybe I'll get another chance to see the Yardbirds sometime.*

Steve Seymour lived near La Crescenta in Pasadena, California, and like me was a big enthusiast of British rock bands. When his mom decided that she and Steve would go visit his aunt on Catalina Island, she didn't stop to think about who else would be on the boat. This was a family trip, and it was as simple as that, or so she may have thought. But when she and Seymour arrived at the dock in Long Beach, they were greeted by throngs of people lined up to go on the boat. They were dressed like British mods, with flowered shirts and striped bell-bottoms. These people were contestants who had won the KFWB contest. Once everyone went on board, the boat left for Catalina.

Seymour's mother went inside to the bar and he went along. All lined up along the counter were the Yardbirds, drinking and talking. Relf had on his dark sunglasses he was famous for, and Beck was sitting there, not expecting to be bothered by anybody. Seymour boldly went up to Beck, this was a chance of a lifetime! "The security guards were watching some contestants, who were looking in the bar but were too young to get in," Seymour laughed. "I was too young to be in there, but it was okay because I was with my mom. So I came up to Beck, my hero in the band, and asked for his autograph. He gave me one, but acted like he was doing me a big favor. Like I was wasting his time. In fact, he didn't even look happy, like he didn't want to be there. Then security came up and told me to go join the crowd outside."

Once on the island, Seymour talked his mother into buying him a ticket for the concert, which was being held at the Avalon Ballroom. He went to the show, which lasted just over an hour. Relf had on slacks, a turtle neck sweater with a sports jacket over it, and Beatle boots. Beck was most casual of all, with jeans, a T-shirt, and a jacket. Overall, the group didn't seem that together; the set was sloppy.

"The PA was too loud, and Relf drowned out everyone with his harp," Seymour said. "I thought Beck played real sloppy because it seemed like he came in at the wrong times. He looked real temperamental, like he wanted to be elevated above the rest. After the band played a song, they'd sort of stand around and talk about what to do next. It wasn't like they played one song and then go right into another. It almost seemed like they couldn't decide, like they were having an argument."

Some of the numbers jelled after sloppy starts, and Seymour remembered that there were a few times when the band got really tight and into jamming. One time this happened was on "Here

'Tis," when bass and guitar riffs were traded, almost like they were having a war. Other songs included "For Your Love," which had Relf on bongos, "Heart Full of Soul," "A Certain Girl," "Train Kept A-Rollin'," and quite a few others. Another reason that it was hard to hear the music well was because the audience, mostly fourteen- to sixteen-year-old girls, was screaming its brains out. That may have even made the band upset, along with not being able to hear each other because of the poor PA. Seymour left the partially filled ballroom, glad that he went—more for the experience than the music. There had definitely been some tension onstage.

Despite personality problems with Beck, 1966 saw the band break new creative ground with the release of the album *Over Under Sideways Down*. It consisted of many spontaneous first takes. At the time, there was a vogue for Indian music like Ravi Shankar, which the band enjoyed, so there was that influence, along with psychedelic doses of Beck's fuzz tone and feedback. There had been a version of "Heart Full of Soul" with a sitar recorded the previous year, but it had gone unreleased. Beck had proven what he could do with his Toneblender fuzz pedal on that song, and he took it even further with how he played on "Over Under Sideways Down." The album was released in England as *Roger the Engineer*, with a humorous cartoon of Roger Cameron on the cover. The group found themselves working with an engineer who knew what to do with four-track equipment.

If there was any record that helped pioneer psychedelic rock, *Over Under Sideways Down* was it. The Beatles released *Revolver* the same year. The entire album spanned various types of music, including the mystical, sitar-laden sounds of India. The Yardbirds were in the same vein with their new release, with a heavy emphasis on guitar sound effects and improvisation. From the slow-building intensity of harmonica and guitar in "Lost Woman" and Beck's searing leads in "What Do You Want" to the wild, untamed progression of the title track, there hadn't been anything quite like it before. Change was in the air, and in more ways than one.

Gomelsky gave up working for the band. He felt no one wanted to consider his ideas, like bringing in an Otis Redding, Memphis–type sound and more of an emphasis on keyboards. In addition, the band was working hard, playing many gigs, and felt they weren't seeing much money out of it. He handed over managing the band to Simon Napier-Bell, who had trouble managing personality problems. Beck showed up late to sessions and would be lax in the studio. Being a player of emotion, he would let the notes express what he felt at the moment and not always refine the work he produced. He sometimes flew into rages from disliking what he played, and sometimes this transferred over to the stage. Hence, there would be great performances as well as bad ones. Napier-Bell brought in a new person, Peter Grant, to share his duties. A London native, Grant already had a colorful career as a professional wrestler and had worked in the 1950s with Little Richard, the Everly Brothers, and Chuck Berry during their English tours. When a split management deal didn't work, Grant assumed control. He would handle the Yardbirds from the later part of 1966 until their breakup in 1968.

The aptly named *Over Under Sideways Down* album not only traveled new musical avenues but it also showed the Yardbirds at their zenith in the studio. When I finished hearing it for the first time, I was dazed from all the different sounds. For the next two years, this group would have a tremendous impact on fusion music that West Coast groups would play. Near the end of their career, the Yardbirds were still highly admired in America. It appeared that American audiences were open to new ideas that groups came up with and interested in seeing what a group could create. As a contrast, in England after the Yardbirds stopped being a people's band and playing at rhythm and blues clubs, their following changed. The psychedelic music created with Beck became too much, and the last album with Page, *Little Games*, didn't even come out in England.

Page was still doing studio work in 1966 but was getting

burned out on it by now. He felt like he had become one of those players whom he hated, someone who just went in and played the same thing over and over. "Eventually, it became boring," Page said. "Especially when they started calling me to do muzak sessions. That was the last straw." Also, the session scene began to change. With less of an emphasis on guitar and more on brass and orchestral arrangement under the Stax Records label, Page was playing fewer solos. Finally, when he went to a rock-and-roll session in France, he was shocked when he discovered how rusty he'd become. He now knew there had to be a change.

His chance to drop session work and get back on the road came in June, when he went to see his old friends the Yardbirds at Oxford University. The band was on a hectic, five-week English tour, riding around the countryside in Relf's father's van and having to share space with bricks, sand, and cement bags. The Oxford show was supposed to be a formal affair. However, it turned out to be everything but that.

Everyone was dressed up in dinner jackets to see the Yardbirds and the Hollies each play three sets. The Yardbirds' first set went well, but to the annoyance of Relf the crowd hardly responded, and he began to drink between sets. When he returned to sing, all hell broke loose. "Keith Relf was rolling around the stage, grabbling with the mike, blowing his harmonica in all the wrong places, and just singing nonsense words . . . but it was great, just fantastically suitable for the occasion," Page said. But Samwell-Smith was after musical precision and it was just more than he could take. He blew up at Relf and said that he was leaving the group.

With Samwell-Smith gone, and Relf staying, the group was stuck with playing commitments. Page offered to play bass until a regular replacement could be found. Everyone asked him to stay on, and he played bass for two months, with Dreja supporting Beck on guitar. Beck claimed that the story was different than this: to make up for the loss of Samwell-Smith's contribution to the

Yardbirds sound, Beck thought it would be great to have two lead guitars. So Page was asked and of course accepted the guitar spot. About his reasons for joining, Page commented, "I never desired stardom, I just wanted to be respected as a musician." Dreja switched to bass so Page and Beck could work out a dual lead combination. This would be the ultimate lineup for many Yardbirds fans.

Page had first taken over on lead during an American tour in August 1966, when Beck couldn't play a gig at San Francisco's Carousel Ballroom. He'd gotten a sore throat, which in the past meant bad news, and there had to be a guitar in there for leads. So Page handled all of them, and wild demonic notes cascaded from the twin amps and zoomed around the ballroom, adding a bizarre effect to the already otherworldly light show. The rest of the band was impressed—even if Beck didn't last much longer, Page could still keep things going.

Back in England, Beck visited Page at his Victorian boathouse on the Thames, which had been redone for Page's musical needs. Two lead guitars steaming away at once was a new idea in rock at the time, and the musicians rehearsed together. They worked on unison and harmony patterns for dual guitar parts, drawing from blues players like Freddie King. The idea was potentially classic, for if the two players had perfected the concept and gotten along over a period of time, the results would have been explosive and dynamic. It was a musical marriage made in heaven, but it wasn't destined to last. "Don't forget there was no stereo mixing equipment," recalled Napier-Bell. "In those days, you put the amps up on the stage, and the sound came from the amps. There wasn't a mixing unit . . . you put Jeff on one side and Jimmy on the other and suddenly all these famous solos of Jeff's were coming out in stereo. It was fantastic. It was certainly the best rock sound I'd ever heard at that time."

As coming shows would prove, sometimes it worked, and other times it didn't. There were times when it actually became more than frantic—dangerous is a better word. During a show in a New Mexico club, something went wrong and Beck's fragile temper flew out of control. He kicked over a stack of amps, which smashed through a nearby window. Luckily, no one was walking under the window at the time, or he or she could have been killed. The pressure continued to build within the Yardbirds, and it would eventually explode. Relf complained that the combined guitar onslaught of both Beck and Page was too loud, and the two guitarists continued to have their on and off nights. With two such talented guitarists' egos competing and trying to outdo each other, there was bound to be conflict. By now, the Yardbirds were in the big leagues, playing with the Rolling Stones and Ike and Tina Turner on an English tour. The stakes were higher than ever now.

The band left to play in America again. Beck went along, but he was now very fragile, and an upcoming Dick Clark Caravan of Stars Tour finally sent him over the edge. It was a chaotic, punishing American tour that had thirty-three shows in twenty-seven days over sixteen states. Along with other bands like Sam the Sham and the Pharoahs and Gary Lewis and the Playboys, the Yardbirds were shuttled on a bus from show to show and slept in seats or on luggage racks. Half the bands would leave one show and go to the next, then trade places with the performers who had just finished. After three nights of this, Beck finally lost it. Page recalled, "I walked in and Beck had his guitar over his head, about to bring it down on Keith Relf's head, but instead smashed it to the floor. Relf looked at him in total astonishment and Beck said, 'Why did you make me do that?'"

Shortly afterward, Beck said he had swollen tonsils and was going to see a doctor, then instead caught a flight to Los Angeles. Once again, he'd gone AWOL during a tour. It was the last straw for everyone in the band. Two days later in Los Angeles, Page found Beck at the Whisky a Go Go with his girlfriend, Mary Hughes. Beck apologized to the band, but instead of being taken back he was fired. Beck asked Page if he was going to leave with him. Page said no, and the group continued as a four-piece until it broke up in 1968. The dual guitar experiment ended, perhaps because of a feeling of intimidation on Beck's part or, as Page claimed, "The thing is, prior to my joining the Yardbirds, apparently he had pissed around onstage quite a lot—knocking over his amps, just walking off, and whatever. At the time I came in, he was in a rut—I think he felt a bit alien in a way."

Dreja thought the dual guitar concept was a good one, but with two talents like Page and Beck it was destined never to work. Dreja found that the performing attitudes of the two guitars set them apart. "Jimmy's always been a real pro, whereas Jeff was always much more a man of emotion. So I think Jeff found it much harder than Jimmy, because he was always prone to play according to how things were and how he felt, whereas Jimmy's idea was always, 'We're professional entertainers, we must go out there and do it properly.'" Beck would overreact to Page being there, for the talent that Page brought was hard for Beck to deal with. Along with this, the band had always put Beck under pressure. Dreja claimed, "We'd expect him to sound like a chicken and a tank at the same time, and because he always managed to do it, you never thought twice about asking him to become a giraffe as well. And when Jimmy was there, there was another huge added pressure, because he had to do it even better then, and do it all the time."

Mickie Most and Peter Grant completed the buying of Napier-Bell's share in the Yardbirds. Most had the greatest interest in Beck, so Grant took control of the Yardbirds. Napier-Bell told Grant to watch out for Page because of his constant questions regarding the band's earnings. Grant asked Page about this rumor of him being a troublemaker, and Page replied, "Troublemaker! You're dead right. We did 'Blow Up' five weeks in America and a Rolling Stones tour of Britain and we got just 118 pounds each."

Grant would look after the Yardbirds, and after the Dick Clark tour he scheduled them for a tour of Singapore and Australia, going with them and experiencing all the hassles the band had to put up with, and it was the first time the Yardbirds made good money on a tour. Having the intimidating London manager around certainly helped. Napier-Bell had done one good thing for the Yardbirds by getting them cast in Michelangelo Antonioni's *Blowup* film. One scene needed a rock band in a club. The Who were supposed to appear in the scene, but they declined, so Napier-Bell hired the Yardbirds for it. In the scene, Beck pushed his guitar neck right through his amp. The song they played was "Stroll On," a variation of "Train Kept A-Rollin'." This was one of the only two documentations of the dual-guitar Yardbirds. The other was a single released in October 1966, which was one of the band's most progressive songs ever.

"Happenings Ten Years Time Ago" was brought in by Relf on tape, Page worked on the riff and structure, and the entire song was soon organized. Beck showed up for the session, and he put some guitar parts on top of what else had been recorded, and the bass was played by John Paul Jones. The song re-created a guitar war zone, complete with howling sirens and feedback explosions. The feedback-laden guitar part was so dynamic that when Jimi Hendrix came to England in 1966, one of the first things he did was ask Beck how in the world he got those guitar sounds on the song. "Happenings" became a perfect example of what American radio stations like KHJ and KFWB were calling "the futuristic sound of the Yardbirds." There was one other track that Beck and Page worked jointly on: "Beck's Bolero."

Shortly after Beck left the band, he and Page got together and worked on the instrumental. But the accounts differ: Beck claimed that he heard Page play Ravelian rhythm on a twelve-string guitar at his house, which gave him the basic idea. Beck supposedly added the melody line, then went home and completed the song later. Page said that it was all done in the studio with Page supervising, since the producer had left. He insisted that "Jeff was playing, and I was in the box [recording booth]. And even though he says he wrote it, I wrote it. The idea was basically built around Maurice Ravel's *Bolero*. It's got a lot of drama to it; it came off right. It was a good lineup too, with [the Who's drummer] Keith Moon."

Others on the track included Jones on bass and Nicky Hopkins on piano. Although the group name hadn't been invented yet, there was talk of forming a group since Moon and the Who bassist John Entwistle were sick of the Who. Page had wanted Steve Marriott of the Small Faces as vocalist until Marriott's manager asked Page how he'd like to play guitar with ten broken fingers, then Beck and Page quit speaking to each other for the time being, and that ended the possible Zeppelin-prototype band. But Page and Jones's paths would cross again very soon, during the recording of the last Yardbirds' studio album, *Little Games*.

Grant had brought in Mickie Most as the producer to get the Yardbirds back into the singles market. During the recording, there was an emphasis to produce hit singles. Most's approach with the Yardbirds was ineffective. Page was appalled that Most told the group to go ahead and get ready for the next song without hearing the playback of the last one. When Page asked Most how his guitar solos would play a part, Most answered that the purpose of instrumental parts was to fill in when there wasn't any singing, guitar work wasn't to be at the forefront throughout a song. This countered everything the Yardbirds sound had been about up to that point. Despite everything, there were still some unique innovations put down: Jones arranged a cello section for the title song, and Page used his guitar bowing technique on "Tinker, Tailor, Soldier, Sailor" and also on "Glimpses," a psychedelic instrumental that had Far Eastern–type chanting, the voices of little children, and Godzilla roaring on it.

There were two singles that emerged from sessions for the record, which Page later said the band was conned into doing. Most suggested the group record Manfred Mann's "Ha Ha Said the Clown" in the Yardbirds style, which everyone thought was a ridiculous idea. Page recalled Most wouldn't give up, telling the group, "It'll be an interesting experiment, and if it doesn't work, we'll scrap it." Of course, it was released shortly after it was recorded, despite the fact that it was terrible.

The first time that I heard "Ha Ha Said the Clown" I was hanging out with Clyde Johnson on a foggy morning on Thalia Street, hoping it would clear up so I could see the ocean and paddle out to catch some waves. We passed the time by switching stations on the AM radio in my mom's 1967 Pontiac. The disc jockey on KFWB announced, "Here's the new single by the Yardbirds. We hope you like it! It's bound to go somewhere fast!" I frowned as I heard Page's opening riff, jangling away on the dashboard speaker, but I kept listening, hoping that it would get better. It didn't. The lyrics were ridiculous, about some guy getting laughed at because he messed up a romance. Even though Johnson was intrigued with the new jangling guitar sound, he also didn't like it. What had happened to the gutsy, rocking to the end punch of "I'm a Man" and "Train Kept A-Rollin'"? He asked me how I liked the new Yardbirds song, and I replied that it sounded really stupid and lame, like a soft drink jingle on the radio or an ad for dry cereal on television.

When I later bought the *Little Games* record, I was a little more pleased. The first two songs, "Little Games" and "Smile on Me," were interesting for Page's guitar parts—they sounded more raw and distorted than Beck, but the notes still carried the tunes in a more wild, primitive-sounding manner. "White Summer" was a complete contrast—an acoustic number that sounded like it had come straight out of India; melodic and mysterious, the guitar lines weaved around the tablas like a cobra. The whole instrumental was very refined and every note by Page sounded perfect. "Drinking Muddy Water" was also interesting—it was a driving, over-amped workout. But the rest of the record didn't hold up much when compared to the energy and different music styles represented on *Over Under Sideways Down*.

Even the cover looked thrown together: the Yardbirds' faces were cut out and pasted over a colorful array of dice, playing cards, and a slot machine that said "Fun" on it with coins pouring out of the hole. It looked like a bizarre advertisement for Las Vegas, Nevada. I remember the single "Ten Little Indians" told a story about these Indians that all died because they did some kind of different sin. The humming guitars that rose in volume at the end with accompanying tape loops created a wild, electronic, demonic frenzy. But neither this single nor "Ha Ha Said the Clown" were any kind of success compared to the single done with Beck. But there was still one thing that the band kept afloat with Page's help: a reputation for some very spectacular live performances, especially one performance in Detroit, Michigan, at the State Fair Coliseum called "Mod Wedding" put on by Andy Warhol.

Thomas Weschler, an employee at Artist's Music, was contacted to supply equipment for the gig. His store was the "go to" place for all Vox equipment, which was the official sponsor of the Yardbirds. He reminisced, "Beck had quit and went to England the day before, leaving Jimmy to do all the guitar work. This is no shit—sometimes I don't believe what I was charged with doing—our store provided the amps for the show, Vox SuperBeatles. They were notorious for blowing at full volume. Vic, the owner and my boss, told me not to let these guys turn the amps past 7 on the scale. I said okay boss, and as I set up the amps Jimmy Page came up to me with Beck's Telecaster and said, 'Hello, mate.' I know it was Beck's because it said so in magic marker on the back of the white Telecaster. I mumbled hi and turned around to see my boss glaring at me. I gave him a thumbs up as Page, with his right hand little finger, pulled all the pots [potentiometers] up to 10 and then smiled and winked. I couldn't bring myself to tell Page to turn the amp down, so I didn't. I turned back to Vic and waved, then prayed the amp wouldn't blow . . . I got lucky. So did Jimmy."

After Beck's departure in December 1966, the entire Yardbirds sound underwent a transformation. Page helped bring this about when he played live by bringing in new material like "White

Summer," the solo showpiece that foreshadowed Zeppelin's "Black Mountain Side." Also important was the fact that the band had a different format, and this improved the musicianship. "When Jeff left, it got a lot more tight, really, it became a more workmanlike unit with just the four of us," McCarty observed. With Dreja now on bass, Page grinded out both rhythm and lead parts. His scope on guitar zoomed to new heights at concerts. He played with a violin bow and used the wah-wah pedal to give the group a complexity that they had heretofore lacked. Page recalled, "The Yardbirds allowed me to improvise a lot in live performance, and I started building a textbook of ideas that I eventually used in Zeppelin."

In 1967, perhaps the epitome of American rock music blasting forward was the San Francisco sound. The city became a mecca for the hippie movement during the "Summer of Love." Energy and excitement was in the air. It seemed everyone was plugged into what was going on. Free concerts at the Panhandle and Golden Gate Parks gave exposure to bands that lived in the Haight Ashbury District, including Big Brother and the Holding Company, Jefferson Airplane, and the Grateful Dead. On many walls in San Francisco were scrawled what the term *Hippie* may have meant: Help In Promoting Peaceful Individual Existence. In no time, there was enough of a hippie subculture to support two concert halls: the Fillmore Auditorium and the Avalon Ballroom. For tickets starting at $1.50, you could see three bands and dance all night, with a psychedelic light show projected down from the balcony.

While many were taking psychedelic drugs and gyrating to explosive rock concerts up north, I was ecstatic for other reasons. I'd finally gotten my driver's license and lost no time in driving up and down the coastline, losing myself in cascading walls of water with my surfing friends and enjoying hot, lazy summer days on the sand. In the mornings I'd get the keys to my mom's 1967 Pontiac, strap my new custom Hobie nose rider on the racks, and head to San Clemente or Doheny, where you could surf all day. There used to be some psychedelically painted vans at Doheny that blasted music of the day: Cream, Bob Dylan, the Beach Boys, and the Beatles. I'd pursue music at home later that evening, where I was prompted to buy artists that I'd heard on the radio. "White Rabbit" was always played on KHJ and KRLA, so I got the Jefferson Airplane's *Surrealistic Pillow*, which pretty well blew my sixteen-year-old mind. Another radio standard was "Light My Fire," but I already knew about the Doors from seeing them play on Senior Day at Crescenta Valley High earlier that year. I'd gotten the first Doors album back in January when it had come out, and it sounded better each time—each song seemed to have its own aura of celebration, fun, and slight tinge of menace. Earlier in April, I remember a walk that I took along the Coast Highway toward the main part of Laguna. It was Easter break, and there were wild parties everywhere. I stopped by the oceanfront Vacation Village Motel, leaned on the railing, and stared at the spectacle below me as the first Doors album punctured the night through one of the open doors. Drunken college students clutched beer bottles and jumped into the swimming pool next to the building. I decided that it was time to continue my walk. Laguna was always a good town for parties and wildness. But you could only watch for so long!

The one record that seemed to sum up that summer was the Beatles' *Sgt. Peppers Lonely Hearts Club Band*. The record was seemingly spinning on everyone's turntable. Even my mom and older brother liked it, and we must have played it every evening. The Beatles were clearly more accessible than other bands to my family, especially to my mom, who was a music teacher. She said that they had brought real art into rock music, and later even taught a unit on the Art of Rock at Woodrow Wilson Middle School in Glendale, California. Unfortunately, I didn't do anything to educate myself about live shows that summer, although my friend Clyde Johnson did. What was he up to that summer of 1967? Why, going to see a group that he'd always wanted to experience: the Yardbirds!

It was in July that Johnson and Shannon Dixon, a neighbor

friend, went up to stay in Santa Monica for about a week. Johnson had a godmother there, and for about a week he and Dixon body-surfed and watched the girls on the beach. Nearby was the Santa Monica Civic Auditorium. Johnson and Dixon went up to the Civic, a venue that had been built in the early 1960s and held about 3,000 people. The two teenagers saw a pile of posters in the lobby, designed in the San Francisco style of wavy lines and letters. The psychedelic, swirling words told of the July 22 show that included the Yardbirds, Iron Butterfly, Moby Grape, Captain Beefheart and His Magic Band, and the West Coast Pop Art Exper-imental Band. Johnson and Dixon grabbed some of the handbill-type posters, walked up to the ticket window, and paid for two tickets to the concert.

This show was intended in the spirit of what was going on at the same time in San Francisco, sort of like an Avalon Ballroom type of event. There had been other concerts there already: the Doors had played the Civic on July 3 and were about to hit the circuit of dance auditoriums up north, swirling light show and all. The Civic offered a larger scale of events than the small clubs like the Whisky in Hollywood or Huntington Beach's Golden Bear could offer. But it was still fairly small when compared to the expansive Hollywood Bowl, which was perfect for the huge large draws like the Beatles, Rolling Stones, or Jimi Hendrix. With the Santa Monica Civic Audi-torium, there could still be a feeling of intimacy, a "love-in," or a "happening," like what was present in San Francisco. People were drawn tighter for a powerful, positive experience.

"It was a gathering of tribes kind of thing—there was a festive mood," Johnson remembered. "It had the feeling of a Griffith Park Love-In. Everybody would go to the park and bongos, flutes, and acoustic guitars would be playing. People would be blowing bub-bles and smoking doobies. But as far as many drugs being taken at this concert, there weren't very many drugs being passed. Every-body was there to hear the music."

Everyone filed in the large glass doors of the Civic on the day of the show at around 2:00, for the afternoon show. The talk in the crowd was about Beck, not Page. One guy said that Beck had flipped out on LSD and was in a mental hospital, and another disagreed, saying that Beck would be there for sure, and Page might play backup guitar. Most everyone seemed to have a positive attitude about things, that Beck would be there and re-create all the fantastic songs that most people there knew by heart, such as "Heart Full of Soul," "You're a Better Man Than I," and "I'm a Man." Magic could happen—the Summer of Love was still on, and music was the potent force that helped drive it. The feeling was perhaps that things were so good that they would never come to an end. This was right before many supergroups like the Beatles, Cream, and the Yardbirds would splinter and reform, changing the music scene. Many American bands would suffer the same fate: Moby Grape, Love, and Buffalo Springfield. But the magic was still in the air—for now.

The majority of the teenage audience was still in school or had some kind of job. Hence, the longest hair for most guys was like a pageboy type of cut. One small group of "freaks" in American flag uniforms came in with fuzzy beards down their chest and hair down their backs. Many people saw these genuine hippies and gave them a standing ovation before the show.

The show started off with the West Coast Pop Art Experimental Band, followed by Captain Beefheart, after which the announcer came out and told everyone that Iron Butterfly couldn't make the show, but the Strawberry Alarm Clock would play instead. After this, the Experimental Band's PA system was taken down and the rest of the concert suffered through substandard equipment. Most of the vocals were lost in an electronic muddle. In fact, a few days later the *Los Angeles Free Press* wryly commented, "I understand sound is endemic to every single show in that house. Knowing months in advance that you are going into the Civic and that it has a PA system from an Alabama bus station, one would think."

It was almost an hour's wait for the Yardbirds. People talked about Beck and their favorite Yardbirds songs. Johnson was out in the lobby when he heard the announcer begin talking. "And now, what you've all been waiting for—the group whose songs you've heard; whose songs you've played!"

"The guy said that because the Yardbirds influenced the Sunset Strip scene to the max," Johnson pointed out. "If you didn't do at least two Yardbirds songs in your set, you wouldn't be hired at the Hullabaloo or the Whisky. It was a big deal—you had to play the Stones, the Kinks, and the Yardbirds. You had to put that hard edge on it."

Everyone was told that Beck wasn't there. Many up front murmured their disappointment. What kind of concert was this without Beck? The announcer went on to say that the rhythm guitarist would play guitar instead, and that his name was Jimmy Page. Then the curtain rose, and the first bars of "Train Kept A-Rollin'" thundered out across the auditorium. Before the song was over, all discussion of Beck ceased for the rest of the concert. Page had taken over, and Johnson's reaction was, "Lord, help us, we were in another land! As a rhythm section, it was probably the tightest one, live, I've ever seen, ever. Period. You couldn't stick a needle between the riffs. So what it did was give Page a lot of room to move. He could go anywhere he wanted—he coulda gone to the moon with his leads, and that's what he did in concert."

Johnson got up to take some photos; he was over to the left of the stage, and couldn't get over to the right, where Page stood. Everyone sat in folding chairs, and the middle section went all the way through the orchestra pit right up to the stage. People in the front had their feet against the stage, and Johnson would have had to go all the way up his aisle, through the lobby, and down the next aisle to the right to get over to Page. But then he ran out of film and decided to stay where he was—he could still see everyone onstage pretty well, anyway. Pure electric energy blasted through the poor, outdated 1950s-vintage sound system.

The Yardbirds thundered on for sixty or seventy minutes.

During "I'm a Man," Johnson noticed Relf's Nehru jacket was drenched in sweat. "They were all wearing Nehru outfits, natural-knit Indian-style, except for Page. He was wearing a silver Nehru jacket, which made him look like an alien from outer space. There were no colored lights onstage, just white lights. So when Page was in the spotlight it looked like there were the Yardbirds and this silvery alien from space playing Beck's licks, but better than Beck." Despite the insufficient sound system, the bass and guitar could be heard all right and even Relf's harmonica broke through the din every now and then, but the vocals were lost in distortion.

When Page got out his bow and started working the strings of his guitar, his head down, his black hair swinging across his face, the Yardbirds never sounded so otherworldly. The song lasted close to fifteen minutes. This was a tour de force for Page's bowing in the show—a song no one had ever heard before, "I'm Confused." It was dramatic and scary. The original idea had been borrowed from Jake Holmes, a folk singer the group had seen perform at New York's Café a Go Go. His version of the song was called "Dazed and Confused," and Page would make full use of it later on with Zeppelin. The Yardbirds had different words to this tune, written by Relf, and, of course, an eerie, menacing guitar solo by Page that droned forth from his bow and then exploded into a furious lead that he also used on the last Yardbirds single, "Think about It." This was progressive rock, Yardbirds style. They sure had come a long way from the local London band that played rhythm and blues.

The audience was surprised when a rough version of "You Go Your Way and I'll Go Mine" was played. But the hits were there, too—"Heart Full of Soul" made everyone remember the good old Yardbirds days. McCarty's drums could be heard in all their crashes and rolls. He played so loud that it didn't even seem like he needed microphones, even though the drums were up on a riser and miked. The show ended when Page tore up the place with a frantic version of "Over Under Sideways Down," his fingers taking off on a whirlwind lead that turned the song upside down, and when it was over everyone filed outside, their ears ringing, babbling about Page. When they walked in, he'd been a nobody, and now, he was a legend, bound for the stars.

I got a little gift from Johnson that summer of 1967. When I'd gone up to visit him after the show, he raved about it and gave me an extra handbill from the Santa Monica Civic Auditorium, its psychedelic letters swirling into curved points like hookah smoke. My dad had helped me airbrush similar letters on the side of my new surf vehicle that I got a year later—an old 1955 Dodge mail truck I named "Mirage." The little Yardbirds memento went up on my paneled wall back in Laguna, next to some of my other psychedelic posters from downtown head shops. The next year when Johnson tried to talk me into going to a concert, I didn't think twice about it. It was the best show I ever saw during my teenage years, in Hollywood at the Kaleidoscope Club, the former home of the Hullabaloo and the future site of the renowned Aquarius Theater. This particular show was a benefit for KPPC, an underground FM radio station in Pasadena. A large assortment of bands showed up to raise money: Clear Light, Steppenwolf, Sweetwater, H. P. Lovecraft, the Peanut Butter Conspiracy, Buffalo Springfield, and Jefferson Airplane. Like my surfer friend Bill remembered about San Francisco, we were able to go right up to the edge of the stage and watch the bands in action.

At the start of 1968, Grant put together what would turn out to be the final Yardbirds tour in America. He and Page had become good friends, for Grant traveled with the group and experienced their ups and downs, as well as making sure that they were well paid. Page was happy to be on the road again and proud to be in a band that he'd known and seen for years. The psychedelic music scene was in full swing, and Page laid down the ground rules for the classic British rock guitar hero look. He fit right in with his crushed red velvet pants, white ruffled shirts, reddish-brown embroidered jackets, and love beads. To top it off, Page's art college background came in handy when it came to his Telecaster's look. Page said, "I painted it and I had reflective plastic sheeting underneath the pick guard that gave rainbow colors." There would be many loud, spellbinding performances from New York to the West Coast, where the Yardbirds had built up a fanatical following. In January, the last single was released: "Good Night Sweet Josephine" backed with "Think About It." It certainly wasn't a poor effort. The A side had some hair-raising guitar work by Page through a kind of phasing unit, which gave the notes a sonic space-age sound. "Think About It" was actually the more interesting of the two songs, for it had a number of various leads that foretold what was to come with Zeppelin. It was a pressure cooker of riffs that slowly rumbled, then exploded like a volcano. Page was already blazing new ground.

The band arrived in New York during late March and played New York's Anderson Theater while still suffering from jet lag. Epic Records recorded the show for a possible live album, but the fellow the company sent to record the gig didn't know what he was doing. He miked the drums from above, so the bass drum didn't come through. Worse still, Page wasn't recorded through the amplifier he was using, so all the fuzz and sustain were lost. Page was assured that miracles could be done later in the studio via the world of electronic wizardry, but the finished product appalled him. The record was doctored up with bullfight cheers dubbed in at places, like on "Shapes of Things" when Page broke into a solo, making the show sound like it was played before a rowdy group of sports fans. And slower parts, such as the end of "I'm Confused" just before it became "Heart Full of Soul," had clinking cocktail glasses in the background to give a more "live" feeling. Everyone in the group was outraged. The band had the final word on what was put out, so they made Epic shelve the project. This recording proved it was the final nail in the band's coffin. It briefly resurfaced in the fall of 1971 to cash in on Page's popularity with Led Zeppelin. The cover artwork had the title *Live Yardbirds* with a giant

Yardbird standing over a city holding a banner that read FEATURING JIMMY PAGE. I was lucky enough to pick up a copy of the original album in a Hollywood record store before it was pulled off the shelves.

Leaving the East Coast, the group booked some Los Angeles appearances. The Shrine Exposition Hall put on numerous shows through Pinnacle Dance Concerts, and on May 31 and June 1 the Yardbirds were featured with B. B. King. Tickets cost $3 in advance and $3.50 at the door. People could get them at lots of different locations, such as Walichs Music City, Free Press Bookstores, and Laguna Beach's Sound Spectrum. By now the Sound Spectrum had relocated about a mile south of downtown, on the Coast Highway near the Pottery Shack off Cress Street, where it still exists. I'd go there and see some new Yardbirds promotional photos. They announced the band was now on Mercury Records. I knew about the new single, and judging from that I decided that the next album would be a lot better than *Little Games*. There was also a funny poster out that showed the Page version of the Yardbirds dressed up in fur coats, as if they'd just come in on the boat from Alaska. It was a weird contrast to the other posters high on the wall: the Stones in Beatle boots all sitting somberly on the floor, the Grateful Dead on Haight Street, and Jimi Hendrix on a hill, hands on hips and his legs spread, with some girls peeping out from behind him. The tickets were available at the Spectrum, but once again I was to miss a Yardbirds show. I was still too hooked on surfing to think about going up to Los Angeles if I got to hit the beach over the weekend. I was around Los Angeles during the week in La Crescenta, so if I could get away over the weekend, I'd jump at the chance. I hated the heat and smog that seemed to get worse every year.

The Shrine show would prove to be my last chance to see the Yardbirds, and I passed it by. But my friend Norwood Price went, and he had his camera with him, too. The shows used festival seating, so that meant no chairs and more people could attend. Price wanted to photograph Jimmy Page, so he had to guess where he would stand in relationship to the other members of the band. From the first explosive notes of "Train Kept A-Rollin'," the band displayed their new sonic musical heights that they had reached. Armed with only a 50 mm lens, Price snapped away with his camera at Page, who was wearing red crushed velvet pants and a white frilled shirt. He guitar-bowed his way through an early nine-minute "Dazed and Confused," wrenching notes from his psychedelic painted Telecaster guitar. Then as the set progressed, their rave up consisted of a twelve-minute-plus version of "I'm a Man" and medleys of "Smokestack Lightning" and "Beck's Bolero," as well as a frantic, electronic exploration of "I Wish You Would" going into Donovan's "Hey Gyp." To top it off, there was an intense "I Ain't Done Wrong" with Relf like a modern pied piper, blowing out harmonica blasts that intertwined with Page's power chords.

The furious playing enraptured the crowd. Not unlike a crashing tidal wave, the music conjured up an enormous wall of surging sound that was full of wildness, roaring, crashing, and moving up and down. The energy was epitomized in the lyrics of "Drinking Muddy Water," with Relf crying out, "I've been runnin' and a-hidin', trying to lose my mind." It seemed like the group was buoyant and as strong as ever, but appearances were deceiving—just like the new Yardbirds promo photos that I'd seen. The band's days were numbered.

After the highly successful American tour, the Yardbirds returned to England. On July 7, 1968, the skies cried in a depressing rain-soaked summer night as the group played its final show at Luton Technical College. The Yardbirds were history. Relf and McCarty quit for good. Relf felt that he was at a dead end; it had been a long, tumultuous road since 1963, and he was physically and emotionally exhausted. Also, Relf wasn't happy with the direction the Yardbirds had gone. There was way too much volume now, and it had gotten too far away from it original roots. "It continued developing with Jimmy," Relf said, "but quite honestly for me the real feeling, the kind of guts of the Yardbirds came to an end when it became a commercial band with 'For Your Love.' My happiest days, my memories were with Eric . . . the happiest times were playing London clubs like the Marquee and the Crawdaddy Club. With Eric it was a blues band."

Relf wasn't interested in the same type of music as Page. While Page was getting into longer, free-form pieces like "I'm Confused," Relf preferred shorter teen romance songs like "My Baby," which the group would also play at shows. There was a real contrast in material and style. And there was the problem of the records being poorly produced. For example, if Most hadn't produced *Little Games*, it might have been better. As far as Relf was concerned, trying to cash in on the so-called psychedelic sound was a total waste. What the producer came up with was not always what the band had in mind. By now, the Yardbirds were just getting off on sound and feedback. Relf pointed out that musical and member changes made the band more and more crazy. "So, you got a pretty schizoid kind of sound. I mean the band can't undergo those changes without bearing some kind of shock—without direction being sort of blurred."

Due to this lack of clear direction, being worn out from tours, and wanting to start something new, Relf and McCarty had enough. On the contrary, Page was fresh and enthusiastic and still wanted to rock out on the road. He was also much more disciplined than Relf and McCarty, who simply didn't care anymore. At twenty-four, Page was already a seasoned professional. As far as Page was concerned, the show always must go on, which was an attitude that Relf and McCarty snickered at. No one obviously wanted to work together for a common goal anymore, which disappointed Page. "When I joined the Yardbirds, my main reason was to give myself the opportunity of playing my own music," Page stated. "Before that, my only interest was session work. I began to feel limited not being able to express myself. When I left, it was for almost exactly the same reasons. The group split because everyone began to feel the need to go in his own direction. The pity is, there would have still been great potential."

The group's end happened in disagreement over an upcoming gig. The incident was symbolic of how some members had lost the enthusiasm for playing together. Grant remembered, "It was the end of a tour and there was a day off and they were offered five thousand dollars to do a gig in Miami. Jimmy and Chris Dreja said, 'Yeah, we'll do the gig,' but the others said, 'Screw that.' Five thousand dollars was a hell of a lot of money in 1967, so there was a row and the others said, 'We quit!' I said okay, but I drafted a letter and had them sign it. It gave Jimmy the name the Yardbirds."

Grant called Page up and gave him the bad news: the Yardbirds were finished. It was the end of a unique music era. Page was left standing at the crossroads. He could resume his session work, return to art school, or seek out musicians for a new group who could at least follow his ideas, if not elaborate on them. Grant added that he and Page now had ownership of the name and that there were some Scandinavian dates for the fall if Page was interested. He replied that he was.

There were some considerations in forming a new band. First was the type of music: Page had taken a liking to quieter, acoustic folk music like Pentangle and Joni Mitchell. But after Beck's first album *Truth* came out in July 1968, and seeing Cream's success, it looked like there was potential for another heavy-sounding British blues band. Next was how the group was to be managed and produced. Page had seen what had happened to the Yardbirds, with the exploitive Epic label, the parade of managers, and the bungled record production. Many teenagers had discovered the magic of listening to stereo mixes on headphones, and Page knew it. This time around there would be complete artistic control, from the recording studio down to the advances and touring fees. Grant and Page knew from experience what they wanted, and they were very determined to get it. This paved the way for the Led Zeppelin master plan. During their final year together, the Yardbirds had made money from tours because of Grant's presence, so Page had complete faith in his abilities. Now they needed to find the rest of the group.

The three former teenage music freaks who would join were now musicians who had paid their dues. John Paul Jones, a family man, was tired of arranging forty to fifty scores a month and was more than ready to leave studio work. It had gotten to the point where he would put a piece of score paper in front of him and just stare at it. Then Jones heard that Page was starting a band. Their paths had crossed before in sessions with Donovan. Page remembered the rest this way, "He got wind of it from somebody, and called me up and said, 'Are you starting a group?' And I said, 'Well, yeah—thinking of getting something together.' 'Well, I'd like to get involved in that.' I said, 'Great—you're in.'"

Page also told Jones that he was going to see a singer that Terry Reid told him about. The singer sang in a not too promising band named Hobstweedle. Also, the singer had a funny name: Robert Plant. Page went up to see Plant sing at a teacher's training college outside of Birmingham. There was an audience of about twelve, and the prime reason they were there was for the drinks. But what Page saw in the singer intrigued him. In his hippie caftan and beads, Plant shrieked out Moby Grape and Jefferson Airplane songs and bounced around the stage. The material wasn't such a big deal to Page, because he'd seen the actual bands whose songs Plant was singing. But the wild range that this singer reached was incredible. Page walked up to Plant after the show and introduced himself. He invited Plant down to his Pangbourne boathouse to talk about music and exchange ideas. Plant accepted the offer.

When Plant showed up at Page's house, Page told Plant that he was going to the store and to just pull out some records to play until he got back. Afterward, Page and Plant began to laugh when they found out that Plant had chosen the same records that Page was planning to play for him. Among them was Joan Baez's version of "Babe I'm Gonna Leave You," and the two threw around different ideas. Maybe they would be more like a band that sounded like the Incredible String Band, an acoustic Renaissance-style group, or one that was more heavier sounding, with a blues emphasis.

For the latter concept, Plant said that he knew of a drummer who was perfect. He was so enthusiastic that he hitchhiked up to Oxford to run down the drummer, his friend John Bonham. He was on tour with Tim Rose and was making steady money for the first time. When Plant asked him to drop everything and join the Yardbirds, Bonham shook his head. Here he was, finally earning good money to support his family, and here comes his nutty singer friend asking him to join a band that had become lost in American pop history. The Yardbirds were now largely ignored in England, and it looked pretty much like Page was creating a new Yardbirds lineup, modeling the format somewhat on the old group. It was a gamble, and a risky one at that. It wasn't only the 30 pounds a week Bonham was earning either; the success of the Tim Rose gigs brought in other offers to Bonham. Joe Cocker wanted him, and so did Chris Farlowe. Bonham turned down Plant for the time being.

Page decided to go see Bonham play at a Tim Rose gig in North London's Country Club. After he heard the drummer's relentless, heavy pounding, Page knew what his new band would emphasize. Bert Jansch's Pentangle had been a stylistic consideration for Page before—the softer, intricate folk rhythms that recalled the English countryside. But now with Bonham's approach, the group would instead have a blues-rock punch that would leap out at audiences. There was no doubt about it, the new Yardbirds had to get Bonham. But it wasn't easy because he didn't have a phone. Plant tried to help by sending eight telegrams to Bonham's favorite drinking haunt in Walsall, the pub Three Men in a Boat. Then Grant sent no less than forty more telegrams! But getting the heavy-handed drummer seemed nearly impossible.

The breakthrough came when Bonham thought about the music

that he wanted to play. He knew that Page was a top guitarist and that his syncopated, rock-steady rhythms would fit in well with Page's riffs. Bonham also enjoyed Plant's wild, unrestrained style. Plus, Plant was an old friend of his, so it might be fun, and Bonham finally decided that playing for enjoyment was most important. Page had clued him in on what the music would sound like, and Bonham compared that to what Farlowe and Cocker had to offer. There was no doubt: what Page's group had to offer sounded like the best music. He wired Grant and accepted the offer. Everything was in place at last and Page planned a rehearsal. But no one had any idea of the power that was about to be let loose. It was time to carry the Yardbirds torch forward. It was time for the launching of Led Zeppelin.

CHAPTER 2

"You Shook Me"

Jimmy Page, Robert Plant, John Paul Jones, and John Bonham gathered together for the first time in a small, stuffy London basement filled with wall-to-wall amplifiers during the fall of 1968. It was a curious mix of the two experienced session musicians and two untried talents from the Midlands. This was the big test, or tryout, and every one of them was nervous. After some discussion, Page suggested the Yardbirds song "Train Kept A-Rollin'." "It's basically a twelve-bar blues. Easy: just G to A." He counted it out. It began a little rough, then the room exploded from behind the wailing chords and howling vocal pouring from reverberating amplifiers. Jones and Bonham were absolutely locked together as a rhythm section. At the end of the power onslaught, there were a lot of silly grins around. Maybe it was from the relief, or maybe from the knowledge that they were onto something. They were so turned on that they jumped to other numbers like Garnet Mimms's "As Long As I Have You," some old blues, rhythm and blues favorites, and finally back to the Yardbirds with "Dazed and Confused." The session was amazing, electrifying, and stunning. They were barely able to conceal their excitement of what lay ahead.

In that first hour, they found their identity. The prototype Led

Zeppelin was baptized: the rock guitar of Page, the blues vocals of Plant, the jazz-bass of Jones, and the power drumming of Bonham. Each one was strong and the chemistry of the four together was awesome. Faced with a prior Yardbirds commitment, the four musicians began rehearsing a stage act at Page's house. After only fifteen hours of practice, the foursome had hammered out a set of material on double quick time. Along with old Yardbirds numbers and ancient specimens of the blues, there were also brand new compositions to complete the playlist.

Leaving Britain, the quartet shot out to Scandinavia for a week's worth of gigs. Thus, it was a nervous, but highly expectant new lineup that took to the stage on the evening of September 7 at the Gladsaxe Teen Club, which was actually a school gymnasium on the outskirts of Copenhagen, Denmark. As a teenage Yardbirds fan, Jorgen Angel just happened to be there the first night that Led Zeppelin played together as a group. Angel had secured a position as house photographer at this club that would become the launching pad for careers of some of rock's biggest bands. The club came alive with enthusiastic music fans who wanted to find out about emerging talent in the rock field.

Said Angel, "They had this place in a school hall and they made an evening for young people every Saturday night. No alcohol. The hall could hold about one thousand people. I was told the Yardbirds were coming and I thought, 'Ah, that sounds great.' I was really looking forward to it. You could actually say I was disappointed even before the concert started because I was looking forward to seeing the Yardbirds again, and what we were getting was one Yardbirds member and three totally unknown guys."

When September 7 finally came around, it didn't take long for Angel—and many others in the small crowd—to be won over by the exciting new band. The day of the show, Angel remembered, "They turned up at the school in the afternoon when the people from the club were hanging up the decorations—colored light bulbs and so on—to make the gymnasium look a little less like a gymnasium. The band asked if they could rehearse while the decorations were put up. So they rehearsed." When fans showed up, they didn't know what was to come, but they paid the cost of admission, $1 to $1.50. The hall slowly filled up. It was time for their first live performance as a band.

The New Yardbirds opened with "Train Kept A-Rollin'"—a nod to Yardbirds fans like Angel. Then the band blasted through a set containing embryonic versions of the songs that would become their first album: "I Can't Quit You," "You Shook Me," and "Dazed and Confused," as well as the blues chestnut of "The Hunter" that evolved into "How Many More Times." Armed with his mom's vacation flash camera, Angel cruised up to the side of the stage, took close-up pictures, and also worked his way into the crowd and got some shots as the band sweated away. Their set lasted about forty-five minutes or so. The band was still green around the edges and the notes were not all correct, but the feeling was there. Even though the speakers broke down, Plant's voice was so powerful that you could still hear him at the back of the auditorium.

Most importantly, the first tour taught them how to play together for maximum effect and gave them a taste of audience reaction to their songs. There was an outrageous volume, along with a freshness and invigorating spirit on the cover songs. But it was the new, original material of "Good Times Bad Times" and "I Can't Quit You Baby" that flung out a barrage of Page's psychedelic solos and electrifying, powerful blues. Plant said later that when the band broke into "You Shook Me," he hadn't planned to moan along with Page's descending notes during "You shook me all night looooooooong." It simply happened. Within seconds, the music was transferred to the audience. The four musicians felt it, built on it, and then madly threw it out to the crowd. Crunching notes were hammered into everyone's heads. The sheer attack of volume definitely shook some brains loose, whether it was a segue of "Train Kept A-Rollin'" into "Communication Breakdown" or the crashing, ominous climax to "Dazed and Confused." The instantaneous combustion of that first rehearsal was now being whirled around in an electronic testing ground. Willie Dixon's "You Shook Me" was the perfect musical metaphor for what had just been born with this new band. Zeppelin's sound was a raw, loud, unbridled onslaught that attacked European audiences and shook eardrums like never before!

On their return to England and with contract obligations out of the way, the Yardbirds were no longer necessary, except as a name to draw attention at the first British shows. This was a new band with a different identity from the Yardbirds, so a new name was vital. Some strange ideas were at first tossed around, names like the Mad Dogs and the Whoopee Cushion. Then Page remembered a talk that he had with Keith Moon. Moon and the bassist John Entwistle were unhappy with the Who and were toying with the idea of forming a band with Page. In his typical British humor, Moon commented that the band would probably be a flop and go down like a "lead zeppelin." The name stuck, Page said, because "it seemed to fit the bill. It had something to do with the expression about a bad joke going over like a lead balloon." To avoid mispronunciation with *lead*, the *a* was taken out.

With the name settled, Led Zeppelin quickly began assimilating the heavy rock lessons of the Yardbirds, John Mayall's Bluesbreakers, Cream, Jimi Hendrix Experience, and the Jeff Beck Group with unerring precision. Fresh off the first tour and bursting with emotion, Page immediately wanted to go into a studio and commit the group to vinyl. In spite of their brief time together—only one month since their first rehearsal—Page was convinced they were ready. The manager Peter Grant booked an October session at London's Olympic Studios. The band wasted no time in completing the work. The album took only thirty hours total, spread out over two weeks, to put down on tape, an incredibly short time for an entire album. (Normal production time for albums then ran 150 to 250 hours.) They basically recorded their stage act from the Scandinavian gigs, which featured most of the songs they had played on tour.

Serving dual roles as musician and producer, Page captured the energy, the youthful enthusiasm, and the raw hunger of a band ready to take on the world. In the studio, he became the mastermind of the Zeppelin sound. Page explained, "I wanted Zeppelin to be a marriage of blues, hard rock, and acoustic music topped with heavy choruses—a combination that had never been done before. Lots of light and shade in the music." The quartet had taken advantage of Cream's recent demise and upped the blues-metal sweepstakes by making the music heavier and more ominous than it had ever been before. Even the Jeff Beck Group's hugely influential *Truth* album sounded thin compared to the booming Zeppelin debut.

Since the group's appearances would be to support the record, it was an effective approach for the music to have a "live" feel to it. Most tracks were cut with little overdubbing. Theirs was a sound that didn't overwhelm or engross the listener, but rather snuffed out any possible distraction. When listening, one had a sense of being surrounded. Page had heard that distance made depth, which in turn gave you a booming sound. In addition to close miking amps—just putting the microphone in front—he'd have a mike at the back of the band as well, and then balance the two. Page also knew that the drums had to sound good because they were going to be the backbone of the band: if you only close miked them, they sounded like someone hitting cardboard boxes. Page created the innovation of backward echo. This was reversing the tape, recording the echo, and then playing it back the right way again so the echo would precede the signal. The results of this technique can be heard at the end of "You Shook Me."

Page's sonic attack from thunder to distorted tones to echo were, incredibly, done with only a little, battered old Supro amp with a twelve-inch speaker, a wah-wah, a boost pedal, and a Fender Telecaster guitar. Plant recalled, "That first album was the first time that headphones meant anything to me. What I heard coming back to me over the cans while I was singing was better than the finest chick in all the land. It had so much weight, so much power, it was devastating. I had a long ways to go with my voice then, but at the same time the enthusiasm and spark of working with Jimmy's guitar shows through quite well. It was all very raunchy then. Everything was fitting together into a trademark for us."

It was clear that a whole new school of rock and roll had arrived. Wild, crunching power chords would play off more delicate passages. Plant's vocals would shriek, moan, croon, and then rise again to a sexual frenzy as Page's guitar began to cry out higher and higher notes. "Babe I'm Gonna Leave You" showed how arrangements could have slower, softer moments as when one floats downstream on glassy sheets of water—but then a change happened. The hard rock passages were like musical spaces that become bouncing rapids. Other mental pictures were conjured by "Good Times Bad Times." With the first few notes of Page's Telecaster, a slowly moving zeppelin came into view, its giant, dark shadow blotting out the sky as it floated overhead. Then with the middle guitar break, a great explosion flashed out in blinding yellow light. Like the *Hindenburg*, the great sky behemoth collapsed in flames. The cover art depicting this incident couldn't have been better. Led Zeppelin's debut album undoubtedly had no precedent.

I discovered this as a teenager, thanks to my friend Clyde Johnson, who'd had his interest in popular music ignited by seeing the Yardbirds Santa Monica Civic Auditorium show. Since then, he'd fanatically kept up on any new interesting rock albums through the 1960s. He had been in various bands in high school and now played guitar in a local band called the Warlock Convention, covering old Fleetwood Mac, Cream, and Yardbirds songs. Clyde's band often played at parties and at a La Crescenta church teen club, the Neutral Zone. Songs like "I'm a Man" got the full workout, and "Spoonful" was played for twenty psychedelic, jamming minutes. Whenever any new groundbreaking album came out, I'd usually first hear it at Clyde's house, which is exactly what happened with Zeppelin's debut release. He was pretty excited about it when he showed me the wild-looking cover, with its stark, black-and-white image of the *Hindenburg* about to crash. I commented to him that the guys on the back looked like they'd just come in from the woods, especially Plant and Page. I asked, "What kind of a name is 'Robert Plant'?"

"You gotta hear this! It's the new band Jimmy Page has," my pop music tutor declared. There was no turning back now, the record had already fallen onto the turntable. I heard most of the songs with my eyes closed. The first notes of "Good Times Bad Times" created a sort of musical hypnosis that changed with each song. On "You Shook Me," Page and Plant made like brawling alley cats in a call-and-response that brought the blues classic to a shrieking conclusion. When "Dazed and Confused" ended, there was a mind-paralyzing, threatening feeling in the room. The dark, menacing world painted by Page's echoing crashing guitar notes and Plant's wild cries drifted into memory as side two played.

Jones's brilliant organ introduction on "Your Time Is Gonna Come" created a vision of dawn's first rays. They broke over distant hillsides and slowly splintered the darkness into the brightness of morning. The remainder of the record rang with eclecticism. As Page strummed the first notes of "Black Mountain Side" and tablas came into play, one thought of either crowded streets in India or a quiet place where one could light the nearest stick of incense and meditate. An abrupt stop to "Black Mountain Side" brought a sizzling, rock and roll original that shook the walls, "Communication Breakdown." This one often opened shows on the 1969 tour. Perhaps Zeppelin was best at strong, heavy blues, as on "I Can't Quit You Baby." Intense organ, harmonica, and guitar solos showed that the different members excelled in this format. I opened my eyes for a second to see the clock, and saw that it was past midnight. It had been a long day, and I wondered if I was hearing things when "How Many More Times" came through the speakers. Plant's voice rose and fell with Page's guitar. The strange moans seemed to evolve out of the guitar's electricity. The voice wove around Page's notes like a spirit invading the record's grooves. When the guitar and drums reached their crescendo at the song's climax, I knew that it had been a first listening I would never forget!

After the overwhelming exuberance felt by the group when they recorded their album, the next couple of weeks were a complete letdown. England did not seem ready for them. British promoters greeted them with indifference. They played a few gigs at universities and at the Marquee in London, but failed to ignite the audience. America had to be the answer—it was ready and waiting. Page told Grant to take Led Zeppelin to the bank. So in November the ruthless Grant, standing over six feet tall and weighing over three hundred pounds, flew to New York with tapes and jacket artwork in hand. He was a heavy dude in more ways than one!

Using the guitarist's reputation with the Yardbirds as bait, he worked out a deal with Atlantic Records. Atlantic's check for a $200,000 advance—an almost unheard of sum in those days—signified the label's commitment and belief in the band. Under its landmark terms, the band was promised total creative control: their records would be produced independently, without any label interference. The group would also control all jacket artwork, press ads, publicity pictures, and anything else related to their image. In return, Atlantic would have world distribution rights. The unique cover design was by George Hardie, who was hired to create a facsimile of the photograph from the 1937 *Hindenburg* airship disaster. On a sheet of tracing paper, he drew a dot stipple interpretation of the zeppelin going down in flames, which became a striking image in black and white. This was the inventive spark of creative design that made a statement and joined musicians and cover artists together in the 1960s.

This kind of artistic control was virtually unprecedented for a rock band that was negotiating its first contract. But for Page, it was critical for Zeppelin's success. He saw how the Yardbirds had been poorly represented in their music and record covers, particularly with *Little Games*. Nothing like that was going to happen with Zeppelin; he knew how he wanted this new band to come across and he strove to make sure that it would happen. Page had complete confidence in his direction. With Grant's help, this would become common practice during the band's lifetime.

For the band members, it was like winning the lottery. But the music press was less ecstatic. Atlantic Records had promoted the deal to such an extent that jealousies were aroused. The press asked who was this "hyped" and unknown band that had popped out of nowhere? Who did this Led Zeppelin think they were? How could any artist be so important? Those questions would soon be answered. The Atlantic press release of late 1968 stated that "Zeppelin will be the next group to reach the heights achieved by Cream and Hendrix." As far as Atlantic's support went, Page stated, "I think the group can live up to everything Atlantic's done. I don't think they've made any outrageous statements."

Grant's strategy was to take a chance and unleash this unknown band on the great American public, even though the album had not been released. The United Kingdom had turned down its chance and if the group cracked it in America, they would almost certainly make it big back home. His previous experience in the United States as tour manager for the Animals served him well. He knew which venues would be most effective toward breaking the act and mapped out a one-month tour from December 1968 to January 1969 to hit key sites like the Fillmores East and West in New York and San Francisco, respectively, the Boston Tea Party, the Grande Ballroom in Detroit, and the Whisky a Go Go in Los Angeles. It was time to shake up the senses of both the audience and the music industry.

Led Zeppelin invaded America on Christmas Eve 1968. They would support headline acts like Vanilla Fudge and Iron Butterfly. At their first concert in Denver on December 26, they were not even listed on the bill. There was a risk factor in being the unknown opening act, but at the same time there was intense excitement in playing on American soil for the very first time. Also, they learned from Vanilla Fudge, who really improvised onstage a lot; they were great musicians with a very confident delivery. Fudge encouraged Led Zeppelin to open up, too. John Bonham saw the Fudge's drummer twirling his drumsticks, grabbing the cymbal on the left side, and attacking his drums and took notice.

On December 30, the group played at Gonzaga University, in Spokane, Washington, second on the bill to Vanilla Fudge. The gymnasium they played in was freezing. Plant told the crowd, "You won't believe this, but I don't think either ourselves or the equipment is used to the temperature. It's taken about three hours of gas stoves under the equipment before we can ever get it together." Since the debut album had yet to come out, there were covers interspersed throughout the set for the audience to relate to. The set opened with an explosive "Train Kept A-Rollin'," which flowed right into "I Can't Quit You." Next came Garnet Mimms's "As Long As I Have You," which became a vehicle for a medley of Spirit's "Fresh Garbage" and Otis Redding's "Shake." The show continued with Page showpieces: "Dazed and Confused" and "White Summer." Plant introduced "Dazed" by letting the crowd know that the song was from the upcoming album that would be out in three weeks.

The music reached its zenith with "How Many More Times" and Bonham's solo "Pat's Delight," named in reference to his wife and later to be renamed "Moby Dick." Just before the band erupted into this tune, Plant commented, "I think we're getting warmed up now." As the crowd filed out after the show, many probably thought to themselves that the opening band wasn't too bad at all.

Leaving the cold and snow behind in Denver, Seattle, Spokane, and Portland, the band almost didn't make it to sunny Los Angeles. Following the Portland show, Zeppelin began to drive back to Seattle to catch a flight to Los Angeles. They drove through a snowstorm so powerful that a state patrolman pulled them off the road and told them to stop driving. But Grant was determined to make it through and forged on despite the protestations of the band's road manager and driver, almost sending the car over an embankment. Panic-stricken and arriving in Seattle four hours later, they realized the reason the airport was so deserted: it was New Year's Eve! Someone suggested getting drinks, but Plant and Bonham were both under twenty-one years old and were denied entrance to the bar.

The following day the weather had cleared and they flew to Los Angeles, which warmed to Led Zeppelin and offered the band leisure opportunities. The news was already out on the street that Zeppelin would be playing at the Whisky a Go Go from January 2 to 5. This location was already a historic place: many other acts had played there before going on to superstardom, among them Frank Zappa and the Mothers of Invention, Jimi Hendrix, Cream, and Janis Joplin. The Doors appeared there as the house band in the summer of 1966 before they had even put out a record.

Rodney Bingenheimer, affectionately known as the mayor of Sunset Strip, was there when Zeppelin hit town. His involvement in the music business was varied: he was a stand-in for Davy Jones on the Monkees television show, later he had his own club, Rodney's English Pub, and he became a radio host on KROQ. He had later been partially responsible for David Bowie getting signed to RCA—and even had wild times with Page during the Yardbirds. He and Page first met at a teenage fair in San Jose, and then later they ran into each other at a Los Angeles party. Bingenheimer recalled, "I met him at this guy's house named Earl Lee, who was the happening photographer at the time. He always used to throw parties up at his little house. And I remember Earl Lee, myself, and the Yardbirds going to a love-in at Griffith Park. There was a riot there and the cops were chasing us all around. So we went back to Earl's house and hung out with a bunch of girls and things."

When Zeppelin played at the Whisky with Alice Cooper, Bingenheimer was again at the center of events and emceed the show. Zeppelin was second on the bill and was given the smaller of two dressing rooms. Afterward, Bingenheimer noticed Page backstage practically turning green from a bad case of the flu. A doctor was called in, who told Page that he was insane to do the set. But Page always believed that the show must go on, so he played anyway with a temperature over 104. He was given some shots that helped him get through that night's set. Despite any shortcomings, the Whisky shows became legendary.

Located on the Sunset Strip, the Whisky held about 300 people. It was like a large, teenage insane asylum on the small, cramped dance floor. There was no age limit, and once the band started playing in this smoky, beer-soaked environment, almost anything could happen. Unlike an asylum, the Whisky had a cover charge, and it was inhabited by people who thrived on crowds, excitement, and loud music. People who hung out there included rock stars, any other hardcore music freaks, and various other assorted Hollywood characters. Without a doubt, the Whisky was the premier club on the strip. There were also a variety of wilder-than-life groupies. These women were the type who would literally do anything to get to meet and spend the night with their favorite musician. Page noted, "Playing music is a very sexual act. . . . Groupies are a better ball, by and large, you know; they've had more experience and they're willing to try more things. The sex angle is important. But no more important than girls who are also good friends and make you feel like family." An interviewer asked Page who's been their best lay and what names come up most often. Page laughed and replied, "They all say *I'm* the best!"

Pamela Des Barres, née Miller, known as "Miss Pamela," was

queen of the Los Angeles groupies and the Whisky was her very own personal living room in 1969. Led Zeppelin did more than get her attention. According to her, "The band stormed onto the stage and swept me up in the hard, *hard*, twisting, turning, churning, thunderous, heaviest of all metal, until I was a sopping, wrung-out, gleeful basket case. Majestic Robert Plant was the haughty wailing prince. John Paul Jones, enigmatic and elegant, epitomized a British musician. John Bonham was busy melting his drums down to liquid fire, steam pouring out of his sticks. The divine Jimmy Page wore pink velvet, his ebony curls clung to damp, flushed cheeks as he created guitar licks that redefined rock and roll."

There was another Yardbirds fan in the audience that night who had met Page after the Yardbirds Santa Monica Civic Auditorium show in 1967, an amateur photographer, Norwood Price. He asked Page what made the band's distinctive sound, and Page replied by asking Price if he owned a Telecaster. Price said he did, which wasn't actually the case since a Fender like that cost $220 new, a huge amount for a teenager in those days. Page then told Price that he set the guitar toggle switch between the detent positions. This meant that more pickup combinations could be activated and different sounds could be created. (Fender would later incorporate this revision in later versions of the Telecaster.) Price appreciated the Yardbirds' innovative style and would see and photograph them in 1968 at L.A.'s Shrine Auditorium and then Led Zeppelin twice the following year. At the Whisky, he was able to work his way around the dancers up front to take pictures of the band. He got right next to Page during "White Summer" to capture him playing his Danelectro, and then moved a little farther back to take some group shots.

Price heard some rumors that Page was staying at the Chateau Marmont, an ancient hotel resting on a hill off the Sunset Strip. It is one of the most famous Hollywood landmarks. Actors, writers, and producers all called the chateau their home away from home; now the rock musicians had taken it over. Since he used his own darkroom, the next day he made eight-by-ten photos of the Whisky concert and drove over to the hotel. Page was registered under his own name, so Price called him on the hotel phone and offered to give Page the photos. The two agreed to meet at the hotel pool. Page lounged poolside with a young lady friend and a bottle of wine and viewed the photos. Price asked Page why he still used the Telecaster, as more rock and blues players were now using the Les Paul. Page succinctly responded, "It gets the job done." After a few more minutes of conversation, Price left the photos with Page, who seemed pleased with the gift.

Page had a good friend that he knew from the Yardbirds days, photographer Chuck Boyd. He was the premier photographer in the L.A. music scene throughout the 1960s and had taken photos of anyone and everyone, from the Beatles and Rolling Stones to Jefferson Airplane, the Doors, Jimi Hendrix, and the Yardbirds. Page handed Boyd a test pressing of the first album, and with a sly grin told him there was some "garbage" on it. The garbage sure sounded pretty good to Boyd once he got home and spun the record. He would be given total access to Zeppelin—in the dressing room, onstage, and in the recording studio. Not at all pushy, Boyd was just down to earth and blended in with everyone else. Being a fan of rock music, he'd travel to the shows and became one of those rare people that Zeppelin trusted and believed in. As a result, Boyd was able to take some incredible and intimate pictures of the band in 1969 and 1970.

Before leaving L.A., the band members took on the sights and sounds of Hollywood. It was an experience they would never forget. "Bonzo and I were amazed," Plant recalled. "We'd barely even been abroad, and here we were. It was the first time I saw a cop with a gun, the first time I saw a twenty-foot-long car. The whole thing was a complete bowl-over. . . . I went wandering down Sunset Strip with no shirt on. . . . Frank Zappa's girl group, the GTO's, were upstairs. We threw eggs, had silly water battles, and had all the good fun that a nineteen-year-old boy should have."

An indelible mark had been made on the Hollywood crowd. After the Whisky gigs, word spread like a spark in a dry tinderbox canyon. Here was a band that had something new to deliver in heavy blues, played their asses off, and delivered the goods onstage. The futuristic sound of the Yardbirds had been thrust light years ahead! And this was only the beginning. Local music visionaries wondered what was to come next, but no one could imagine the creative twists and turns the band would take.

Their next set of dates from January 9 to 12 was at the Fillmore West in San Francisco, where they would support Country Joe and the Fish and Taj Mahal. It would be a significant breakthrough if they could crack San Francisco, the home turf of the Grateful Dead and Jefferson Airplane. Zeppelin realized the moment was theirs to seize. Page was nearly over the flu, and the band was getting used to American audiences. "Everyone else in the group was happy to see me better, and we really started to play from that point on," Page noted. "That's the nice thing about American audiences . . . they just want to see what you can do."

"If you're going to San Francisco, make sure you wear some flowers in your hair," sang Scott McKenzie. The band almost wore seaweed in their hair from a hilarious experience while being on the road there. The road manager could never find anything. Plant recalled, "We were in San Francisco looking for the Fillmore. We were down somewhere by Fisherman's Wharf in the fog in this Oldsmobile Cruiser, me and Bonham fooling around in the back and Jimmy saying, 'Close the window. My hair, my hair!' The road manager was backing up and suddenly the car wasn't going anywhere, but he was accelerating really hard and he backed up on the capstan [those things that tie up the boats]. Had he missed that by nine inches either side, we would have reversed quite merrily into the San Francisco Bay."

On their first visit, the band electrified the mellow Fillmore hippie crowd by going straight into "Communication Breakdown" with a ferocious attack. You could almost see people's jaws drop and have puzzled looks, wondering what was the deal. The audience was stunned. By the third night, there was total intimacy with the audience. Plant remembered, "I looked over at Bonzo and thought, 'Christ, we've got something!' That was the first time we realized the Led Zeppelin might mean something." Just like L.A., San Francisco was conquered by the Zeppelin attack.

Bill Erickson was a fan who witnessed one of the early shows and had the chance to meet the band between sets. Wearing a Yardbirds T-shirt and a black leather jacket like Page's, he had just had his senses pulverized from the front row. Bill and his brother, Richard, hung out for a while in the concert hall in an effort to regain their senses. Then, as they went down a hallway they saw an open door, looked in, and saw Page there alone. Both went in and Bill said to Page that he liked Zeppelin better than the Yardbirds. Page replied, "You're very kind . . . actually, we've been a bit nervous about coming here."

Then the rest of the band came in, and the brothers nearly went into shock. Introductions went around. Then Richard told Page that he was better than other acts going around—Jeff Beck, Pete Townsend, and Jimi Hendrix. Bonham replied, "That's what I keep telling everybody. He's better than all that lot." Page asked the brothers how they thought the band came across to the crowd, and Richard said, "You guys are cool, man!" Bill added that he'd enjoyed seeing the Yardbirds but thought that Zeppelin was more balanced. Then Page commented that he put a lot of thought into getting the band together and wanted the top musicians. To which Bonham said, "But he stumbled on us instead!" Everyone laughed at that comment.

Then before the conversation ended, Bill told Page that he couldn't believe what he had heard in Yardbirds songs with Page, like "Think about It" and "White Summer." Page quickly responded by saying that the impact of those songs was present more than ever with this new band. In short, with this tour there was now a wild new music that shook audiences from coast to coast. Led Zeppelin had arrived, there was no turning back, and rock entertainment would never be the same again.

In spite of the positive response from audiences, Zeppelin's first U.S. visit was conducted under less than optimal conditions. The group traveled by station wagon between West Coast shows and were paid an average of $700 a show. Plant operated the band's PA system from the stage with a 150-watt amplifier, which was about as loud as a television set that only had a treble and bass control. The sound box was placed in front of the bass drum to change the volume of Plant's voice. Page's equipment was minimal: his psychedelic painted Telecaster, a Harmony acoustic, a bunch of Rickenbacker cabinets left over from the Yardbirds, and a mix of amps—mostly Vox and Fenders. Jones used his 1961 Fender jazz bass, and Bonham played, for the most part, without miking his drum kit.

Still, from that point on, Led Zeppelin took off. Their debut self-titled album was released to teenage ears on January 12, 1969, and would remain on the charts for a remarkable seventy-three consecutive weeks! The group's popularity was achieved primarily through word of mouth that started spreading everywhere across the States. Plus, Grant had sent out test pressings to underground FM stations. After San Francisco it was on to Detroit. The Grande Ballroom had a gaudy midwestern hippodrome look and was the mecca of the Detroit rock scene. Almost everyone of musical importance in the city was in attendance. It was once the site of stately waltzes and high-priority social affairs. Now, the neighborhood was run down, but if you were over fifteen and able to pay, you could still dance.

Led Zeppelin had about one hour's worth of original material. When the multiple encores started, they reached into their grab bag of cover tunes. There was a large sampling of songs the band liked and many audiences knew. Zeppelin whipped up quickie versions of, among other things, the Isley Brothers' "It's Your Thing," Spirit's "Fresh Garbage," the Beatles' "I Saw Her Standing There," and "As Long As I Have You."

The Boston Tea Party's four-night run near the end of the month was another milestone. Jones fondly remembered "playing for four hours on the last night and if anyone knew more than four bars of any tune, we would go into it. It was the greatest night. I will never forget that. It was unbelievable. Peter Grant was in tears at the end of it, putting his arms around all of us. We were all crying in the dressing room. That was it. We knew that we had definitely done it by then." The packed house demanded and received seven encores.

Another triumph of their first tour went down at their New York debut at Bill Graham's Fillmore East. This venue had become the center of the rock universe in America; it was practically the church of rock for fans and one of the most important gigs for any artist. It had been an old movie palace, a gothic hall that held 2,500. Graham had already hosted numerous shows with the likes of Jimi Hendrix, Janis Joplin, the Who, and the Doors. Now it was Zeppelin's turn. Perhaps nothing is more telling with regard to the changes that were about to happen in popular music than what took place on the evening of Led Zeppelin's first appearance there, January 31, 1969. Iron Butterfly was the headliner on the strength of their hit "In-A-Gadda-Da-Vida." Zeppelin was only an opening act. But Butterfly appeared dated and old and it would only be a matter of time—actually that evening—before Zeppelin would lead rock into the 1970s.

Howard Fields was "thrilled beyond belief to be seeing Led Zeppelin. If you weren't a Yardbirds fan, it's unlikely you knew Jimmy Page's name and no one knew at all who Plant, Bonham, and Jones were. Being in the first row didn't hurt either. I remember the first song, 'The Train Kept A-Rollin' like it was yesterday. It jumped right out at us right at the start—very exciting! I also remember Plant's beautiful blues singing on 'I Can't Quit You Baby.' Of course, for some years I had a tape of the show which I recorded with a Wollensak cassette recorder. However, the *most* vivid memory to me, as a fledgling drummer, was of John Bonham's animalistic approach and awesome bass drum ability that had never been done before."

By the third song, the audience was already worked up when Page looked at Plant, and said, "Now let's really get down to it." From that moment on it was pure magic. Page led the band through two hours of nonstop TNT rock. Each song built to a resounding climax that left the audience absolutely breathless. At the conclusion of the performance and after several encores, the emcee came out and said, "I think we have just witnessed the new kings of heavy metal!" All you could hear in the hall were shouts of "Zeppelin, Zeppelin, Zeppelin."

Another spectator at the Fillmore East show was Hugh Jones, the future editor of the Zeppelin fanzine *Proximity*. He remembered this event as one unlike anything before. As a young teenager who lived fifty miles north of New York City, the Fillmore was a little piece of heaven on earth for him. Since he'd just turned twelve in late 1968, Jones was fortunate that his parents let him go with friends to some early shows. For him, going to the Fillmore was literally entering another world. He remembered, "From the moment we walked into the Fillmore's crowded lobby, the whole scene was blowing my impressionable young mind. Longhairs and freaks from wall to wall, the hip and the hipper seeing and being seen, and beautiful bra-less hippie girls casually smoking joints and smiling at what must have been a stunned, open-mouthed gape on my face."

As Jones entered the concert hall, he was greeted with the light show screen that welcomed him by saying, "Welcome to the Fillmore East, Joshua Light Show." As always, this prestigious visual treat would offer swirling, psychedelic light patterns that went along with what was played. Jones remarked that the opening number created something real, nearly physical, "The drums sounded like thunder and you could feel the bass; the guitar was like a physical presence in the hall, and within this thunderous muddy roar came a wail that pierced through it all. It took a couple of seconds to realize it was the vocalist."

Jones's further recollections describe a band of musical intensity that elevated the audience to a new musical realm. After Plant's slow opening line of the next song, "I Can't Quit You," the band slammed into the slow blues with a vicious wall of sound. People took sideways glances to see others' reactions—everyone was mesmerized! In skin-tight velvet pants and a ruffled open-necked shirt, Plant whirled around the stage, singing off Page. In crushed velvet bell-bottoms and a leather jacket, Page attacked his Telecaster with hair hanging in his face. Jones stood stock still, stared into space, and created solid bass lines. And thundering through it all was Bonham, whom Jones described as a maniac, "Bonham is flailing away, arms flying above his head, and creating these syncopated things between snare, tom, and bass drum that defy description. He plays so loud it shakes the walls, and then he brings it down to a whisper as Page does the same, just for a few phrases and then they crash into the final guitar solo and 'I Can't Quit You' comes to a close."

As the spectacle went on, more surprises were unveiled: Page dragged his violin bow across his Telecaster's strings on "Dazed and Confused" as Plant moaned in unison. Bonham drove the audience wild with his drum solo on "Pat's Delight." Plant introduced the band in the jazzy bass line intro during "How Many More Times," then Page threw in some "Smokestack Lightning" riffs for the Yardbirds fans. A frenzied encore of "You Shook Me" had a duel between Page and Plant. They leaned into each other, and Page's guitar shrieked as he ran his slide up the neck, and Plant mimicked each note until Page lost—since he ran out of guitar neck to go up on!

The audience was shaken into ecstasy, and everyone screamed for more as the song crashed to a close and the house lights went on. When the light show screen flashed "More?" in big letters, the roar became deafening. Out went the house lights. The band came out and exploded into a frantic "Communication Breakdown." The excitement and energy going back and forth from performers to audience was inescapable! Jones summed up the night by concluding, "The lights went up again and everyone was grinning at each other, shaking their heads—the buzz in the hall was tangible. We'd all been witness to something very special, something we'd never forget."

On their first tour, Led Zeppelin stormed across America like an army possessed, taking no prisoners. They started off not even on the bill in Denver, and by the time they got to New York City they were second to Iron Butterfly, who didn't even want to go on. Zeppelin's massive, overpowering sound was in no small way due to perhaps the most important instrument in rock: the drums. Without Bonham, there is no doubt that Zeppelin's sound never would have made the unbelievable impact on audiences that it did. But no one realized the influences that certain bands of the time had made on Bonham. Vanilla Fudge was another band that specialized in a heavy sound. The drummer Carmine Appice had a drum setup that Bonham liked so much that he wanted the same setup for himself. Appice explained it this way, "John was really freaked out by the Vanilla Fudge albums. One of the things that really freaked Bonzo out was the drum set which I had, which, at the time, was two twenty-six-inch bass drums, a twelve-by-fifteen marching tom, a small tom-tom, a sixteen-by-eighteen tom, a twenty-two-inch bass drum over on its side as the big tom, and a six-and-a-half-inch snare. I mean, it totally freaked him out as it did a lot of the English drummers. He wanted the same drum set I had. I remember to this day calling up Ludwig [the drum manufacturer] and telling them about this group, Led Zeppelin, that I thought was going to be big, and that the drummer wanted a duplicate drum set. Six months later Vanilla Fudge and Led Zeppelin went out together on an equal bill, and we both had the same set of drums—the first maple set in rock and roll."

Bonham's playing technique definitely deviated from the mainstream pop music that had a stronghold in England at the time—surf music like the Beach Boys and the Ventures—as well as the English equivalent that the English threw back to America—Herman's Hermits, Dave Clark Five, and the Searchers. To develop his style, Bonham had done a careful study of twelve-bar blues and listened to Cream's drummer, Ginger Baker, whom he respected. Bonham was drawn to Baker's straight-eighth feel, the open bass drum work that gave a ringing sound, and especially the flashy stage presence. Baker pushed the drums to the front of the limelight. Gene Krupa, a jazz drummer of the 1950s, considered drums more than just a backing instrument and took percussion to a higher level. Bonham noted that "people hadn't taken much notice of drums really before Krupa. And Ginger Baker was responsible for the same thing in rock. Rock music had been around for a few years before Baker, but he was the first to come out with this 'new' attitude—that a drummer could be a forward musician in a rock band."

Because of his solid, exuberant style, Bonham became more than noticeable at shows. He was anything but content to plod along in the background in straight time. His sound was as important as the vocals or guitar, whether on record or in concert. His drums were the hard drive of the band. However, his drum kit ended up being quite a simple affair. As Zeppelin hit the road, what Bonham took with him was a fourteen-by-twenty-six bass drum, a twelve-by-fifteen small tom that was first mounted on a snare stand and then later on a Ludwig bass drum rail mount, sixteen-by-sixteen and sixteen-by-eighteen floor toms, and often a Supra-Phonic six-and-a-half-by-fourteen snare that had a Speed King foot pedal with a wood or hard felt beater. For cymbals, he had a Paiste eighteen inch on his left and a Paiste twenty inch on the right, as well as a sixteen inch farther to the left and fifteen-inch Sound Edge high hats. He always used Ludwig drum shells, although they changed from wood to stainless steel. As time went on, he added a timpani and a thirty-eight-inch gong. With this setup, Bonham set out to revolutionize rock as never before. He always experimented, challenging himself and the band. Most of all, more than any other drummer he was a contributor to the music, shaping the songs.

With Plant's stunning voice, Page's guitar virtuosity, Jones's solid musicianship, and Bonham's intense drumming, there have been few rock groups who hit the United States with as much impact as Led Zeppelin. The music always came first. "Once we were onstage, we all assumed equal status," Jones said. There were no egos, but a genuine respect was built up between the members for each other. After their conquest in America, the band should have had a triumphant homecoming. Their album had reached Number 90 and was steadily climbing up the Billboard charts, and their live shows were resounding successes. But back in London, Page was unhappy. The critics, and in particular the influential rock magazine *Rolling Stone*, had knocked their tracks, even though rock radio stations in the United States had made them underground hits. In the March 15 issue, John Mendelsohn wrote, "'Good Times Bad Times' might have been ideal for a Yardbirds' B-side. . . . 'Babe I'm Gonna Leave You' is very dull in places (especially on the vocal passages), very redundant, and certainly not worth the six-and-a-half minutes the Zeppelin gives it." And Mendelsohn came down hard on Page by saying, "He is also a very limited producer and a writer of weak, unimaginative songs."

When Page read the review, he couldn't believe it. In his naivete he thought the band had done a good album and were doing all right, and then all this venom came flying out. He couldn't understand why or what he'd done to deserve this type of review. After that, the band was very wary of the press. To hell with critics. I had also bought a copy of that issue at 35¢ and couldn't believe

the review of their first album either. I thought that it was a masterpiece. Were Mendelsohn and I listening to the same album? By
the year's end, Mendelsohn would eat his words.

Zeppelin's debut album, although released in the States two
months earlier, still hadn't reached the shelves in England. The
English press had taken only a small amount of interest in Led
Zeppelin, and the English audience had not yet embraced Zeppelin
in quite the same way that Americans had. As a platform to present their music to British listeners, Zeppelin performed a variety of
radio shows for the BBC. This was the first exposure for many to a
band that was causing such an uproar in all the music papers.

American audiences were much more aware of what was happening musically. And the United States was so massive (a vast
teenage wasteland) that there would be more chance of airplay and
more places for them to gig where their type of music would be
appreciated. By the time Led Zeppelin set off on its second U.S.
tour in April 1969, their album had reached Number 10 on the
American charts and already they were a headline act. The fans
kept coming. In a sense, the press backlash was a compliment to
the band. They'd arrived with such force and such confidence that
they'd rendered the approval of the press unnecessary.

Their schedule was heavy. Nearly thirty shows in as many
days and yet they devastated audiences night after night with dazzling performances at which fans screamed for more. Their stage-
craft would involve Page taking a violin bow and beating it across
the strings to hypnotize the crowds in grand sorcerer tradition.
Plant would develop an overtly sexual wolf as he howled at the
moon in that distinctive primeval wail. Bonham blistered through
the drum solo for twenty minutes, sometimes using his bare hands.
Jones was usually in the background, shunning the spotlight, but
always steady and sure, always coming through on bass and keyboards. He was content to focus his energy on anchoring one of
rock's most dynamic rhythm sections. "I would listen to the bass
drum and be very careful not to cross it or diminish its effective-

ness," Jones said. "I really wanted the drums and bass to be as one unit—that's what drove the band along. It was important to be rock solid so Jimmy and Robert could be more free to improvise and experiment." City after city surrendered to the power of their onslaught and not a spare ticket could be found.

At the Fillmore West in San Francisco on April 27, Page and Bonham kicked off "Train Kept A-Rollin'" with drums and guitar interplay that warmed up for Page's first train whistle notes. Then the song exploded into the chugging progression before the first verse. When the tune "I Can't Quit You Baby" slammed to a stop, next came a song from Plant's Band of Joy era: "As Long As I Have You." Zeppelin proved that this wasn't just another plain old rock concert, with a predictable set of songs in a neat package, like the Beatles and Rolling Stones shows had become. A long jam ensued, with both new and old tunes: "Fresh Garbage," "Cat's Squirrel," "I'm a Man," and "No Money Down." Each song led into the next one.

Plant sang verses from different songs, and Page at times just played the chords. There was a real feeling of spontaneity, and this part helped stretch the set out to about two hours. Later on, "Sittin' and Thinkin'," a classic blues from Buddy Guy, caught everyone by surprise. Plant moaned out the first lines, showing the tormented soul of a man who knows that his woman has left. Page banged out some descending heavy chords. Then Plant screamed about her messing with his mind and going out on him, and a screeching note blasted from Page's amplifier, sounding like what happens when the mind snaps. But Plant ended the first verse with the feel of a man still in control, "I don't think I'm gonna move into your neighborhood." The audience was surrounded with Zeppelin's form of blues: slow, menacing, and very effective.

The evil that women do became a common theme for Zeppelin. Robert Johnson's compelling messages about the Devil's troubling presence was updated into songs about relationships, as heard in "Dazed and Confused," "Your Time Is Gonna Come," and "How

Many More Times." This type of songwriting cemented Zeppelin's image as a hard-rocking band that had machismo to spare. Blues songs were a perfect vehicle to say how the woman "did in" the man. But with Page's personal relationships, it was just the complete opposite. As Pamela Des Barres became increasingly romantically fixated on Page, she would begin to live out the first four lines of "Dazed and Confused" more and more. Page completely controlled their relationship. To hear Des Barres describe it, Page had a woman's emotions wired like a television. He could flip to any channel, turn up the sound, do a little fine-tuning, and then watch the results of his actions.

"He knew what to say all right; he could have given a master's course in how to turn a fairly sane girl into a twittering ninny. . . . I could feel myself falling apart and turning into one of those gooey unrecognizable substances. . . . He liked to be in control, and didn't take many drugs or drink much alcohol. . . . When I told him I missed him, he came out with, 'Oh, Miss P., really? Are you telling me the truth?' My melting heart wasn't ready for this guy. I swallowed it all whole, and it was . . . delicious." For her, it was a wonderful romance, even if Page called the shots by seeing her only when Zeppelin was in California. She had experiences that other women could only dream of. She held the band's jewelry during concerts—they would hand it to her as they walked onstage. As the band played, she sat on Page's amplifier and watched the crowd go crazy.

But Page didn't do all the bad things to her that he was capable of, according to Des Barres. Shortly after Zeppelin had played its Los Angeles gigs during the second tour, she discovered something. Inside one of Page's suitcases she saw some whips, curled up like sleeping snakes. He came up behind her and assured her that he would never use them on her. Page went even further, she claimed, when he told her that "he would throw the whips away to show how much I meant to him. After ripping off my antique-lace dress and making raging, blinding love to me, he wrapped the whips round and round his forearm and slid the leather coils into the plastic flowered wastebasket, where they remained until he left for Somewhere U.S.A. a week later."

This dark secret of how Page conducted some of his personal affairs is one example of the lurid stories about the band that began to circulate during the 1969 tour. The press would sensationalize each new rumor. Undoubtedly, the most wild, sinister, and well known one of all is that Page made a deal with the Devil to make sure his group got famous.

The idea of a deal with Satan for gain isn't unprecedented. It was believed by many that the brilliant tours de force on the violin by the ingenious, yet eccentric Niccolò Paganini were due to satanic powers. Paganini said that he had an experience that "revealed to him the secret of everything one could do on the violin." He even had a strange, ghoulish appearance: tall, thin build, long arms, spidery fingers, and even transparent skin. After his death in France in 1840, too many commoners were frightened for the Catholic Church to bury him.

Robert Johnson also has stories about a deal with the Devil connected to him. Perhaps the greatest blues player of all time, Johnson's influence still echoes today, even though he only recorded twenty-nine songs in his brief career. He contributed to the repertoire of Cream, Led Zeppelin, the Rolling Stones, and Eric Clapton. Johnson, like Paganini, had a fatal attraction for women. It would lead to Johnson's death in 1938 by poisoning from a jealous husband. Johnson was only twenty-six years old. The deadly whiskey bottle passed to Johnson on that fateful night was supposedly how the Devil had Johnson pay his due.

The Faustian bargain that Johnson struck was supposed to have happened in 1931, when he was on one of his many wanderings alone. He would drop out of sight for weeks, but this time he returned to the Mississippi Delta and his playing was now downright scary. Some of the old blues masters who had seen Johnson before as a novice were now shocked. When bluesman Son House heard Johnson's new playing, he turned to Willie Brown and exclaimed, "Well, ain't that fast! He's *gone* now!" To these other players, Johnson had some musical powers that just couldn't be due simply to the months he was gone. The playing didn't just sound like the product of study and practice, there was some other reason behind the percussive, rhythmic chords and clear, bottle-neck notes that rang like a bell. Like a fire doused with gasoline, word spread throughout the delta: Little Robert had sold his soul to the Devil. It would be later said about Johnson that "he became a phantom, the ultimate composite of the perfect blues hero: doomed, haunted, desperate, driven, dead at an early age."

Johnson lived and died the mythic life of the traditional blues singer: hard drinker, womanizer, and drifter. But more important, he did little to downplay the satanic rumors about him; rather, he wrote songs about life's brevity, impending doom, and the Devil. The story of Johnson meeting Satan at the crossroads of Highways 61 and 49 at Clarksdale, Mississippi, one dark and lonely night, having the fallen angel tune his guitar, and striking the fateful bar-gain is what makes legends. Whether the story is true or not is irrelevant. The important idea here is that Johnson did his best to add fuel to the fires of controversy about him. Blues was branded as the Devil's music in the Delta, just as Paganini's music was in Europe before Johnson.

In his own way, Johnson would also have his own mystique. The only two known photos of Johnson both show long, curved fingers clutching the fret board, not unlike Paganini's. His songs complete the picture: "Cross Road Blues" (where he is said to have met Satan), "Ramblin' on My Mind," "Me and the Devil Blues," "Hellhound on My Trail," and "If I Had Possession over Judge-ment Day." Other artists, such as the Rolling Stones, built on this theme with their song "Sympathy for the Devil."

Another guitarist known for his fantastic ability on guitar, wom-anizing, and dying before his time was Jimi Hendrix, who was no stranger to this concept of supernatural events happening to the bluesman. At one of his concerts, he talked about the idea when he said, "It's about this cat runnin' around town . . . a whole lotta people from across the tracks are puttin' him down. They don't want to face up to it that the cat has something, but everybody's against him because the cat might be a little bit different, so he goes up the road to be a Voodoo Child—come back and be a magic boy."

In Johann Goethe's *Faust*, Mephistopheles brandished a violin; Paganini played staccato notes precisely his own way; Johnson sang emotional, scary Mississippi blues; Page drew a bow across his strings and created haunting, electric sounds. Even though the satanic rumors about Zeppelin grew with the band's popularity, part of the influence was carried over from distant winds of past tradition. Page did little to discredit any rumors. In fact, his own activities, like his interest in black magic and Aleister Crowley, helped build on the Satanic image.

Crowley had written his personal code of conduct titled *The Book of the Law*. In it, he said there is no law beyond "do what thou wilt." This was an elaborate version of the hippie saying, "Do your own thing." Crowley believed in self-liberation and in finding one's true destiny. This is what Page did when he discovered the guitar and forged ahead with all his energy. Crowley was a rebellious mystic who outraged Victorian England and who was obsessed with the occult, a hedonistic lifestyle of adventurous sex, and a blind devotion to various drugs such as cocaine and heroin. He also practiced black magic, trying to summon demons.

Page was interested in collecting Crowley artifacts, and eventually he purchased Crowley's supposed haunted mansion, located on the shore of Scotland's Loch Ness. Des Barres got involved with Page's interest by purchasing a Crowley book in Hollywood for Page and sending it to him. She said that Page was definitely involved with magic; "He was *really* into that stuff. I believe that Jimmy was very into black magic and probably did a lot of rituals, candles, bat's blood, the whole thing." Rumors such as this would be played up by the press as time went on. However, bad publicity tended to increase interest in Zeppelin.

Curiosity would prove to be an effective magnet to draw people to concerts. Once there, few were disappointed by what they saw and heard. By now, interest in the group was at a fever pitch. Everyone around the Los Angeles music scene knew about the excitement at the concerts, with Zeppelin's Whisky gigs already legendary. The band not only had genuine fun playing when they rocked the crowd to extremes but they also commanded attention during quieter moments as well, like when Page picked up his Danelectro, sat on a stool, and played "White Summer" by himself.

My four-track tape of Zeppelin's first album got played to death in an old half-ton panel mail truck that I bought from the postal service. It was an old 1955 Dodge that had a tired flathead six-cylinder engine that got up to 55 miles per hour on the free-way. My tape player and speakers immediately went on the dash, and I threw a couch and pillows in the back area, which was big enough to stand up in. And I had to change the lettering on the truck because of a run-in I had with the Montrose post office. My friends and I thought it'd be fun to drive through the post office parking lot and freak out the workers. We drove into the lot with "Communication Breakdown" going full blast from my metal box speakers on the dash. Some mailmen jumped out of the way of the crazy truck that had teenagers hanging out the backdoor. We waved, screamed, and sang. A fat, crew-cutted supervisor guy ran up to the truck in a fury, jumped on the driver's side, hanging on to the window. Plant's words about having a nervous breakdown flew into his angry, red face

"Hey! What the hell are you kids doing? Turn off that racket!" he yelled.

"No! Why? We're just driving around!" I screamed back.

"It's noise, noise, *noise*! Stop this thing! *Now*!" he barked. I kept driving, so he reached over, turned off the engine, and yanked out the keys. That ended the music, right during Page's crazy guitar solo.

The police were called, and I was forced to paint over the U.S. mail letters before I got my keys back. On the way home, one of my friends commented that the supervisor had seen a mirage because my truck looked like something it really wasn't. So at home, my dad made a cardboard stencil and we spray painted the name "Mirage" in large, swirling rainbow letters across the side. It was now a red, white, and blue psychedelic mail truck. This became my Sunset Strip cruiser, and the Mirage joined the parade of crazily painted cars on weekends.

When I blasted Led Zeppelin's first album at La Crescenta's Hindenburg Park love-ins, a crowd would gather around the Mirage. The music became a kind of soundtrack for everything else that was going on—somehow it fit right in. The hippie movement was a few years old and not dead by a long shot—or at least it seemed that way—as Zeppelin swept into town. They played two nights on May 2 and 3 in a reconverted warehouse in Pasadena, the Rose Palace. This was where the floats for the world-famous Rose Parade were decorated, and now it was also a southern California version of the Fillmore West. Lots of groups played there, including the Spirit, the Grateful Dead, and John Mayall. My high school always had little fliers with psychedelic artwork advertising these shows strewn across the hallways and plastered on the lockers.

Mirage had broken down with a bad transmission, so I was driving my mom's Pontiac when I heard about the shows on KRLA radio. The ads started with the first notes of "Good Times Bad Times" and then an announcer cried, "See Led Zeppelin now at the Rose Palace—May Second and Third! Two shows! Get tickets before it's too late!" About 4,000 people drove up for the Rose Palace shows. They were a must, so I went to a night of the intense music and insanity. The band's equipment was driven up to

Pasadena by roadies in an old van. They unloaded the amps, guitars, and drums at the rear of the building, where floats were always lined up for the Rose Bowl parade.

Craig Folkes was a photographer and fan of the band who knew some of the entourage, like disc jockey Rodney Bingenheimer. "It was still early, before the show," Folkes recalled. "I arrived at Rodney's place, just off Hollywood Boulevard behind the Aquarius Theater. Next stop on Sunset was to pick up a musician friend of Jimmy's, Screamin' Lord David Sutch. He'd known John Bonham, John Paul Jones, and Robert from various bands in England. Jimmy at one point had been a member of Screaming Lord Sutch and the Savages. He'd relocated to LA with his famous Union Jack Rolls Royce. This night he had it parked in the rear of his apartment building and didn't feel like showing it off. So I became the designated driver and photographer. We all piled into my Volkswagon and started off to the Rose Palace. David was looking forward to their reunion, as that was all he talked about on the drive over."

People drove psychedelically painted vehicles from the wildest sections of Hollywood. There were cars with fluorescent rainbows, stars and comets, and MAKE LOVE, NOT WAR plastered on them. One van had COMMUNICATION BREAKDOWN written on its sides, the curved letters slightly weaving like cobras about to strike. The outside of the Rose Palace wasn't much to look at—just a large, long building with a sign over the double doors saying this was the place. But the inside was a different story, mainly because of the people. The interior had a high ceiling, Astroturf on the floor, and a stage that was small in comparison to the ones Zeppelin used later. The smell of marijuana drifted through the air. Individuals with painted faces wandered about, handing out sticks of incense. At the side of the building was a strange, wide-eyed woman in a scarf and buckskin shirt. She flailed her arms and screamed some weird poetry about men, gods, and nature. A small group stopped to watch her, and then yelled at her to shut up and go sit down. I passed up this little conflict, for I didn't relish seeing the outcome. There were no chairs, so I inched my way up toward the stage. I wasn't sure what would happen next. But what happened I'll never forget—it was some of the most electrifying, powerful music I had ever heard.

The lights finally flashed out, and then some spotlights brightened the stage. Yells and cries rose out of the crowd, which had pushed up against the stage. "The band came out onto the stage one by one, with Sutch and Rodney following close behind," Folkes recalled. "They gave me the obligatory head nod and hand wave. Rodney went to the far side of the stage and stood behind the amps. Lord Sutch walked to the microphone. 'Ladies and gentlemen,' he announced, 'it is my exteme pleasure to present to you from England . . . *Led Zeppelin!*'"

The band blasted into "Train Kept a-Rollin'." Sheer energy, electricity, and spontaneity were thrown out to the crowd. For over an hour and a half, the audience surged to the music like an ocean current. Near the show's climax, everyone went wild when the first notes to "How Many More Times" boomed from Jones's amplifier. Page followed with his wah-wah introduction, and arms flew up all over the audience. After Page and Plant interacted with rising and falling cries and guitar notes, it all broke loose. The progression to the first verse thundered out in electric fury. Bonham's cymbals somehow rang out above the din. The audience first began to sway, then some up front and at the sides began to dance. Some others up front tried to climb up on the stage, but bouncers pushed them back into the swirling crowd. One teenage boy made the ascent with the help of a few friends who pushed him up. He scrambled up next to Page, and some of the crowd cried out in surprise. Page glanced over and smiled at him, and the boy tore off his striped velour shirt, threw it into the crowd, and began dancing around Page. The guitarist responded by leaning over slightly and shuffling his feet. Before the ecstatic kid was dragged away by stagehands, he and Page stood together and did a few side steps, a funny dance duet created in a psychedelic, electric pressure

cooker. It wasn't hard to see then how Zeppelin's energy had captured American audiences.

Like Plant, Page loved to interact with a crowd. He would use
thrilling guitar theatrics. With his Telecaster slung so low, he flung
it one way or the other without missing a note. He would saunter
across the stage and strike power chords, break into a Chuck Berry
duckwalk, slam his strings, and hold his guitar over his head,
feedback screeching. With his face half hidden by a black mass of
hair that hung down, he often had his eyes closed in concentration. He had to be the coolest looking musician around. Teenage
guitarists everywhere emulated Page's style. Suddenly, he had
taken over from Eric Clapton as the leading guitar idol of millions.

Photographer Robert Knight followed Zeppelin around on the
West Coast. He was responsible for them playing in Hawaii on
May 13th and was able to hang out with the band during their
visit. "Having hooked up with Led Zeppelin at the Whiskey A Go
Go in early January 1969 and traveling up the Fillmore West gig in
San Francisco and flipping out of how great this band was, I
phoned back to Honolulu my hometown and told the local promoters they needed to book this band now! They would be the
biggest band in the world, which they did straight away. Since I
knew the band and the promoter did not, he sent me out to the
Honolulu Airport to greet the band. As they came off, I got them
all to do a group shoot with recording tapes of *Led Zep II* in their
arms. The next week was fabulous fun, as I photographed Led
Zeppelin running up and down the beach and learning to surf and
totally destroying their multi-million-dollar rental home with garden hoses and water fights!"

He caught on film Robert Plant and John Bonham playing
around in the home's swimming pool. When either Plant or
Bonham attempted to get up on the inflatable raft, the other tried
to pull off his bathing suit. Plant even tried to hang ten on the
surfboard but kept falling off. He did, however, manage to sit on
the board—waiting for the perfect wave? Not catching any waves,

Plant and the rest of the band decided to go out to dinner. Tagging along, Knight saw a typical evening with Zeppelin. He remembered: "The dinners out of Buzz's Steak and Lobster were way out of control as the various bottles of wine that lined the wall seemed like logical targets for John Bonham to throw various objects trying to knock them off the walls!"

A local review reported that this was the best rock show ever in Hawaii. (Zeppelin was one of the few British rock groups to hit Hawaiian shores.) According to Knight, the promoter got the band for only $5,000. The Zeppelin mentality of fun had been brought to Hawaii.

The band was working hard with sold-out venues in Detroit, Minneapolis, Chicago, and Boston. The tour's closing dates were at the Fillmore East on May 30 and 31, where the band made a spectacular return. Backstage access was easy at the Fillmore because no passes were needed and no security guards stood at doorways. Groupies wandered back and forth and photographers like Jeffrey Mayer caught their action on film. Zeppelin stalked onstage and let loose an earthquake of sound and frenzy. As the echoes of the final power chords dissipated, concertgoers filed out of the hall, ears still ringing, dazed by the meteoric power of the onstage musical carnage they had witnessed. Who could forget Jimmy Page's thunderous power chords, Robert Plant's vocal histrionics, the pulsating ability of John Paul Jones, and, finally, John Bonham's dynamic drumming?

Unlike the end of their first tour, Led Zeppelin was now returning to England as a band one had to see. Word now spread fast, just like it had in America. Zeppelin's first proper scheduled United Kingdom tour from June 13 to 29, 1969, included stops in Birmingham, Manchester, London, Newcastle, Bristol, Portsmouth, and the Bath Festival. Reviews from Birmingham read, "Led Zeppelin showed just why they have taken America by storm."

The band may have been creating more than just musical headlines—a very weird event took place, captured on film by famous photographer Ron Raffaelli. His work with Zeppelin occurred mostly in 1969 and included accompanying them on several tours throughout Europe, England and briefly in the United States. He also shot striking images of them at several sessions in his own studio in Hollywood and on at least one occasion at Quantum Recording Studios in Los Angeles during a session for *Led Zeppelin II*. His affiliation with the band began when he photographed them at a show at the town hall in Birmingham, England, on June 13. It marked one of the strangest experiences of Raffaelli's entire career as a photographer.

"I had another commitment and had to get back to the United States right after that concert, so I packed up all my equipment and flew back the next morning," he recalled. "The first thing I did when I got back was develop the film, and I was shooting with a Nikon 'F', which is a 35mm single lens reflex camera that you can't use to shoot a double exposure. Some of my studio cameras you can double expose with because the advancing of the film and the cocking of the lens are two separate things, but with the Nikon it's all one thing and you can't disengage it.

"As I developed the film I found pictures on that roll with 'ghost' images on stage with Led Zeppelin. And I remember being backstage with the group before the concert and they were talking about how this concert hall had been built on top of the ruins, or foundation, of what was once a medieval prison where there was a lot of torture and executions going on. I hadn't thought of this until I saw what looked to me like double exposures—there was one with a large face and you can tell that its been mangled—it's a deformed human face—and it looks like it's in pain or something."

For the band, posing in a studio was like pulling teeth. So one time, to get the band's full and undivided attention, Raffaelli recalled, "The group showed up and I immediately posed them on my set and clapped my hands for my assistant to bring me my camera. From the back of the studio a tall, beautiful, completely nude blond model appeared, carrying my camera on a silver tray.

Needless to say, I had the group's complete attention for the duration of that session!"

England was now listening more closely to Zeppelin. On June 29, they played London's prestigious Royal Albert Hall, the site of other memorable shows by the Beatles, Rolling Stones, Cream, and Jimi Hendrix: Britain had finally accorded them the recognition they deserved. The British press reported that "when Led Zeppelin came out and played at a good ten times the volume of everyone else, the audience very nearly freaked completely."

At the end of Zeppelin's excellent set, and an encore, it was after 11:00 P.M. The house lights had gone up and a portion of the near-capacity audience had filed out. Those who remained clustered at the foot of the flower bedecked stage first started to clap and then shifted to stomping their feet before crying out for more, until the whole cycle began over again and continued. Some of the crowd who had left poured back into the auditorium to see what all the fuss was about. It was obvious they weren't going home till they got more, but when the group returned to the stage they found the power had been switched off. "Hey, put the power on," demanded Plant as the group stood around. Plant took up a harmonica and wailed on that and all the others could do was clap until a few minutes later when the power was back on. With the first few bars of "Long Tall Sally," the audience was on its feet dancing in the aisles and in the box seats. The air around the stage became thick with paper airplanes (symbolically) thrown from the boxes along with a ticker-tape reception of handbills, balloons, and petals of the flowers from the foot of the stage.

The success of Led Zeppelin was getting out of hand. All they wanted was to play what they wanted to play, to have a hit album or two, if they were lucky, and to have moderate success in both England and the United States. Out of small ambitions had come overwhelming acceptance from the United States, a first LP that soared to the top 10 in the English charts, and packed audiences wherever they played in Britain. "I was just amazed," said Page.

"I never expected much to happen in England and what has happened was beyond everyone's wildest hopes." The major problem,
however, was that not all the fans could get in to the concerts
because tickets went so fast.

Seeing them play live was becoming an essential experience,
but Zeppelin began making some real noise when their U.S. coast-
to-coast summer tour kicked off on July 4–5 at the Atlanta Pop Festival. It was just one of many being held that summer around the
country, and the first one ever in the Deep South. Over 125,000 of
America's underground subculture had made the pilgrimage there
for fourteen hours of music each day by such groups as Joe Cocker,
Canned Heat, Grand Funk Railroad, and Led Zeppelin. Zeppelin
sounded just as loud outdoors as indoors.

The Rolling Stones sounded loud outdoors, too. During a trip
to Europe, my brother Steve and I saw the Stones at a gigantic festival setting in England. They gave a free concert on July 5 at
London's Hyde Park. This would become the British equivalent of
the Atlanta Festival or Woodstock. Graced with grassy, rolling hills
and sky high trees, the place was huge, and had about 250,000
people there. Now bigger than ever, the Stones wanted to say
thank you to their many fans. The Stones were also about to
embark on their U.S. tour and wanted to try out their new lead
guitarist Mick Taylor, who'd replaced Brian Jones. When the Stones
came out, I was surprised to see that gone were their Beatle-type
haircuts—they'd all grown their hair down to their shoulders.
The stage was decorated with displays that showed the band's
medieval feast from the inside of their last album, *Beggar's Banquet*.
Jagger, in a white laced Renaissance outfit, read a short tribute to
Jones, who had drowned in his swimming pool a few days before.
Then a huge cloud of butterflies was set free from the stage and the
Stones let loose with raw versions of "Jumpin' Jack Flash," "Stray
Cat Blues," and "Street Fighting Man" as well as their current hit
song, "Honky Tonk Woman."

They also played some new songs, "Love in Vain," from the

upcoming LP, *Let It Bleed*, and a long, jam type excursion called "Midnight Rambler." The show's climax had a wild ending with African conga drummers and a tribal dancer with a spear who pranced around the stage during "Sympathy for the Devil." The Stones had gone back to some pretty primitive roots. No doubt about it—the English music scene had really changed from the days of the first British music invasion to the States in 1964.

There were no violent incidents anywhere in the crowd. People stood around me, yelled, and waved their arms but no one was out of control. Security for the show was provided by a British version of the Hell's Angels, motorbike riders who mostly just watched people and walked around the edge of the crowd. I ended up about twenty feet from the front of the stage, where I took some pictures with my Instamatic camera. Up front there were celebrators—hippies in headbands, long hair and granny dresses as well as exotic black guys in flowing robes—all dancing and twirling around, oblivious to everyone else. England really swung in 1969!

Led Zeppelin was still in America.

Meanwhile, On July 18 and 19, the band played at the Kinetic Playground in Chicago. Thomas Weschler, the road manager for Bob Seger at the time, was able to make it to the show. Seger was in Milwaukee playing with the Beach Boys and had Saturday night off. "Bob and two other guys on the crew and myself went down to Chicago to see some bands," Weschler recalled. "Seger went to the Aragon Ballroom to see Jefferson Airplane. Bob was a big Grace Slick fan and not just for her singing. I went to see Led Zeppelin, Jethro Tull, and Savoy Brown, all on the same bill at the Kinetic Playground. The venue was loaded with beautiful girls, which I focused my camera on, as photography was a favorite thing to do then and now. So instead of doing what I should have been doing—photographing the rock stars—I shot photos of various girls! I still got to practice my craft, just on more interesting subjects to me at the time."

Because of the female distractions, Weschler was able to get only one picture of Page when he was bowing his guitar. Later that night, both Seger's group and Zeppelin stayed at the Holiday Inn at Center City. Weschler had a brief, yet humorous interaction with Plant there. "I was in the lobby getting some pop and of all people Robert Plant came up to me and asked if he could have a quarter for cigarettes. Of course, I said 'yes'!"

"Music, Love, and Peace" was the announced theme of Seattle's first annual Pop Festival held the weekend of July 25–27 in a farm valley northwest of Seattle. The orgasmic moments of the festival were Led Zeppelin. They followed the Doors on the last night with a sexual ferocity and rampaging energy that literally blew the hinges off the Doors.

As Zeppelin's status grew, tales of tour debauchery quickly spread and were given wide currency. No band had more groupie tales told about them than Led Zeppelin. As exaggerated as many of the stories about them obviously were, there was usually some truth on which they were founded. The notorious shark episode happened in Seattle at the Edgewater Hotel, where the band was holed up. The hotel sits right on Puget Sound, and the hotel used to loan rod and reel to the guests so they could FISH OUT YOUR WINDOW as a big sign on the side of the building boasted. Bonham was fishing out of his hotel window the day before and had caught some red snappers and mud sharks. After the show, the band had been drinking with members of Vanilla Fudge and a seventeen-year-old groupie. According to legend, the girl was tied naked to a bed and had unspeakable things done to her with a shark's nose during an orgy of lust, which was only a little exaggerated.

Carmine Appice, the drummer for Vanilla Fudge, was there when the whole depraved event started. He was hanging out with Jones, the girl, and the Fudge keyboard player Mark Stein, who happened to be making movies with an 8 mm camera. "It was *my* groupie," recalled Appice. "She saw the camera and said she wanted to play around." Then Bonham and two members of

Fudge's road crew entered the room with the catch of the day: a mud shark. "We moved to my room, and it got pretty gross," Appice continued. "I decided to leave, and then I realized I was in my room already." It was the single, most famous sex act in rock-and-roll history. Although there have been variations on this tale, Appice's account seems to have most corroboration. Frank Zappa wrote "The Mud Shark" song, which accurately reflects Appice's story. And Plant was at the filming and confirmed that the groupie enjoyed the entire shark affair. "I was there in the room with Bonham and his wife and my wife," Plant remembered. "She loved it. Not my wife—the woman. She was not complaining whatsoever. She got up, thanked everyone very much, and that was it."

Back on the road, the band continued to work on their next album, *Led Zeppelin II*. Atlantic Records was pushing for an autumn release. As a result, the group wrote and recorded the album in hotel rooms, dressing rooms, and studios all over America throughout the tour. It would be a genuine road album, with ideas and experiences from the tour influencing the writing. "The Lemon Song" was a rewriting of Howlin' Wolf's "Killing Floor." It included the phrase "squeeze my lemon 'til the juice runs down my leg," which was borrowed from Robert Johnson. There were obvious sexual overtones like these about groupies. "Living Loving Maid (She's Just a Woman)" was written about an aging groupie. Equally significant was the part Plant was taking in lyric composition. He wrote the lyrics of "Thank You" for his wife, Maureen. Jones recalled the album's recording on the run, "When you're playing every night, you're hot and your brains are working quickly, as are your fingers. We were quick at getting our parts, then we could work on a performance, get the best take, and say 'that's it,' and we all knew that was it. There was none of that uncertainty that inexperienced bands have of not knowing when they'd got something."

They received a gold record for a million dollars' worth of sales from their first album. Then, before the band left for dates on the West Coast, their record company informed them of the unbelievable 400,000 advance orders for the new album. *Led Zeppelin II*'s success was guaranteed. The steady buildup in popularity for the band was now underway.

Two weeks after Woodstock at the former site of the 1964 World's Fair in New York City, the renowned rock photographer Joe Sia was onstage with Led Zeppelin. "It was an absolutely gorgeous summer night at the huge outside venue and I was probably on assignment for *Rolling Stone*," recalled Sia. "Sometime during the opening act I approached the stage from the audience's side and was able to walk up without any problem." As he firmly positioned himself at stage left armed with his camera, Zeppelin's powerful assault would be felt on his ears. "Led Zeppelin were great to see and photograph," remembered Sia. He would capture onstage moments a few feet away from the action—Plant throwing out a barrage of blues wails as Page, in a white cowboy hat, ground out explosive notes from his Les Paul. Inside, 10,000 fans saw this spectacle, and there were 3,000 who had been turned away and were listening outside.

Forget the Rolling Stones, the Beatles, or the Who. No other rock band owned the concert stage like England's masters of high-volume mayhem, Led Zeppelin. Their third American tour ended as a complete success, performing in front of 120,000 screaming fans, over the Labor Day weekend at the Texas International Pop Festival in Dallas. This show included such performers as Janis Joplin, Ten Years After, and Sly and the Family Stone. Jones remembered, "My wife was there for that one, and I recall how Janis Joplin taught us how to drink tequila with salt and lemon. There was just the three of us in her trailer—memories don't come much better than that." Zeppelin received a first time ever tour high of $13,000 for their one-hour set. Happy and exhausted, the group returned to England for a timely rest. Page embarked on a

The Yardbirds Last Rave-up in L.A., 1968.

Mr. Big, manager Peter Grant.

The First Performance, Copenhagen, 9/7/68.

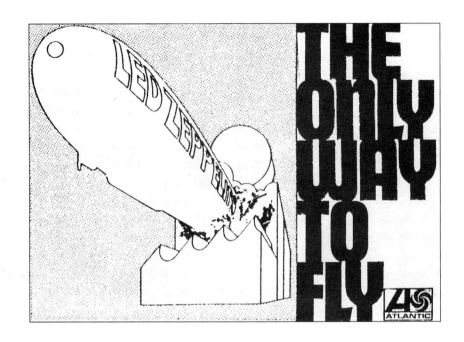

This show is rated "H" (for Heavy).

ZEPPELIN, ZEPPELIN, ZEPPELIN.

Telecaster guitar hero.

Jimmy Page, the mastermind behind Led Zeppelin.

Coming across the ocean in an uproar of guitar and vocal mayhem.

Kawabonga
—Robert Plant in Hawaii, May 1969.

She's Just a Woman.

Ghost

"Let the music be your master."

Full Flight Over Canada.

Bring It On Home.

In the days of my youth . . .

trip to Spain and Morocco and the other three members decided to spend time at home in the country with their families.

By now, they had also finished their second album. On October 12, they appeared at the Lyceum Ballroom in London. During the concert to a capacity crowd, Plant introduced some of their new numbers. Five days later they were off to the United States on their unprecedented fourth tour, starting at the famed Carnegie Hall in New York City, as one of the first rock bands since the Beatles to grace the stage there. The American audience didn't just take the band to their hearts, but treated them as one of their own.

A rock and roll fan from New Jersey named Ron Kellerman did just that. Through luck or fate, his path crossed with that of a guitar player from England who was destined to eventually become the legendary lead guitarist of Led Zeppelin. His incredible story is one that most fans dream about. In the early 1960s, Kellerman had written to Sun Records and eventually got both to meet Jerry Lee Lewis and a job answering his fan mail. This linked him up to the British rock scene through letters from England, and Kellerman got to know Screamin' Lord Sutch. From here, Kellerman began to correspond with an up-and-coming musician, none other than Jimmy Page.

"As I recalled, it was a very pleasant evening in late October 1969," Kellerman said. "We were enjoying the last remnants of Indian summer. It was around 5:30 in the evening and I was sitting in my living room with Screamin' Lord Sutch." He decided to call up Page and bring him over to Kellerman's house to show Page his record collection. Page was available and said to come on down and pick him up. "Within fifteen minutes we were streaming down the freeway in my 1968 burgundy Chrysler 300 with 'Whole Lotta Love' blasting off the FM hard-rock station. In those days, not an hour went by without a Zeppelin song being aired." Kellerman added he was "en route to one of the most amazing moments of my life." At the time, Page was interested in the early Sun Records as well as many old rock and roll records on obscure labels like the defunct Excello label, which Kellerman had. "One of the items Jimmy picked to listen to was my original Sun 45 of Elvis Presley's 'Mystery Train.' We continued listening to much of my Sun 45 collection. Jimmy was knocked out by the full-echoed sound of the recordings, which were made in a studio not much bigger than my living room."

As the evening wore on, Page sat in front of the light-wooded RCA Victor cabinet model record player, playing records and discussing his varied musical tastes with Kellerman and Sutch. "Jimmy went from Jerry Lee's angry piano pounding to bluegrass banjo to black R&B back to country artists like Merle Travis," Kellerman recalled. "His exploration of different musical forms was endless, which may account for all the varied musical compositions and styles that would transpire in the near future for Led Zeppelin. His tastes were not rooted in just American music but international music as well, especially the Far East." The conversation continued from music to horror movies and world affairs to what growing up in England was like. Page also said that he had an interest in art and sculpture but that it was overshadowed by his involvement with Zeppelin. Kellerman's teenage sister was barely able to control her excitement over having a real rock star at her house. The down-to-earth Page asked her if she liked high school, to which she replied she didn't. But she did honor her brother's request—although just barely—not to call up any of her friends and tell them about the special visitor.

Kellerman gave Page some rare records, which Page tried to turn down but finally relented and accepted. Kellerman's mom offered everyone some homemade cakes, donuts, and coffee, then they finally turned in at 4:00 A.M. Later that morning after some more coffee, the three music fans headed down the New Jersey turnpike toward New York City. On arriving at Page's hotel, he thanked Kellerman for the evening, got out of the car, and disappeared through the front door. Kellerman's unbelievable time with Page ended.

By the time *Led Zeppelin II* came out in October, Page had begun using Marshall 100-watt amplifier stacks and a late 1950s Gibson Les Paul sunburst guitar that would become his trademark. Page cited several reasons for his switch to Marshall. "Besides being one of the best drummers I've ever heard, John Bonham was also one of the loudest. He was the reason we started buying bigger amps. Also, at that time it was state-of-the-art reliability. Marshalls were really good for going out on the road. I was always having trouble with amps—blowing fuses and whatnot." Page said that he "was quite happy with his Telecaster, but once he started playing the Les Paul, that was it. The Les Paul was so gorgeous and easy to play and seemed like a good touring guitar."

Led Zeppelin II announced the birth of a new monster sound of high-decibel destruction that combined the torrid, animalistic raunch of old Chess and Sun Records with the progressive scream of rock's latest technology pushed to the brink. It would blow teenage minds for years to come. It also blew the mind of the *Rolling Stone* reviewer John Mendelsohn, who had put down their first album, "Hey, man, I take it all back! This is one fucking heavy-weight of an album!"

The album was not all about volume. But even the softer moments, like the lazy jazzy-blues interludes in "What Is and What Should Never Be" and the lighthearted acoustic trot of "Ramble On," sizzled with anticipation of the atomic blast sure to follow. And when it came, there was nothing like it on record any-where: the pelvic grinding of "Heartbreaker" suddenly erupting into a full psycho, Yardbirds gallop; and the rousing martial stomp of "Bring It on Home," with a massed chorus of Page guitars blast-ing the riff like Roman trumpets.

The best-known track from *Led Zeppelin II* was undoubtedly "Whole Lotta Love"—from the staccato machine gun sound of

Page's opening guitar riff to Plant's howling declaration of sexual prowess ("every inch of my love") to the rampant Jones-Bonham rhythm attack. Midway through the song, the band jumps into an experimental section of studio tape effects, string grinds, and the eerie wail of Page's electronic wizardry. To get these spaced-out sounds, Page and engineer Eddie Kramer spun just about all the dials on the control board. Finally, the crack of Bonham's snare signals the climax: a burst of short, machine gun guitar licks that still constitute one of the great metal solos ever, despite its brevity.

The riff for Zeppelin's first anthem came from Page. On the solo, he used a depressed wah-wah pedal to give him a really raucous sound. Page stated that "the amp was turned up very high. It was distorting, just controlled to the point where it had some balls to it." If you played the album on your stereo loud enough, your parents would probably run screaming from the house—this record should have been X rated! *Led Zeppelin II* became the band's first album to reach Number 1 in America and England, knocking the Beatles' *Abbey Road* off the top of the charts.

"Too many groups sit back after their first album, and the second one is a downer," remarked Page. "I wanted every album to go one step further—that's the whole point of it." The album was exactly what Page wanted: a consolidation of the best ideas found on Zeppelin's first album, with just enough experimentation to show that the band was determined to grow. *Zeppelin I* and *II* ushered in a whole new era of music, with the impact of the two albums growing stronger with each passing year. The second album became affectionately known by fans as the "Brown Bomber" because of its sepia-toned cover. It boasted superimposed faces of the band along with some German war aces. Known as the Flying Circus, the original scene came from an old World War I photo. Part of the now familiar Zeppelin blimp image was also evident, all of which jumped out at the viewer when the jacket was opened.

Before the year was out, the band took a detour to play some gigs in Canada. Toronto's Rockpile show was August 18, followed by some return visits a few months later to some larger arena venues. On November 4, Zeppelin performed at Kitchener's Memorial Auditorium. The photographer Dave Richardson saw both the Rockpile and Kitchener shows and noticed the radical difference a few months had made. The Rockpile was in a smaller, more crowded building than the Memorial Auditorium, and the set was performed at a much more frantic pace. Richardson also noted something else new at the Kitchener show. In the lobby was a big display heralding the release of *Led Zeppelin II*. The record itself wasn't in stores yet, so this was the first sign of it anyone had seen.

As Richardson went into the concert hall, he found another surprise: the place was only one-third full. This could be because the show was booked as an afterthought, since there had been little publicity about it. But Richardson didn't mind, after remembering how hot and crowded the Rockpile had been in a masonic lodge that had a capacity of barely 2,000. There had been a much bigger buildup time wise for the Rockpile show, which sold out and had thousands outside trying to get in. But to Richardson, Kitchener was a better show, and it was now a lot easier to get pictures with fewer people around. "It was really easy to move around and get near the stage," he recalled. "Zeppelin seemed better rehearsed than at the Rockpile. There was less banter between songs and a more expanded set list. It featured some songs from the new album including 'Heartbreaker'." Plant stormed about the stage in furry winter white boots. The band unleashed their usual sonic onslaught, although the set was cut short by a faulty PA system. The show's promoter Dick Wendling said, "I ended up doing the sound that night with my PA system. It wasn't big enough, so I had to get a friend of mine from Buffalo to bring up some more gear. . . . I'll be the first to admit that it wasn't the greatest."

The crowd was estimated at less than 2,000 people at Kitchener. Along with last-minute, minimal advertising, another reason
for the low turnout was because numerous other shows were being
held that week, with appearances by Iron Butterfly, Vanilla Fudge,
and Johnny Winter. In spite of growing popularity, Zeppelin wasn't
as huge as they would later become.

Peter Grant had probably made the decision to play a larger
venue, as he anticipated that the band's popularity was about to
skyrocket with the second album. Kitchener was the eighth and
final Canadian concert that year; it would also be one of the last
places Zeppelin would play to such an intimate audience. A few
weeks before there had been Carnegie Hall; a few months later
would come the Royal Albert Hall. In the space of just one year,
Zeppelin had accomplished remarkable feats in not only where
they performed but also in how they played.

Zeppelin's blazing stage frenzy hit people hard from New York
to San Francisco. Pamela Des Barres described the phenomenon in
her book *I'm With the Band*, "Led Zeppelin live in 1969 was an
event unparalleled in musical history. They played longer and
harder than any group ever had, totally changing the concept of
rock concerts. They flailed around like dervishes, making so much
sound that the air was heavy with metal. Two hours after the lights
went out, as the band sauntered offstage, the audience was a deliri-
ous, raving parched mass, crawling through the rock and roll
desert thirsting for an encore. Twenty long minutes later, mighty
Zeppelin returned to satiate their famished followers."

The final American dates were at San Francisco's Winterland
on November 6, 7, and 8. This celebrated venue was actually an
abandoned ice skating rink that could hold up to 4,500 people,
more than the Fillmore West's 1,800. It was on this particular trip
that Des Barres says Page broke off their relationship permanently.
At the airport she expected to be flying to England with Page but
instead he left her there. "Jimmy flew off to England," she said,

"and he didn't offer me the seat next to him on the plane. Instead, he told me at the airport, 'P., you're such a lovely little girl. I don't deserve you, I'm such a bastard, you know.' I felt like I had just been handed a one-way ticket to Palookaville. Alone at the airport, I knew what it was like to be crippled."

For Jerry Prochnicky, 1969 was a great year for music. The proof was in the vinyl. Not only had there been the first two Zeppelin albums but there was also the Rolling Stones' *Let It Bleed*, debut albums by the Stooges and Santana, and MC5's live set *Kick Out the Jams*. During the Christmas season, Prochnicky went to his underground record store to search for rare bootlegs and imports. There on a carousel rack he spotted a twelve-by-twelve hardcover Led Zeppelin fall tour book. It was only $1. Flipping through the pages, he was amazed by the great onstage and offstage photos by Ron Raffaelli. To his surprise, there were nine more copies behind it. So instead of picking up just the one, he scooped them all up and gave them as Christmas gifts to his Ledhead friends. Today, in collector's circles this book goes for over $100.

The band had spent an exhausting fifteen months touring and needed a break. Plant bought an old farm near Kidderminster. Bonham got one in West Hagley. He said, "It will be the first Christmas at home for me with my son, Jason. Last year I was away and before that he was too young to know. He's music mad and I bought him a great set of miniature drums. It's an absolutely perfect replica, down to the bass drum pedal and high hat. Even I can play them." Jones had his family move to Hertfordshire. All were getting ready for Christmas at home. The country life that the members began to lead would play a role in their coming efforts on record. It was a time to reflect on life and slow down a bit, after rocking and shaking audiences on both sides of the Atlantic. The big impact had been made. Now with 1969 at an end, Zeppelin would enter a new decade and realm for its music.

CHAPTER 3

"Over the Hills and Far Away"

As the new decade dawned, no one could foresee the changes that would happen to American culture. The 1960s utopian hippie dream of peace and love had turned sour. We believed that music could set us free—that rock and roll was bigger than our lives and that it could raise us above the problems of growing up, of society, of violence and war. But the curtain came down on the 1960s with the Rolling Stones' free concert at Altamont Raceway outside of San Francisco. On that strange day, in the midst of 200,000 people, Hell's Angels hired as stage security stabbed and killed a member of the audience not far from the stage. Let it bleed . . .

On a larger scale, violence continued in the form of the Vietnam conflict. The war in Southeast Asia dragged on. We had a front row seat in front of our televisions to the killings, atrocities, and body counts on the nightly news. It was the first televised war—one in which parents had actually seen their sons killed during the news broadcasts. If you were a male and had a low draft number, life was pretty scary. Country Joe's antiwar anthem, "Feel Like I'm Fixin' to Die," had become too uncomfortably real for any draft-age guy. He realized that his mom could be "the first one on your block to have your boy come home in a box."

For Jerry Prochnicky, it didn't look too bad as far as being invited into the army was concerned. After he'd gone to college for two years, he still didn't know what to major in or what he wanted to do. But he had gotten enough units to get an Associate Arts degree in Liberal Arts. "So I got the piece of paper to show something for my time," he recalled. "Beyond that, I stopped going to school. My lottery number was something like 212, so there was little chance that I'd be drafted and sent to Vietnam. The world heavyweight boxing champion at that time, Muhammad Ali, was unjustly stripped of his title for refusing induction into the military. He said it best for us all: 'I got nothing against those Vietcong.'"

America was at war with itself over Vietnam. Tension was in the air. Generational and cultural clashes at home intensified. Antiwar protests spread on campuses all over America. Then in 1970 President Nixon sent troops into Cambodia, escalating the war instead of ending it. What was going on? The fall of Saigon in 1975 finally closed the book on an ugly chapter that should have never been written—at the cost of 55,000 American lives.

The Watergate hearings in 1973 and 1974 were great televised theater. The collapse of the corrupt Nixon administration was far more globally entertaining to many than O. J. Simpson's flight and trial would be two decades later. Nixon's eventual resigning—or chickening out—of office was a disgrace to many Americans.

Growing up in the 70s was a comedown from the 60s. Most young Americans were angry, frustrated, and bored. One needs to remember that there were no MTV, no cell phones, no Internet, no reality shows, no DVDs or videos, no Game Boys. More than ever, the biggest popular cultural thing was music. But the music had changed.

The Beatles, the most influential band of the 1960s and perhaps of all time, announced their breakup in April 1970. Jim Morrison and rock and roll went on trial in Miami that August, the aftermath of the Doors concert there on March 1st, 1969. Morrison was charged with four counts: 1) Lewd and lascivious behavior 2) Indecent exposure 3) Open profanity 4) Drunkenness. There then followed three major deaths in rock within the next twelve months—Jimi Hendrix, Janis Joplin, and Jim Morrison. The Miami trial had "killed" Morrison's spirit and his body wasn't too far behind. For fans Hulett and Prochnicky, who had both seen Morrison onstage, it was a sad end to what had been a talented rock performer and gifted poet. Jerry said, "I would have followed him to the end of the earth. He was a special friend of the music, and a part of me died with him." But it was dangerous to be a rock star, to act like one, to be treated like one.

Music throughout the 1970s was fragmented, mirroring America's dissatisfaction with the real world. There would be country rock, hard rock, easy listening, disco, funk, glam, metal, reggae, punk. Above it all rose Led Zeppelin. They appealed to both sides of the dividing line. Zeppelin had that hard edge, but didn't drive you nuts. They were sort of cosmic and heavenly at the same time, too. It was a balance that people were drawn to, one that they really liked.

Led Zeppelin would become rock gods, arguably bigger than the Beatles. Just when music and big money came together, they gave new meaning to "sex, drugs and rock 'n' roll." Led Zeppelin ruled the decade and no one did it bigger, badder, or wilder. They were tailor made for the louder, faster, post-hippie rock kids. Going to a Led Zeppelin concert was a rite of passage. To be a fan of this band was like being a member of an exclusive club. Zep news traveled in the back of cars, over the telephone and on the radio.

Zeppelin kicked off 1970 with a seven-city British tour. The news about the band's appearance at London's prestigious Royal Albert Hall spread quickly. Stuck with high taxes and unemployment, young Britons were also angry, frustrated, and bored. But on January 9th, all their troubles were left outside the hall, as inside, there would be some good rockin' tonight. Albert Hall was stark and simple, so intimate that it was almost like you were alone in a living room with the band. There was nothing flashy. The show had no special lighting, dry ice clouds, fog machines or smoke bombs. There were just four hardworking musicians that concentrated on delivering an explosive performance.

Robert Plant's face was all but obscured behind his mane of hair, but his voice was heard loud and clear. John Bonham was all muscle and moustache behind his ferocious drumming, while John Paul Jones clutched his bass guitar like a machine gun and threw out the lines with fitting strength and speed, holding together the volume that cascaded from the stage. Jimmy Page's sleeveless harlequin sweater made a vivid contrast to his coming guitar theatrics. *New Musical Express* said that he looked like he had just come out of a department store. "The slight frame of Jimmy Page, clad like a Woolworth's sales counter in Alf Garnett shirt, jeans and white plimsoles, belies the fearsome aggression of his guitar."

"We're gonna groove!" Plant cried to the packed hall, and Zeppelin did just that. The audience became so excited that many people were dancing around the stage. Plant incited this frenzy with his stage motions that made him appear as a whirling dervish. He wildly shook his head and hips, wailed and groaned to Page's echoing volume, and strutted about the stage with complete confidence and arrogance. But he also was an accomplished vocalist in the best blues-soul–shouter tradition. As he leaped in the air, energy seemed to first ripple, then bounce off his body. Plant said about this show, "We had no expectations, but we knew we had something between us that was special." As Page jumped, he unleashed a frenzy of climactic notes. Jones' bass rumbled throughout the building, and every crack of Bonham's snare or kick of his bass drum bombarded the audience. This was a band that was very much the sum of all its parts.

It was a two hour-plus blitzkrieg, a dynamic showcase that blew everyone's minds. Page's lightning-fast guitar breaks flew out on "I Can't Quit You, Baby." His Danelectro sounded like an army of guitars on "White Summer/Black Mountain Side." And Plant went into part of one old blues song after another during "How Many More Times"—from "Boogie Chillun" to "Traveling Riverside Blues." Plant led into "squeeze my lemon" by moaning, "One thing that everyone needs and wants so bad . . . We're gonna do it in Birmingham and Glasgow . . . Glasgow needs it!"

And then John Bonham really got down to it with "Moby Dick." His drum solo got a standing ovation. Near the end came "Whole Lotta Love" and "Communication Breakdown," which provoked a response that easily could have been a flashback to an early Stones concert. Fans packed against the stage pounded it with their hands, shook their heads in wild, electric ecstasy. Then Page came out for the encores with his custom Gibson Les Paul Black Beauty model. The band devastated everyone with Eddie Cochran's "C'mon Everybody" and "Something Else," then ended on the blues with Plant on harmonica for "Bring It On Home." And Zep sure as hell brought it on home that night! The entire spectacle was originally filmed as a one hour television special, but the idea was later scrapped. In 2003, Page finally had the show released on DVD, and fans can experience the event for themselves.

The Albert Hall show was a significant moment in Zeppelin's history. First, it was a hugely triumphant return to London for the band. Even people like John Lennon, Jeff Beck and Eric Clapton had requested tickets. Second, it had taken place on Page's birthday. And finally, Page met someone who would become very important in his life—French model Charlotte Martin. The two were introduced backstage and were instantly attracted to each other. After the tour ended on January 24, the two new lovers settled down at Page's Pangbourne riverside house. Page would eventually marry Charlotte and have his first child with her, a daughter named Scarlet.

About this same time Page bought Boleskine manor, Aleister Crowley's estate on the shores of Scotland's Loch Ness. Along with persistent stories of a lake monster in the area, there were also rumors concerning the estate, including the ghost of a beheaded man haunting the house. According to Page, it was a residence long associated with tragedy. He said, "There were two or three owners before Crowley moved into it. It was also a church that was burned to the ground with the congregation in it. And that's the site of the house. Strange things happened in that house that had nothing to do with Crowley. The bad vibes were already there."

One will hardly be surprised at the vibes of the place when taking a short tour of the grounds. At the entrance to the property hangs a sign that reads PRIVATE—KEEP OUT . . . BOLESKINE HOUSE. Loch Ness surrounds most of the property, and there is a long driveway that leads up to the actual house. The road wasn't lit at night, and there were guard dogs that ran the grounds to keep out unwanted visitors. This sort of scene evokes images out of *The Hound of the Baskervilles*. If you're lucky enough to outpace the dogs, then you pull your car up to the house. The house itself appears like a variety of different-shaped white cottages all pieced together, some with rounded towers and others with square towers. Each section has long, oblong windows made up of twelve rectangular panes of glass. Around the back of the house is an old graveyard containing ancient graves, crypts, and tombstones, many of which are several centuries old. Huge trees stand around the cemetery, silent sentries that also overlook Loch Ness Lake. Inside one of the rooms off a hallway is an old plaque that reads N, ALEISTER CROWLEY, POET, BLACK MAGICIAN, AND IMPRESSARIO.

Why was Page so fascinated with a character like Crowley? Part of the reason dates from Page's schoolboy days, when he first read about him. (It's useful to keep in mind the time in which Zeppelin became a phenomenon. By 1970, the 1960s' dream of peace and love was faltering. Perhaps the revolutionary spirit and mysticism of the era darkened with the times. Page said that the first book he read about Crowley was *The Great Beast*, and this aroused a curiosity.

Born in 1875, Crowley said that he was driven to rebellion from his parents, who belonged to a strict Christian cult. He also claimed that he was visited by an ancient Egyptian spirit in 1904 who dictated *The Book of the Law* to him.

The basis of Crowley's belief was rooted in personal liberation, to "enjoy all things of sense and rapture." He wanted to use rituals and magic to create individual change. How did he specifically try to do this? With ritual orgiastic sex and drug taking. This credo fit right in with the 1960s philosophy of sexual liberation and drug-crazed behavior, one that Page lived in to the hilt.

Crowley viewed the Devil differently. Rather than seeing him as the complete personification of evil, he saw him as the bringer of intellectual and spiritual freedom—hence his saying "Do what thou wilt." However, Page said, "I do not worship the Devil. But I am interested in magic. I feel Aleister Crowley is a misunderstood genius. Because his whole thing was liberation of the person, of the entity, and that restriction would foul you up, lead to frustration which leads to violence, crime, mental breakdown."

The emphasis on personal achievement and fulfillment no doubt appealed to Page's hopes and desires for the band. Indeed, he said, "When you've discovered your true will you should forge ahead like a steam train. If you put all your energies into it there's no doubt you'll succeed. Because that's your true will."

Although this point of view is obviously unapologetic ambition, it can hardly be considered a pact with the Devil. But besides engaging in self-destructive behavior like drug use, how far did Page go in flirting with the darkness? He did have quite a collection of Crowley artifacts like capes, wands, and boots. After Page acquired the ultimate Crowley artifact, the Boleskine House, he attempted to restore it to its condition when Crowley conducted his rituals. He even went so far as to have a satanist paint murals.

The place was pretty freaky and scary, although Page didn't seem to think so in 1970. "It's not an unfriendly place when you walk into it, it just seems to have this thing. . . . I'm attracted by the unknown."

But Page kept much of his occult interests private. B. P. Fallon, who knew the band well as its publicist, humorously explained, "He believed his philosophies and it shaped how he acted, but it wasn't directing every iota of his life. I don't know far he took it. I never observed him conducting any rituals. In my experience he didn't even practice yoga. He certainly wasn't sacrificing any virgins at midnight. He couldn't find any!"

Miss Pamela had her own extreme explanations as to why Page had such an interest in the occult and acquired so much magic paraphernalia. Remembering when he showed her his whips, she claimed, "He was curious about the dark aspects, he carried his whips around and he liked to inflict a little damage on willing girls. . . . I think Jimmy really believed the Crowley stuff. He gleaned a lot from it. It helped create his aura and mystique. Sure there was an element of play-acting, flapping around those big halls in Crowley's cape. But . . . he's a notorious tight wad; he had to be totally into something to pay for it!"

Interest in sorcery and magic stretches back to ancient civilizations that used supernatural means to contact the spirit world in an effort to control life, foretell the future, and gain guidance. But the Bible warns that messing around with magic and trying to tell the future is dangerous, that Satan is behind occult practices, and that only God knows the future. Wizards, witches, enchanters, and those who called on spirits were condemned by Moses. In short, sorcery leads to a dead end.

Crowley's efforts at magic were futile and his life went downhill after an aborted attempt to contact the Egyptian god Thoth, whom he called his Holy Guardian Angel. Crowley made enemies of other occultists like the famous Irish poet William Butler Yeats.

The crazy ways that Crowley lived his entire adult life were as radically opposite as one could get from the greatest commandment given by Jesus—to love both God and people. Crowley's reputation finally went completely sour, his band of followers were gone. He became hopelessly addicted to heroin, and he died in 1947 a lonely, tormented man.

Page now downplays the connection he had with Crowley. For Page, it was merely one part of his formative years while in Zeppelin. He told *Guitar World* that "it's unfortunate that my studies of mysticism and Eastern and Western traditions of magick and tantricism have all come under the umbrella of Crowley. Yeah, sure, I read a lot of Crowley and was fascinated by his techniques and ideas. But I was reading across the board. . . . It was quite a major part of my formative experience as anything else."

Page would make reference to his interests in Tarot cards, Crowley, and magic in his film fantasy sequence in *The Song Remains the Same* from 1976. But although he would share some of his interests, he claimed that he never had any intentions of wanting to get others to follow Crowley's teachings, practice magic, take drugs, or get involved in other types of crazy behavior. "I wasn't really preaching, because it wasn't really necessary," Page elaborated. "My lifestyle was just my lifestyle. I didn't feel the need to convert anyone; it was just the way that my life was taking me at that time. At the end of the day, from this vantage point, it can either be glorified or criticized."

Shortly after the short British tour, Plant encountered some bad luck that would return to haunt him. In February, he suffered a car crash near Birmingham while coming back from a Spirit concert. Both cars in the accident were write-offs. Plant was admitted to Kiddermeister Hospital with facial lacerations and damaged teeth. Later that month came Zeppelin's first full-fledged European tour, which included Sweden, Denmark, Holland, Germany, Austria, and Switzerland.

The band had an unusual, comical experience when it toured Germany. Eva von Zeppelin, a relative of the designer of the doomed airship, had became furious that rock musicians were performing using *her* name and threatened to sue the group if they played as Zeppelin. She even went into a recording studio where the band was recording and tried to get them thrown out. In the newspapers she fumed, "They may be world famous, but a couple of shrieking monkeys are not going to use a privileged family name without permission." She got some publicity, and the band got a temporary name change. For the only time in Zeppelin's history, they played one Copenhagen show on February 28 as the Nobs.

They returned to their name Led Zeppelin on their next date, March 7, at Montreux, Switzerland, a quiet, peaceful mountain community. News spread quickly and fans came from all over Europe. The small casino where they played held only 2,000 people. A review in the local newspaper praised the group, declaring that Zeppelin's music "seduces the senses" and that Led Zeppelin's triumphant show was unprecedented in the small mountain town. The group had enjoyed their visit to Montreux as much as the fans.

The peace and quiet of Montreux was a far cry from what was upcoming on their North American tour from March 21 to April 18. These were troubled times—a battlefield of confrontation as political tensions brought out the cops nightly, especially in the South. At some venues, police employed unnecessary violence against fans. The tour got off to a bad start as the band was on its way to Canada. Page's Gibson Black Beauty Les Paul "disappeared" off the truck at the airport. He seldom took it on the road, but things were going so well that he decided to start using it. The 19,000 screaming fans that greeted the band at the Pacific Coliseum in Vancouver had to ease the loss a little. The crowd was rewarded with two and a half hours of ear-splitting rock.

The March 27 show at the L.A. Forum was pumped! The band played with an enthusiasm and vibrancy that began to set Zeppelin further and further apart from all other rock acts. John Paul Jones now played organ onstage, which added a new dimension. By now, Zeppelin had embraced L.A. as their second home—it was an awesome place to have a great time—and the music showed it! Plant started off the festivities with commenting to the crowd, "Good evening. Everybody feel all right?" Without a doubt, the crowd was feeling all right. There was spontaneity to the max! After "We're Gonna Groove," Plant ad-libbed lyrics to "Dazed and Confused."

During his trademark solo, Page bowed his Les Paul to new heights. With the help of his Echoplex units and wah-wah pedal, his amplifiers emitted sonic howls that swirled around the Forum's round walls. Neil Zlozower was there on one of his first photo shoots, taking pictures from the audience with a telephoto lens. He was amazed at Page's theatrics. He clicked away with his camera as Page went up and down on the strings with his bow. Zlozower recalled, "You know, the highlight for me of any Zeppelin show was you'd always be waiting to see Jimmy whip out that violin bow and be strummin' his guitar with the violin bow, because no one ever did that back in those days as far as I know. He *was* the originator. There was just always something about watching him, where it was like . . . c'mon, Jimmy—whip out the bow—whip out the bow—whip out the bow!"

Everyone was enveloped in an unearthly, mesmerizing mass of electronic effects. But fans weren't just captured by the sound. New material from the second album was added—"What Is and What Should Never Be" was now a permanent addition in place of "I Can't Quit You." Before the band broke into a sizzling "Heartbreaker," people sprang out of their seats and filled the aisles, so Plant told people to sit down on the floor. After a few more songs the aisles began to fill up again, and people tried to crowd up to the stage. In an effort to be humorous, Plant dedicated "Since I've Been Loving You" to "the little men with the suits who keep pushing everybody back down the aisle. It's their big day, y'see."

The show continued with more humor from Plant during "How Many More Times" as the band members were introduced as "the four survivors of the Graf Zeppelin." In a nod of tribute to the Beatles, Bonham was said to perform "for the benefit of Mr. Kite" and Page was described as "the man who made rock, rock!" Plant encouraged everyone, including the police, to clap, but the authorities overreacted when the crowd filled the aisles again. It had become a cat-and-mouse game: police got everyone seated, then backed off, only to have the crowd get up when security was not in sight. There was an "us versus them" mentality in the crowd, the antiwar attitude of not listening to anyone in a uniform. Added to this, the loud, aggressive music would get everyone going. There was no solution in sight. Plant warned everyone again to cool down, "Easy! Easy! I want you to be cool 'cause these men have got big sticks and they don't care! You keep cool and we'll keep cool!"

This helped to quiet things again, and the show went on with a powerful medley that included Maurice Ravel's "Bolero" and the Yardbirds classic "I'm a Man." With this, the crowd again leaped up. This became too much for the authorities, who now feared that the situation was close to an all-out riot. To monitor the situation, the house lights flashed on. The first encore of "Whole Lotta Love" flew out over the Forum crowd—Page ferociously attacked his theremin after the first two verses. He waved his hand over it, and his magic motions drew low moans and shrill shrieks. He used his Echoplex sound boxes atop his amplifiers to full effect, creating pulsating auditory vibrations that rose and leaped out, with life all their own. The audience was mesmerized like never before in the Forum that night. Plant asked in vain to switch off the house lights before the final number, a wildly rocking, frantic "Communication Breakdown."

As the crowd filed out, the emcee announced an upcoming Forum concert, "April 25, the Forum presents Jimi Hendrix. If you wanna mail for tickets, mail for them now!" The Forum in 1970 was becoming *the* place to see unbelievable concerts. The 18,000 who saw this Zeppelin show had been treated to an outstanding performance. The newspaper even reported that 4,000 fans hung around for half an hour in the hopes of another encore, but this was not to be. This show turned out to be bittersweet because of all the crowd problems and police reactions.

A few nights later in Pittsburgh, Zeppelin stopped playing in the middle of the set and walked off the stage to let things cool down. The cheering fans stood on their seats and went wild with enthusiasm, but baton-wielding cops ran into the crowd and pushed people off the chairs. It could have turned out pretty ugly. When you were being bombarded with the Zeppelin sound, it was hard to just sit there. After a short break, the band came back onstage, and there was no more trouble.

The tour rolled on—no opening act, no intermission, just high volume. The band was playing really well together. Although Zeppelin was bursting with adrenaline, the loss of privacy, the endless travel, the highs and lows (musical and narcotic), the sheer hard work, the superficiality of on-the-road relationships compared to home life, all these ground their emotions to a pulp. Furthermore, for all their strutting confidence, Zeppelin did come under fire. As well as loving them, America scorned them. Long hair was still frowned upon, let alone sex, drugs and loud music. Death threats were made at the band, so armed guards rode along with everyone. Like something out of a scene from the movie *Easy Rider*, the band was ridiculed and refused service at roadside diners in the South by rednecks. Upon their arrival in Memphis on April 17, Zeppelin was given the keys to the city. But by that evening, the band was threatened backstage for their long hair. So the band got out of town fast by concert's end.

In part, the American experience had gone bad on them. And

the quartet knew they had neglected their British audience. Now their instinct was to put that right and re-engage with what were genuinely strong elements in their background: country life and folk music. All of them hailed from small towns. Plant pointed out: "That's one thing Led Zeppelin has done for me. It's slowed me down . . . It's exactly what I wanted. It gives me room to think, breathe and live. I wake up in the morning and there are no buses, no traffic. Just tractors and the odd pheasant hooting in the next field."

Alongside their studious passion for the blues, Page and Plant were also besotted with Fairport Convention, The Incredible String Band, and Joni Mitchell. Page's "all-time favorite" guitarist was not a bluesman named Johnson, Waters, or Wolf, but acoustic virtuoso Bert Jansch. Page said that "he tied up the acoustic guitar in the same way Hendrix did the electric."

By late April, the band had completed their fifth stateside trek. They had promised themselves a break when they got back from America. Bonham and Jones returned to the peace and tranquility of home. But Plant was restless and called Page about a remote cottage in the Welsh hills that he fondly remembered from childhood. On summer weekends his father would drive the family up to the wooded Snowdonia area near the River Dovey. As a child, Plant fell in love with not only the mysterious dark forest but also with the tales of sword and sorcery associated with the area. Plant recalled: "When I was little, I dreamed heroic dreams. Most of the time I was the hero . . . the odds were always pretty much against me. Sort of like Davy Crockett, but the English equivalent of Davy Crockett—Robin Hood."

This place had a magic all its own. So in early May, Page and Plant retreated to Bron-Y-Aur to relax and write. This place had a faraway feel because it was halfway up a mountain with the nearest town two miles away. Here at this derelict 18th century cottage, they set up camp. The place was abandoned. It had stone walls, no electricity, and no running water. They collected wood to fuel the open-hearth fire which heated a range. The two worked by fire-light and log fires. Water was fetched from a stream and heated for washing. This was a real contrast to hotel rooms. The stress of the last tour was left behind. A sense of relief and freedom was found in their new surroundings—a feeling that would be reflected in a song later titled, "Over the Hills and Far Away." The Welsh countryside would provide inspiration for songs on the next album and set the mellow tone.

With boots on their feet, backpacks on their shoulders, and a cassette recorder, Page and Plant walked in the spring flower-decked hills. There wasn't a soul for miles—just the privacy of nature. With Page strumming an acoustic guitar and Plant tootling away on harmonica, the songs came—"That's the Way," "Friends," "Bron-Y-Aur Stomp." It was an idyllic sabbatical where Page and Plant just wrote. The beauty of this evolving quieter side of *Zeppelin III* was the band's ability to take traditional English instruments, folk songs and arcane myths and make them speak to the kid in Struthers, Ohio, wearing K-Mart jeans.

Later in May, when Page and Plant reported back, Jones and Bonham needed little persuasion that the band should go acoustic. The group began recording at Headley Grange, an empty, damp, run-down mansion in the country that bore the memory of elegance past. The band chose engineer Andy Johns to assist with the recording because he had a reputation for being top notch. Johns recalled: "I was uptight because these guys were so good. You always wanted to do your best for them. Pagey was really easy to get along with, and I don't remember him having an emotional block, not knowing what to do."

Jimmy Page indeed had complete control in the recording studio and had studio smarts. When more recording for the album was being done in June at Olympic Studios, something got accidentely erased. Page said, "I was very good at salvaging things that went wrong. For example, the rhythm track at the beginning of 'Celebration Day' was completely wiped by an engineer. I forget what we were recording, but I was listening to the headphones and nothing was coming through. I started yelling, 'What the hell is going on!' Then I noticed that the red recording light was on what used to be the drums. The engineer had accidentally recorded over Bonzo! And that is why you have that synthesizer drone from the end of 'Friends' going into 'Celebration Day,' until the rhythm track catches up. We put that on to compensate to make up for the missing drum track. That's called 'salvaging'."

"Since I've Been Loving You" was the first song written for the album, coming out of just a day's rehearsal. It was a "live" take with John Paul Jones playing organ and foot bass pedals at the same time. Listening to Ray Charles got Jones into organ. He loved Charles's blend of gospel with rhythm and blues, his sort of church sound on the instrument. Page explained, "I'd still like to keep trying everything through the framework of Zeppelin, and I think everybody feels the same way, too, because everybody's got ideas and as yet we still haven't reached the full potential of what's there . . . And the organ, the keyboard things that John Paul Jones is doing now, has helped to broaden the outlook of everything."

Richard Digby Smith, often Andy Johns' tape-operator assistant, was awed to sit in on a session when Plant sang "Since I've Been Loving You." Smith remembered, "I can see Robert at the mike now. He was passionate. Lived every line. What you got on the record was what happened. His only preparation was a herbal cigarette and a couple shots of Jack Daniel's."

I loved Jones's keyboard work. It gave the band a fuller sound—not that they needed one. But it added a whole new dimension to the Zep sound. Page is celebrated as rock's heaviest guitarist, but when he reached for his acoustic, his touch could be as light as a feather. So as a result he'd work away on the acoustic. Johns found it much easier to record acoustic guitars and drums instead of a loud rock band. Page would say, "Any set of circumstances can be inspiring, really. I guess a lot of the acoustic songs came after tours, when you couldn't really go home and set up a

200-watt stack and just blast out, and consequently you just work out on the acoustic. That was a good balance, really, because you can explore riffs in other ways."

About this same time, my own life would take a turn toward creativity in music. By now I'd gotten off active duty in the Air Force. In 1970 I'd moved from Laguna Beach and wound up on some bluffs in the south end of San Clemente. My little apartment was a stone's throw from the beach off Buena Vista Street, by the Miramar Theatre, a rock and blues venue over the years. Just north of the pier was a glassy beach break named 204, after the railroad sign next to the tracks. I climbed down the hill and surfed there every day and enjoyed the small yet sometimes tubular waves. Back then it wasn't a well-known break and there were plenty of waves to go around. It was a temporary paradise.

My old buddy Clyde Johnson was still very active in the La Crescenta music scene. He knew that I'd been writing songs and wanted to find out what we could do. So during the last week of July he came down to visit, and brought along a Yamaha nylon string guitar, a harmonica, recorder flute and reel-to-reel tape recorder. The next three days we hung out on the beach, with Clyde on the sand working on riffs while I was out surfing. Then at night we rehearsed, switched on his recorder and created.

We'd bought an old 45 record of the Coasters' "Yakety Yak" at a thrift shop and were amused at the flashbacks to teenage chores the song evoked. So we recorded that first, using guitar, tambourine and harmonica. It was raw, loose, fun. There was also a ballad I'd written about a lonely guy cruising along the beach, sort of like Crosby, Stills and Nash. We started out with fairly normal songs— then we got pretty far out. I had a poem about an alchemist making gold, working away in a secret lab like an early gothic scientist. The words painted a dreamscape of pointed peaks, slowly moving mist, and a purple sky that changed colors over the alchemist's hut. Clyde played autoharp which sounded like a warped harpsichord in a cave, then overdubbed flute sounds. The result was a weird mix—the Moody Blues meets the Incredible String Band. The sessions were pressed onto an EP by Clyde. We designed a cover with our own art that had castles, pointed peaks, flying lizards, UFOs, and lost ships at sea. New doors of mystery had swung open to a musical world for us. It had all been inspired by the sounds of waves and seagulls—nature was our muse. For us, there would never be another summer like that one of 1970.

Led Zeppelin started to itch for life on the road again. But before the band tackled the U.S.A. again they were seduced by a yearning for glory in their native England. So they accepted an invitation to play the Bath Festival of Blues and Progressive Music with the likes of John Mayall, Pink Floyd, Santana, and Jefferson Airplane.

Led Zeppelin's triumphant appearance at least signaled their acceptance by their home crowd. Europe greeted Zep with open arms and ears. In front of 200,000 people, they played for over three hours. The set included new songs such as "Immigrant Song," and "Since I've Been Loving You" and acoustic numbers like "That's the Way." To everyone's delight, Plant did his Elvis impersonation during "I Need Your Love Tonight" and "How Many More Times." Page appeared as a rock and roll farmer with a tweed coat, a hat and a beard. Plant told the crowd, "It's really nice to come to an open-air festival where there's no bad things happening."

The crowd went wild for Zeppelin, demanding and getting encore after encore—a total of five. The performance confirmed their ranking in Britain as equal to the Stones and Beatles, and probably was very much the turning point after which the band never looked back. But they knew America was beckoning, and from August to September they were again touring the states for the sixth time in under two years. In America by now they had become as big an attraction as the Beatles had been in their heyday.

At the Oakland Coliseum, Led Zeppelin blasted nearly 10,000 people half-senseless with music of sheer power, force and emotion. There was an assault on all fronts, from hard rockers to acoustic numbers to blues. The band left the stage exhausted and exhilarated. The basic format was simple as possible: the band, a stage and lights but no props or supporting act, and good, loud, wild music. There was one new addition to the music—an acoustic portion, drawn from the new album. Page said that this part went well overall, although there were some exceptions. "Some places, though, it's been a bit of a shock," he admitted. "I relate it back to the period after we'd done the first album, but the second one hadn't come out. We always try to get new numbers on stage; we used to do 'What Is and What Should Never Be' and it didn't really happen when we first started to do it because there's no association, nobody knew what it was . . . A similar sort of thing has happened with the acoustic things . . . The audience is hearing them fresh and there have been mixed reactions . . . But we always give as much as we've got to give that night. When it comes to the encores, we'll go on and on and on if they want to."

The band's return to the L.A. Forum on September 4 clearly demonstrated this different side to Zeppelin. Located off the freeway by Los Angeles International Airport, the Forum stands in the middle of a vast parking lot. Once inside, one was awestruck by the Zeppelin stage. According to a spectator, it looked like something out of a war zone. He described it this way, "It looked like an open-air attack tank. Or some sort of futuristic altar. I was wondering if my ears would be bloodied by such an array of amplifiers upon banks of amplifiers." The audience quietly waited for the show to start, some people passing marijuana cigarettes. Suddenly the piped-in music stopped, and the entire Forum was thrown into darkness. Many in the first few rows sprang to their feet and began cheering as spotlights flashed on a row of amplifiers. The lights followed Plant as he strode out from behind the amps and entered the glare of center stage. His long mass of blond curls bounced as he smiled and nodded to the crowd. The cries and screams rose higher from the audience as the rest of the band filed out. Hundreds of Instamatic flashbulbs popped throughout the crowd.

A barrage of sound leaped out from the stage with the show's opener, "Immigrant Song." Plant's high pitches swirled around the arena, and within thirty seconds, everyone was caught up in Zeppelin's presence. Even though the band's unity was strongly evident, there were also times when each member was given a spot for individual creativity. One of the moments this was truest for Page was early on during "Dazed and Confused." When he used his guitar bow on his extended solo, the sounds created were hypnotizing, almost otherworldly. Electronic echoes gradually turned into haunting, violin-like notes, not unlike what Paganini may have also played. Also entrancing in his own way was John Paul Jones, who churned out an extended organ improvisation after "Since I've Been Loving You." Through the keyboard, Jones painted pictures of misty Celtic lands, shrouded in myths that echo along the rolling, grassy knolls.

Throughout the performance, Plant was an expressive master of ceremonies. As he introduced the next solo spot, he announced that "You might hear in the background the crash of sticks against skins—yes, it's our own, our very own—John Bonham!" The Forum's walls shook with "Moby Dick," and near the song's climax Bonham demonstrated the influence of rock drummers Ginger Baker and Keith Moon. Frantic cheers and applause broke from the crowd as Bonham simultaneously pounded foot pedal, snare, and tom-tom to create one pounding entity of sound. After he crashed his cymbals at the climax, Plant cried, "All right—what about that? The big B—John Bonham!"

Plant's expressiveness went much further when a medley was played. He strung together one unexpected song to the next, as with "Communication Breakdown," "Good Times Bad Times" and "For What It's Worth"—the last a reminder from his Band of Joy days. He had the audience wildly clapping along. By the time Zeppelin ended with a tribute to England's peaceful, rolling countryside, "Out on the Tiles," everyone was screaming for more. It was delivered with an off-the-wall "Blueberry Hill," Plant sounding like a cross between Elvis and Fats Domino. The response this time was near riotous, and Plant invited all listeners to "get as loose as we are." This could mean only one thing—another medley that used a more outrageous mix of songs than before. This turned into a jam that included Page's echoing theramin on "Whole Lotta Love" and Plant's ramblings on music, love, and sex with "Let That Boy Boogie," "Think It Over" and "The Lemon Song." Plant ad-libbed a few lines on this last number that were both funny and unexpected—"I don't care how you squeeze, mama, just take your teeth out before you get into bed!" The pace changed to accommodate Plant's new lyrics. An excitement was created onstage—everyone felt anything could happen. The magic was there.

Page put it this way, "Not having a set pattern is what does it. The way it's such an invigorating catalyst at times, because everybody feels that way and somebody starts doing something. Everybody smiles and away it goes . . . you've got to keep thinking fast—when it's working well it's really great, four people building something, changing gear without crunching them."

The band didn't always crunch the audience's ears with electricity from the stacks of Marshall amps. There was a definite change of pace when Page played his acoustic on "Bron-Y-Aur Stomp." Plant went out of his way to explain to everyone about the solitude and serenity of the tiles—the British term for rolling countryside. Specifically, Plant mentioned the Bron-Y-Aur cottage in Wales, where the group rehearsed much of the current album's acoustic numbers. "Bron-Y-Aur is the Welsh equivalent of the phrase 'Golden Breast.' This is so because of its position every morning when the sun rises, and it's really a remarkable place. So after staying there for awhile and deciding that it was time to leave for various reasons, we couldn't really just leave it and forget about it—you've probably all been to a place like that." The band enjoyed sharing the new material, whether the hard-hitting electric or the softer acoustic.

L.A.'s Forum was the perfect environment for a Zeppelin show.

When you were in a place as big as the Forum and you looked around and saw 18,000 people jumping around and going crazy and just having fun, you knew that the band must be doing something right. It must have been challenging to get all those people worked up, especially those who were far away from the stage, but Zeppelin managed to pull it off. Few concerts on the tour matched the excitement of the Forum shows. This was the band flying high and taking the audience right along with them.

Zeppelin was voted best group in a readers poll conducted by Britain's most widely read newspaper, ending eight years of Beatles domination. And Led Zeppelin played Madison Square Garden for the first time on September 19. On this date, they could boast of grossing $100,000. The bread was nice, but they didn't let it go to their heads. There was no real "attitude" about them. They were enjoying the fame, but were not drunk with their own self-importance. The members shared a professional state of mind— serious about the music and playing their best. They were always reliable. And Peter Grant believed so much in Led Zeppelin that he got concert promoters to change their agreement from a 50/50 split between them and the act to a 90/10 split in Zeppelin's favor.

Led Zeppelin III was released the beginning of October. It came out in the days when you'd anticipate a record's release, then savor the unwrapping, checking out the artwork, reading everything on it, and just feeling the vinyl. There were no CDs or MP3s, just a 12-inch platter of vinyl. The only decision was whether you'd buy it in stereo or mono.

An ad in *Circus* magazine displayed the front cover with the words: "Led Zeppelin III is here . . . and after you play the album, play the jacket." So I played the album. It presented a very different image of Led Zeppelin from the first two albums. Most importantly, it was predominantly acoustic. Page finally displayed his considerable talent on the acoustic guitar, which he had only hinted at before on cuts like "Black Mountain Side" and "Babe I'm Gonna Leave You" (both from *Zeppelin I*) and "Thank You" and

"Ramble On" (both from *Zeppelin II*). Material like "Friends," "Tangerine," "That's the Way," and "Bron-Y-Aur Stomp" differed greatly from the Brown Bomber's intense aggression. "That's the Way" was my personal favorite of the acoustic material. The song was dreamlike and soothing. Inspired by their surroundings, Plant and Page had written it in the Welsh countryside.

However, the opener, "Immigrant Song," set a standard for medieval imagery of Viking lust in hard rock. Plant's wailing war cries sent chills up my spine the first time I heard it. "Celebration Day" was a funky rocker. "Out on the Tiles" was English slang for "a night out on the town" built by a Bonzo riff. And "Gallows Pole" was perhaps Zep's strangest track ever—a morbid American folk song that Page updated to be about the hangman of a deck of Tarot cards. "Hats Off to (Roy) Harper" was a trip back to the plantation, when blues shouters gathered around a campfire. But for me, the gem of the album was the slow burning, epic blues, "Since I've Been Loving You." Plant did his best Janis Joplin interpretation. And if you've been debating about who is the greatest rock guitar player in history, just listen to Page's tortured solo and move on to another subject.

Overall, *Led Zeppelin III* was an intimate listening experience. The more I listened to it, the more I liked it. I got one of the early pressings with Crowley's motto inscribed in the run-out groove, not only on one side but on both sides of the record. Side one had —Do What Thou Wilt—side two said—So Mote Be it—. Page was able to pull this off in secret by having someone at the studio write the inscription.

After I played the album, I played the jacket. As I turned the wheel, I wondered what was underneath. I bought another copy for the added pleasure of ripping the cover apart to find out what was on the rest of the wheel. The silly cover was meant to represent a crop rotation calendar. There were eleven circular holes on the front that showed different faces of the band members and brightly colored shapes when the wheel was rotated. The final result, created by the artist known as Zacron, wasn't what Page had in mind. Instead of crops, Zacron had splattered the cover with a wide assortment of images such as butterflies, hummingbirds, and flowers. Page wasn't amused and thought that it looked too bubble gum. To me, instead of psychedelia, the cover looked too teeny-bopper for Led Zeppelin. When I spun the wheel, I noticed the band members' faces popping into the holes as well brightly colored shapes and patterns. As I opened up the jacket, I thought I'd see something more like Led Zeppelin, but instead I just got a rehash of the front cover. The only object with an obvious connection to the band was a zeppelin. I thought the back cover was actually more eye-catching and should have been the front. The black-and-white stipple of Jones, Page and Bonham was similar to *Led Zeppelin I*. And there was the crusty, tan image of Plant with his hair wrapped in a halo of tangled sunlight. He looked like a sun god.

Maybe the front cover threw the press for a loop, too. They sure as hell didn't like the record. The album took a critical hammering from the press: "Led Zeppelin Gone Soft" or "Led Zeppelin Tone Down" were the headlines, over comments such as "the wah-wah may be breathing its last screeching breath."

Zep was pissed. They stopped doing interviews. It seemed that Zeppelin was always being put down. It had to hurt deep down inside. It hurt me too, but endeared me more to the band. When Zep was being trampled on, I felt the press was putting me down as well, for being a fan. I was proud to be a Ledhead, and still am today.

Was the press listening to the album, but not hearing it? Didn't they notice the band's broadening range of disparate and sometimes exotic influences, such as East Indian scales on "Friends," American country music in "Tangerine," and traditional English folk on "Gallows Pole"? Today, thanks to the success of MTV's "Unplugged" concert broadcasts by such artists as Aerosmith, Eric Clapton, Neil Young, and Nirvana, the notion of heavy rockers being sensitive balladeers has been accepted as a great step forward. Led Zeppelin were not only twenty years ahead of the pack, but the band still demonstrated that going acoustic didn't have to mean that its hard edge had been lost.

Zeppelin played by its own rules. The members were pleased with the album and that was all that mattered. They felt it was the key to their future progress and showed people that the band wasn't going to be one-dimensional. They were determined to continue the search for new ideas, sounds and direction, a process Zeppelin would maintain until the end.

In late October 1970, Page and Plant returned to Bron-Y-Aur. As before, the pair sat around the cottage hearth with a decent log fire burning and played and sang. They already had a backlog of half-finished songs and fragments of ideas for the next album. Page had begun creating a lengthy instrumental track which had no lyrics, just a nice chord progression and an extended crescendo.

At the end of October a record was released that was acclaimed by critics. No piece of rock music has ever induced more interest in religion than *Jesus Christ Superstar*. For most people growing up in the 1950s and 60s, religion was just a word, or at most, a responsibility. It wasn't about knowing God, just something to do on Sundays. Many churches appeared to be more interested in self-perpetuation and finances than making God known.

John Lennon's remark about the Beatles being more popular than Jesus carried a lot of weight and also created an outcry. For millions of fans, the Beatles were more relevant than most religious leaders. *Jesus Christ Superstar* deglamorized the New Testament version of Jesus. He wasn't portrayed so much as the Son of God but as a human being bothered with such human emotions as self-doubt, conflicting motivation, and confusion. For once, Jesus was more popular than the Beatles. Jerry Prochnicky saw Zeppelin as a positive force: "For me, Zeppelin served as a great escape from a lot of things. I was questioning God, but I believed in Led Zeppelin. Rock music was my religion and Jimmy Page, Jim Morrison, and John Lennon were my messiahs."

During 1970, I was grateful to be in the Reserves, being a medic at March Air Force Base in Riverside, California, instead of dodging bullets in a rice paddy in Vietnam. I also believed that I was serving God and my country. But as time went on, I got very disillusioned as I experienced many angry and frustrated people at the Air Force Base. Their take on serving their country was, "Thank God when I get discharged! I can't wait to get out of this!" I started feeling the same way too after a while. When Nixon began bombing Cambodia, many really started seriously questioning our government's activities in other parts of the world and also started questioning God, too. After all, if I was serving my country, how could this be right? When I finally got off active duty in October, I felt like I had gotten out of jail. By now, I was totally ready to grow my hair long, start listening to more music and do my own thing.

Led Zeppelin had a special type of attraction to me—I seemed to be drawn to their music, almost like a spiritual magnetism. Like many other fans, I would continue to get intrigued with each new record. But no one knew that 1971 would prove to be the year for Zeppelin's most successful album ever. It would also herald the band's most inspiring song.

CHAPTER 4

The Four Symbols

In spite of the Vietnam War and other major societal issues, it was a simpler time and perhaps, overall, a better time for us all—especially for rock fans. At the time there was only one Led Zeppelin, one Black Sabbath, and one Grand Funk Railroad. Black Sabbath was too much "downer music" for both Jerry and me. Jerry though, loved Grand Funk, a remarkable, high decibel power trio from Flint, Michigan. "They were truly an American band," Jerry noted. "Like Led Zeppelin, Grand Funk was constantly being put down by critics as just noise, but I got funked. What's wrong about music so intense that it can be felt physically?"

Stung by critics who thrashed their third LP, Led Zeppelin's response was to plan the follow-up as the definitive killer Zep album, to combine the heavy thunder of the first two Zeppelin records with the folk excursions of the third. The band started work in the new year on their fourth album again at Headley Grange, the huge, dilapidated two-hundred-year old, three-story house outside of London. Page called engineer Andy Johns again. Johns had just done *Sticky Fingers* with the Stones, using their state-of-the-art, 16-track mobile recording truck. So he suggested the truck to Page. Johns elaborated: "Using the mobile truck allows you to have a control room on wheels. It's bit narrow, like a corridor, so your ability to monitor a situation isn't as good as in a proper studio. You end up talking to the band through a closed circuit camera and a microphone, instead of through the studio glass. It can get a bit impersonal, but the advantage is that the band is more at home."

The group began to settle in at Headley Grange. It was the scene of the early 70s—gentlemen rockers at large in the country. Gear was set up. Each day the band would gather downstairs and jam. No one bothered to look at the clock. The place sounded great—within the aged plaster walls the sound was deep and resonant. It bounced around and echoed, so the room sound was pretty much "live." A lot of this was because of the long hallways and passageways. Outside the big double doors was an entrance hall with a staircase and landings all around it. Bonham and Andy Johns made an exciting discovery here.

Andy Johns recalled, "The other guys were out having a drink, and John Bonham and I were at the house. He still complained that he wasn't getting the sound that he wanted. So I said to him, 'I've got an idea.' We got his drums and put him in the hallway and then hung two mikes from the staircase and pointed them toward the kit. The kit was very well balanced internally—each drum's volume was consistent with the others. In the truck I put him into two channels and compressed the hell out of the drums... I remember sitting here thinking it was utterly amazing, so I ran out of the truck and said, 'Bonzo, you've gotta come in and hear this!' And he came in and shouted, 'Whoa! That's it!'"

Once again, Page and Plant brought in some fresh ideas. Plant asked Fairport Convention's Sandy Denny to join him in a duet on the madrigal-type "The Battle of Evermore," with striking imagery of castles and dragons taken from Scottish folk lore. With Denny singing the Queen of Life part to Robert's Prince of Peace, this marked the first time that another vocalist was used on a Zeppelin record. Ian Stewart, sometime piano player, road manager and life-long friend of the Stones, was also used on another track. His boogie piano added a further dimension to the band's trade-mark jam on "Rock and Roll." Bonham had played part of a Little Richard tune, Page improvised a riff over it, Plant came up with words on the spot, and the structure fell into place right away. The sessions had much spontaneity like this. As songs emerged they stayed fresh because they weren't played to death. The way Page put it was, "We were never a band that did 96 takes of the same thing . . . If the track isn't happening and it starts creating a psychological barrier even after an hour or two, you should stop and do something else."

But above their awesome talents there lay an unparalleled understanding of the music itself. The inspiration and energy all came from the band's observations and experiences. At the house was this black dog that was always hanging around begging for food, so thus the title for the album's explosive opening tune. In sessions for "Black Dog," Jones and Page hammered out the progression. Bonham played along and got the percussion down, and the result was a riff-ridden, electronic roller coaster ride. "Misty Mountain Hop" was a bulldozer bomp about a bunch of hippies getting busted. The codeine rush of all the songs had to be "Four Sticks"—named for when Bonham clutched two sticks in each hand and just went for it! And Headley Grange's acoustic echoes roared out to the max on "When the Levee Breaks"—a wild con-coction of Bonham's drums, Plant's monster harmonica, and Page's soaring slide guitar work. As a total contrast, the ballad "Going to California" was inspired by Joni Mitchell, the lyrics of heartbreak beautifully intertwined with guitar and mandolin.

But perhaps the most celebrated, awe-inspiring recording of all was in a longer piece that Page had woven together. He recalled, "I'd been fooling around with the acoustic guitar and came up with different sections, which I married together. But what I wanted was something that would have the drums come in at the middle, and then we'd build to a huge crescendo. Also, I wanted it to speed up . . . So I had all the structure of it, and I ran it by John Paul Jones so he could get the idea of it—John Bonham and Robert had gone out for the night—and then on the following day we got into it with John Bonham."

By firelight, Page ran down the chords in front of Plant. Inspired, Plant wrote down a large part of the lyrics right there. The words told a story of a woman climbing to heaven and painted pictures of a fantasy world with May queens, pipers and forests lit by moonlight. In rehearsals, Jones experimented with keyboard and then recorders to go with Page's acoustic opening. Then the electric buildup fell into place, with Bonham's percussion slowly finding its proper hard-hitting emphasis. "Stairway to Heaven" would prove that the band's style had grown far beyond the heavy blues-based sound of the first two albums.

After recording for several weeks in early '71, Zeppelin did a series of small gigs at clubs and universities in England during March to "get back" to their roots. These were their first British dates since Bath, and could hardly have been more different from that massive event. It was a return to many of the places where they played when they first formed—to re-establish contact with the people who got them off the ground. The Back to the Clubs tour was a shrewd decision by Grant and the band to make points with the only people that mattered to them, the fans. People that had followed Zep since the beginning were thrilled to have the chance to see the band in a small, informal setting. Peter Grant even charged the promoters the same fee as they had done when they first appeared on the scene. And one last great thing happened—the band was totally reenergized.

As the year progressed, they continued to work on the fourth album. The need for several remixes pushed the release date back to November. The band decided that this album would have no title, no mention or photo of the group on the actual jacket, no company logo. The total anonymity of the visual aspect would include only one symbol on it, like a tradesman's symbol—a brand. But then Page decided since it was their fourth album and there were four of them, that each member should choose or design his own esoteric symbol.

Atlantic Records told them that they were committing professional suicide. It just wasn't done this way—it was too different, too radical, and everyone would be confused or just hate it. But Page was adamant. Screw the critics! Page wanted to show them that it was the music that made Zeppelin popular—it had nothing to do with the band's name or image. He wanted the record to stand or fall on its music alone.

About the same time that Zeppelin were recording the new album, Clyde Johnson and I embarked on a musical flight of our own. He'd made his bedroom into a recording studio, and it was there that we began to create more songs for another demo. We were intrigued by the alchemist image, how this little dude tried to create gold and also tried to get to a higher or purer state spiritually by creating. This seemed magical. Clyde played me many records of the artists that he admired in '71—Neil Young, the Stones, T. Rex, David Bowie, Frank Zappa and Led Zeppelin. These became our influences. Clyde wrote the music and I provided lyrics. The songs took us on a mystical journey, illustrated with our own private mythologies, not unlike what Zep came up with on their upcoming album. Some tunes like "Dream Domains" were about flying to unconscious realms aboard a dream ship, sort of like the astral arks of the ancient Egyptians. Others like "Solar Sea Serpents" proclaimed the existence of huge space dragons that flew through the stars and slid to earth on moonbeams. We even had a slow instrumental, "End of Infinity," an electric-acoustic guitar jam that conjured images of space ships gliding along. Most of the songs were pretty spacey stuff, accentuated in stereo sound with Clyde's fuzz tone, wah-wah, tambourines, autoharps, maracas, and an old Chinese dragon drum my mom had lent us.

For the cover, Clyde decided to take some pictures. We drove to a remote area in our hometown of La Crescenta that had all these little hills. Atop the highest one was this old deserted house, half-hidden by trees. It was a falling down wreck, but it had this ancient-looking, tall stone chimney that rose into the air like a castle. I brought along a wizard costume I'd made out of an Air Force surgical robe that had mystical symbols like stars drawn on it with a marker. Clyde clicked away with his camera as I stood next to the chimney. Later we used one of these shots for the cover. For the background I drew this cartoonish dragon that had made all these tracks in the ground. I wrote the song titles inside the tracks. There were fourteen songs so we called the record "Fourteen Dragon Tracks." It really caught the mood of the time for us— being free, looking into our minds as far as we could and creating our own music just for us. We never intended to make money on it. The funny thing was we had no idea that Zep was sort of doing the same sort of mystical thing with symbols and faraway places. Magic was truly in the air.

There was no letup in Zeppelin's schedule in '71, but it was marred by their most frightening gig on July 5 in Milan, Italy. All went well for several numbers at the outdoor soccer stadium, but then the police went crazy. They induced a riot by tear gassing the audience. The promoter ran away. The security also ran off. Zep got trapped in the middle and had to flee the stage to an underground dressing room where they barricaded themselves until everything cooled down. The roadies stayed behind to protect the stage equipment. Zep left Italy never to return again.

But Led Zeppelin did return to Montreux, Switzerland, for two shows on August 7th and 8th. After the disastrous show in Milan a month earlier, Montreux, surrounded by mountains and lakeside air, became the perfect setting for Zep's refueling. And the fans there experienced Zeppelin's supercharged performance, even hearing tracks from the forthcoming album. But it would be the last time Zeppelin played Montreux, because later in the year, during an unfortunate accident at a Frank Zappa concert, the casino was brought down in a burning blaze. The event was immortalized on Deep Purple's classic hit, "Smoke on the Water."

After leaving Europe, the band prepared for yet another tour of America. For Led Zeppelin, every American tour was more elaborate, more expensive and more lucrative than the one before. This time the band brought along with them an amplification system that included a huge variety of speakers and amps—Marshall speakers, Hiwatt amplifiers, Vox echo chambers, and Marshall and Fender Super Verb amps. Page's guitars now included Les Pauls, a Fender Telecaster, and a Martin acoustic and a Rickenbacker 12-string. Bonham had the same Ludwig setup as before, and Jones had his Fender basses, some Farfisa organs and a Hohner electric piano. With all this, the live impact was pushed to the max—crowds were blown away by the sound. And the fans indeed came—the band played to enthusiastic crowds from L.A. to New York. Zeppelin's August-September 1971 tour, with each venue holding over 12,000 people, grossed over a million dollars. At that time, this was an enormous amount of money.

Before the tour started, Page invested in a custom built Gibson doubleneck guitar for performing "Stairway to Heaven." The cherry-red Gibson ES 1275 got different effects during the solo—the 12-string neck got the majestic chime sounds for the rhythm, and the 6 strings for the thick, full solid notes. The extra wide guitar body produced a meatier tone than the standard Gibson SG. The guitar's A/B selector switch allowed for more inclusion for one or both guitars in the circuit. There were master control volume and tone controls for each neck, but only one pickup selector switch that functioned for both necks. Page would leave the 12-string neck open as far as the sound would go, play on the 6-string neck, and get the 12-strings vibrating in sympathy.

At the Forum on August 21, they premiered "Stairway" for the L.A. crowd. By popular demand a second show was added the following night. At Madison Square Garden on September 3, the people stormed onto the stage at the end—it was incredible. That didn't even happen at the Stones concert. Even after the stage collapsed, the band came back on, which was great because it showed that they really did care about the audience—and the monitors were down and they couldn't even hear themselves!

Jerry's sister, Stephanie, saw the band in concert a week later. She remembered, "I got a call from my friends Mary and Bohdan in Rochester, New York, that Zeppelin was coming to their city on September 11. So I told them to get me two tickets, and fast. For me, the concert started as Donnie, my boyfriend at the time, and I pulled out of my driveway in Struthers, Ohio, in his black Cutlass Supreme. As we put on the Led Zep 8-track, the light box began to flash bright colored lights—especially to Bonham's thunderous drumming. As we turned the corner, Donnie's beer can popped and I began to drink my choice of wine, Red Ripple. Five hours later we arrived at our friends' house in Rochester."

Donnie had brought along his 35 mm camera to take some pictures at the show. Once inside, anticipation and excitement grew, joints were lit and the smell of weed filled the sold-out auditorium. Then the lights dimmed, Zeppelin appeared, and everyone started screaming. As the music blasted off with "Immigrant Song" everyone stood up—and stayed that way the entire three hour show. Who could imagine sitting at a Zep concert?

"Robert Plant's opening wail-cry shook me from head to toe," Stephanie recalled. "What a set of lungs. (The rest of him wasn't too bad, either.) I almost cried when they performed 'Since I've Been Loving You.' White boys can play the blues. Then the spotlight hit Jimmy Page who was armed with a cherry red, double-neck guitar. Robert Plant introduced the song as 'Stairway to Heaven,' a title I'd never heard before. Page strummed his guitar lightly, then Plant's dreamlike lyrics came in. It sounded almost classical. It built up and sped along only to slow down once again at the end. Everyone around me was in awe. I was definitely in heaven. Both the band and the audience were in a groove. Page was sweating. They all were sweating. The audience was sweaty. So the band sat down awhile and went acoustic. Time stood still for me, but not for long, as John Bonham's drum solo, 'Moby Dick' brought the audience back to a fever pitch. I thought the 8-track of it in the car was loud, but this sounded like an earthquake. If that didn't bring down the walls in the auditorium, 'Whole Lotta Love' just about did. I hoped the show would ever end. But end it did, with the band leaving the stage to a rousing ovation. What a night, what a band, what a show. My first rock concert—that being with Led Zeppelin! Even today, I still smile when I think of it. Those were the days."

Zeppelin returned to California on September 13th and 14th at the Berkeley Community Theatre. The two shows sold out in record time. Reviewer John L. Wasserman said that the 3700 seat venue was too small for the noise attack. "The concert started late, about 8:20, and continued to around 10:45 without a break. Unless, of course, you count eardrums. Beyond the rather hefty stage monitors, and beyond the numerous Marshall and Acoustic amplifiers hooked directly to the guitar, bass and keyboards, there were thirty-two 15-inch bass speakers and twelve huge horn drivers, driven by God knows how many watts, spewing Led Zeppelin all over . . . It was the perfect system for the Panama Canal. The group's sound amplification equipment—set up for 10–20,000 seat coliseums, was just too much . . . their sound mixer, onstage and behind the speakers, was in no position to bring matters under control. In other words, the group played too loud and I left after an hour and fifteen minutes."

But many fans thrived on the volume attack. In spite of what critics said, fans came away awestruck by the band's energy. They knew that this music was not only loud but also inspiring and exciting. People came to have a musical experience, and the band delivered. Yeah, it was loud a lot of the time—but GOOD and LOUD in a way that left you never forgetting it.

The tremendous impact that Led Zeppelin had on music was

not only felt in the West, but all over the world, including the Far East—especially in Japan, Land of the Rising Sun. On their way back from America, they were one of the first rock bands to play Japan on a three city, five concert tour. The band arrived on September 21, and one of Plant's first words when he got off the plane was, "Where's the Samurai?" More questions were to come the next day, this time from interviewers, when there was a press conference at the Tokyo Budokon. This was a surprise, since Zep was anything but endeared to the press. Based on the questions and answers, this event just reinforced the group's feelings about how dumb interviews really were. One guy asked what rock music was to them, and Page answered that it was useless to define or categorize. Then after that it got really goofy on the questions—someone had the nerve to ask Plant if he was going to cut his hair. Then he was asked if it was "preferable to listen to Zeppelin while under the influence of drugs." Plant flatly answered, "Oh, no! That is a stupid question. It is much more interesting to talk about sex and music than drugs and music."

Interviewers may have thought that these long haired musicians were really a joke. But Japanese fans were completely psyched about Zeppelin. Bonham mentioned, "It turned out that 'Immigrant Song' is our biggest favorite in Japan, and it's the number we always open with." Even with two solid hours of music, the Japanese fans just couldn't get enough. The Beatles had brought screams from fans at Budokon Arena in 1966—but now a totally new explosive rock and roll stormed through Japan. Even though the fans didn't understand all the lyrics, it didn't matter— it was all about the volume and energy. All the shows were hugely successful.

This was really ironic, though, because Zep did away with some of the professionalism they displayed in other gigs in the U.S. Things were more off the wall—the band sometimes kidded around and experimented more like a sound check or rehearsal. Both shows at Budokon Hall on September 23 and 24 started out the same with "Immigrant Song," "Heartbreaker," "Since I've Been Loving You," "Black Dog," "Dazed and Confused," "Stairway to Heaven" and "Celebration Day." But then things started to change after that, especially during the "Whole Lotta Love" medleys. Plant often showed that he could remember the words to old rock tunes, as on the 23rd, with "Hello Mary Lou," "Mess O' Blues" and "Tobacco Road." And the next night Plant sang "Rave On," "I'm a Man," "The Hunter," "Hello Mary Lou" and "Your Time Is Gonna Come."

And it wasn't just Plant's singing, either, that was amazing—Bonzo never failed to capture either the perfect groove with song tempos, and the rest of the band never missed stops or other changes. It was a magical spontaneity, loose and creative, that kept it all flowing. By the time "Whole Lotta Love" was played, the crowds went wild and security guards were kept real busy with fans who tried to climb onto the stage. Other fans got into fights with security when their tape recorders were taken away. Things got out of hand again at Hiroshima's Municipal Gymnasium. Fan Yasunori Naitoh was there and described the craziness: "Bonzo's bass drum was so loud it was like a bazooka! After 'Moby Dick' the audience was getting crazy. During the encore of 'Communication Breakdown' they had to stop in the middle of the guitar solo because the audience attacked the stage."

In Osaka, things were more restrained. Plant became whimsical and tried to fire up the crowd with two Beatles songs, "Please Please Me" and "From Me to You," as well as a sing-along of "We Shall Overcome." Atlantic Vice President Phil Carson played bass and roadie Clive Coulson sang on "C'mon, Everybody" and "High Heel Sneakers." And to top it all off, Festival Hall on the 29th heard some very strange songs during "Whole Lotta Love"— "Tossin' and Turnin'," "Twist and Shout," and "Fortune Teller." There was also the only known live version of "Friends." Altogether, Zep played five medleys that had twenty-plus songs—and half of them were totally unique to this tour. Their '71 Japan visit went down in the band's history like no other tour for its surprises and wildness—onstage as well as offstage.

While in Tokyo, the band wanted to visit a geisha house. Their official interpreter chose not to go along for obvious reasons. When the members returned to the hotel lobby, they made the rock fashion statement of the century! People in the lobby stared in shock as Bonzo strode in wearing a wig, lipstick and ill-fitting kimono. Plant followed, also in a wig and tight-fitting summer kimono. Page chose to have on makeup and a Geisha outfit. John Paul Jones also wore a Geisha outfit, although he looked most embarrassed of everyone. More crazy stunts followed. Back at the hotel room, Plant knocked one of Carson's pillows out the window. Carson explained, "So I thought I'd climb out the window and retrieve the pillow from a ledge. All I was wearing was a towel . . . There was no danger of falling off, but it did take quite a bit of explaining when they phoned the house detective and complained there was a peeping Tom on the ledge outside their room." Zep was banned forever from the Tokyo Hilton after Bonham trashed his hotel room with a samurai sword. Sayonara, guys.

Another time some of the band thought it was time to play a prank on Page while on a train on the way to the next gig. Some stale sake, cold tea and rice were tossed into a bunk. But it turned out to be Peter Grant's bunk, not Page's—and for his size, Grant really hauled ass down the corridor and caught John Paul Jones. Phil Carson recalled, "We had one of the local record people on the train and I think he was about to commit hari-kari. He thought the group was splitting up before his eyes."

But that was far from it—the band just liked goofing around sometimes, and had a great time visiting Japan. They donated proceeds from one of the shows to victims of the 1945 Hiroshima atom bomb blast. The city mayor presented Zep with a letter of appreciation and the city medal. Excited about Japan, the band bought cameras and went around to parks and other places, taking loads of pictures. Fans followed them around for autographs or to talk, and everyone obliged. Zep was accessible, friendly, and outgoing with everyone. It was a trip that none in the band would ever forget.

When Zeppelin flew back to England, they were hailed as heroes. And the standoff between Page and the record company over the cover finally ended. Page withheld the master tapes and forced Atlantic to comply. The new album finally hit the store shelves in November. The cover with the falling down house and the framed picture of the old man carrying sticks on his back provoked a variety of reactions from the retailers, media and fans. In the first few days, merchants had to pull the record from its jacket to make sure they had the right album for the customer. Thumbing through the Zeppelin section at the record store, one might have had a hard time finding the new Zeppelin album. No band or album name was on the front, there was no company logo or catalog number. There wasn't even a song list on the back cover. Fans wondered what this cover was to behold, what new mesmerizing treasures were to come out musically from these four wizards. That was the spell of Led Zeppelin: the breathless anticipation of the unknown.

Over the past thirty-plus years, no other jacket has been dissected more than the one found on the enigmatic untitled fourth album. Page and Plant came up with the design. Plant had been looking around in a junk shop in Reading and found the print of the old man there. Page explained what they decided to do with it: "We then came up with the idea of having the picture—the man with the sticks—represent the old way on a demolished building, with the new way coming up behind it. The old man carrying the wood is in harmony with nature. He takes from nature but he gives back to the land. It's a natural cycle and it's right. His old cottage gets pulled down and they move him to these horrible urban slums, which are terrible places."

Inside the album was the gatefold, which had an ancient-looking bearded man atop a mountain. This was the Hermit character of the Tarot, a symbol of self-reliance and wisdom. He holds out the light of truth and enlightenment to the young man at the foot of the hill. The illustration represented a seeker aspiring to the light of truth. There was also the inner record sleeve, which had song lyrics to "Stairway to Heaven." This was the first time that any lyrics had ever been printed on a Zeppelin record. On the sleeve's reverse were song titles and credits.

Led Zeppelin christened the album with four cryptic symbols, which were also displayed on the inner sleeve. Since then they have become synonymous with Led Zeppelin and an icon for each individual member. To me, the most intricate, mysterious symbol—the Zoso—had to be for Jimmy Page. His symbol was alleged to have a sinister, secret meaning. All Page would say was that his symbol was about "invoking or being invocative." I thought the Z in Zoso stood for Zeppelin. Some others have likened the Z to stand for Zeus, lightning-wielding king of Greek gods, who is the equivalent in Germanic culture to Thor. Germanic peoples believed lightning was caused by Thor's hammer smashing down on an anvil. No one could forget the sound, just like Zep's audiences could ever forget the onslaught of Page's lightning-fast riffs and the thundering music that flew from the stage.

Jones's symbol—three ovals bisecting a circle—represented to me the multi-talented artist that he was—bass player, keyboardist, and arranger. Plus upon further research I discovered that his symbol was also a Christian sign used to exorcise evil spirits. Next, I took the three interlocking symbols to be the drums of John Bonham. The three circles could also be seen as Bonham's triple persona—the hardened Midlands musician, the fun loving extrovert who enjoyed a good drink, and the quiet family man. Lastly, the three circles could stand for the man-woman-child trilogy of life.

Plant's feather in the circle was his pen and quill, since he was the lyricist. Plant claimed to have drawn his symbol from the ancient Mu civilization, which is said to have existed as part of a lost continent in the Pacific Ocean. He added that the feather could be viewed as a symbol that is the basis for many philosophies. For instance, the feather represents courage to American Indian tribes. It could also mean truth, for ancient Egyptians believed in the goddess of truth, who was shown as a feather. Plant said, "I like people to lay down the truth. No bullshit. That's what the feather in the circle is all about."

The fourth album instantly took hold on the U.S. and British charts and would turn out to be Zeppelin's greatest and best selling album. The music did indeed do the talking. In retrospect, the eight cuts seemed like a culmination of all the band's best ideas: the light and shade, the fusion between acoustic and electric. It just sounded like everything had come together on that album—perhaps more than any other one.

It was the sound of *IV* which told most of the story. The opener "Black Dog" set the tone. "Rock n' Roll" was a dose of souped-up '50s boogie. The duet with Plant and Sandy Denny on "The Battle of Evermore" sounded beautiful over the backdrop of mandolins and guitars. It's a shame that they didn't record more together. With the stunning pictures that Plant's lyrics painted and the Renaissance melodies, this was Zep's most mystical moment. Side two's "Misty Mountain Hop" was like a warm up for the closing track, "When the Levee Breaks." Bonzo got real loose again, mercilessly beating his drums. Just when you thought it was safe to have your headphones on! "Going to California" was a sort of Midlands-eye view of the West Coast dream, complete with a jet plane and a girl with flowers in her hair.

The centerpiece of the album was undoubtedly "Stairway to Heaven." Nearly 8 minutes in length, it was a classically structured song, full of poetic images that many fans felt was the pinnacle of the band's achievements. Page agreed: "To me, I thought 'Stairway' crystallized the essence of the band. It had everything there and showed the band at its best . . . It was a milestone for us. Every musician wants to do something of lasting quality, something which will hold up for a long time and I guess we did it with 'Stairway.'"

Engineer Andy Johns seconded the motion: "I knew it was going to be a monster, but I didn't know it would become a bloody anthem."

Year after year, "Stairway to Heaven" is voted the Number One FM radio song in America. What's really amazing is how "Stairway" and the rest of the album have endured, even after years of continual airplay. The imagery of misty forests and pipers is straight out of Celtic myths. And Plant's lady was a unique composite of different mythological women: King Arthur's witch sister Morgan Le Fay, Diana, the Greek white moon goddess, and poet Edmund Spenser's Fairie Queen. From the Zeppelin experience, she could be seen more as a Sunset Strip groupie who's trying to reach higher and leave her mortal life behind in the presence of rock gods. If this sounds silly, how many teenagers followed Zeppelin and found something that was nowhere else?

Page has said that his playing on the fourth album is the best that he's ever done. His solo on "Stairway" is one of the few in history that is as likely to be whistled by the postman as well as played by air guitarists in the bedroom. No '70s high school dance would dream of not ending with "Stairway." And even today, many guitar centers have signs posted that read: "No 'Stairway to Heaven' to be played here." The fourth LP had every indication that Led Zeppelin were here to stay and that the remainder of the '70s would see the band continue to grow and change.

Led Zeppelin IV was one of Page's finest production efforts. No one would ever argue his status as guitar god, but few ever mention Page's brilliant, innovative work in the recording studio as producer—the mastermind behind Led Zeppelin. Unlike the Beatles and Stones, Zeppelin never relied on the outside guidance of a George Martin or Jimmy Miller. Instead they followed the direction of their intrepid band leader, as he steered them through one successful experience after another. Rarely again did he so effectively capture the individual talents of the group on record and push it to the forefront.

Peter Grant booked a sixteen-date UK tour that tied in with the release of the album. The highlight of the tour were two magnificent, five-hour shows at London on November 20 and 21, dubbed "Electric Magic." Over 19,000 tickets were sold and thousands of fans had to be turned away. These unique shows featured more than just Zeppelin. For the audience's amusement there were also circus acts and performing animals. There were also various bands that warmed up the audience, including Stone the Crows featuring Maggie Bell. It was a total rock and roll circus.

For fan Ross Halfin, seeing one of the shows was an experience that he would never forget. It was the culmination of his growing interest in the band that started when he bought the second album. "Led Zeppelin II was the first album I ever bought," Halfin recalled. "I was 14. Although I didn't know anything about the band, I thought the record was amazing. There was a mystique about them. They seemed secretive and they had this aura that no other group radiated. I saw Led Zeppelin at Wembley Empire Pool on a freezing November night, part of the support gig involving pigs jumping through hoops."

A Melody Maker headline screamed out: "Zapped by Zeppelin." The review stated: "This was an English band playing like crazy, and enjoying every minute they stood there on stage . . . They played just about everything they've ever written. Nothing, just nothing, was spared. This was no job, this was no 'gig.' It was an event for all."

Just before the new album came out, I didn't know what to expect from the band. I wondered if they would put out something with both hard rock on it or mainly acoustic material, like on Zeppelin III. In 1971, 8-track tapes were the dominant format, and I played them all the time in my 1964 Volkswagen bug. That November, I picked up the new album on 8-track at Sound Spectrum and checked out the picture of the old man. I figured Zep was invoking an image of the past, like something old-fashioned. It seemed kind of weird—I wondered what it all meant. Would the music tell me? I quickly tore off the plastic wrapper, shoved the tape into my player, and decided to cruise through Laguna Canyon. Although what I heard was definitely new for anything in rock, there were a few songs that really stood out for me.

The first song that really grabbed me was "Rock and Roll"—it had an interplay between Page's guitar and Bonham's drums that was infectious. And Plant's echo on his singing was icing on the cake. Right after that, my Volkswagen passed through an area with gnarled trees, grassy hills and rock formations—the perfect backdrop for "The Battle of Evermore"—Zep at its most mystical indeed. I quickly became enthralled with the Middle Ages world of dragons, battles and castles that was tantalizing and made so atmospheric with the incredible vocals and instrumentation. Right after that, my twenty-year-old mind was blown by "Stairway to Heaven." It went even further with the Celtic sword and sorcery, and as the song grew to its electric climax with Page's final solo I knew that Zep had done something new, fantastic—sort of like a medieval rock mini-opera. Lastly, "Misty Mountain Hop" and "When the Levee Breaks" jumped right out at me—Bonham's drums sounded like thunderclaps. I said to myself, "Listen to this guy—he's kicking ass! This is power drumming!" And Plant's last lines in "Misty Mountain" were intriguing—"So I'm packin' my bags for the misty mountains, over the hills where the spirits fly." What wild, crazy, unreal lyrics. The poetic imagery and the different music styles were too much to handle all at once. But each time that I put this tape in my player it definitely grew on me.

Despite many fans' enthusiasm for the new album, many critics were less than thrilled. Reviews in *Melody Maker* were indifferent and said that the new Zep effort was "Not their best or their worst." Many critics seemed to be stuck in the more traditional days of Elvis, Buddy Holly or even the Rolling Stones. They couldn't seem either to grasp or appreciate what Zeppelin was trying to do. *Rolling Stone*'s Lenny Kaye, who was notorious for ridiculing many bands' latest efforts, gave Zep a backhanded compliment, saying, "Not bad for a pack of Limey lemon squeezers." In retrospect, Kaye's and other reviews should have been better. There were still those who were favorable, though—*Disc & Music Echo* pretty well described how the band had moved forward by saying, "If *Zep II* gave the first indications that their music was by no means confined to power rock, then this new album consolidates their expanding maturity. The eight cuts contained herein follow expounding in greater detail the ideas formulated on the previous collection."

But Zeppelin was a lot more interested in being visionaries and blowing listeners' minds with their musical art than pleasing critics, anyway. Good art breaks through the boundaries of what is commonly accepted. Traditions are thrown out; the mold is broken. It's happened many times in creative fields. Poet and artist William Blake portrayed a flaming, electrically-charged God in his Romanticist painting "Ancient of Days." John Milton gave a radical, heroic perspective of the devil in his literary masterpiece *Paradise Lost*. Using dreamlike imagery, Surrealist painters like Salvador Dali questioned the nature of reality, as seen when Dali hung a melting clock on a tree in his haunting 1931 landscape "The Persistence of Memory." In cinema, Fritz Lang's 1927 unique futuristic epic *Metropolis* was an expressionistic journey about men's motives that molded together space-age architecture and robots with medieval statues, towers and smoking laboratories. Artistic trendsetters must break the norms of their day, outraging many but inspiring others. This holds true in particular for songwriters.

Song crafters like Bob Dylan, the Beatles, and Zeppelin traveled this path. In an interview about songwriting, Dylan told the *Los Angeles Times* that, "I always admired artists who were dedicated, so I learned from them . . . I wanted to do something that stood alongside Rembrandt's paintings." In Dylan's case, his hugest influence early on was Woody Guthrie. Why? It was because Guthrie made a statement. "Woody's songs were about everything at the same time," Dylan continued. "They were about rich and poor, black and white, the highs and lows of life, the contradictions between what they were teaching in school and what was really happening. He was saying everything in his songs that I felt but didn't know how to."

But with folk music Dylan learned fast, and after his huge breakthroughs like "Blowin' in the Wind" and "The Times They Are A-Changin'," Dylan fused folk and rock together in 1965 with "Subterranean Homesick Blues." John Lennon was amazed and wondered how he could ever compete with it. Dylan had bluntly told Lennon that "Beatles songs say nothing." This helped motivate Lennon and McCartney to redefine their songwriting and reach new conceptual heights with the folk-tinged *Rubber Soul*, the experimental *Revolver* and the fully blown psychedelic *Sgt. Pepper* period.

Then Jimi Hendrix came on the scene and reinvented the electric guitar into unheard psychedelic aural dreams. The heavy blues sound of Hendrix and Cream influenced the early bands that John Bonham played in—then blasted off in a much more pronounced fashion in the first couple of Zeppelin albums. Now, in 1971 Zeppelin was radically changing gears and critics weren't ready for it. But in fans' circles the new spontaneity, poetry, unconventional cover and use of the four symbols heightened the Zeppelin mystique, mystery and magic. In spite of the critics, 1971 was a great year for Led Zeppelin, and 1972 would be even better.

After the U.K. tour Zeppelin took the rest of the year off before starting their Australia/New Zealand tour. The band was scheduled to land in Singapore on February 14th for a show on their way to Perth, Australia. But local regulations barred long hair. Unless Zeppelin cut their hair, there would be no concert. There was no show in Singapore. So then Zep went on to Perth, long hair and all, but they didn't have much of a good time there. There was a harrowing drug raid at their motel in the early morning hours.

No drugs were found, and the group was furious. They then flew to Auckland, New Zealand. Three planes brought all the massive equipment across the Tasman. The people awaiting the band probably didn't realize that Zeppelin was going to be so loud. But excitement was at an all-time high. A special Led Zeppelin express train was chartered by five hundred fans to see the band on February 25th at Western Spring Stadium. There was a near-catatonic reaction from the country's rock freaks.

For fan Tim Blanks, the concert was more than a musical experience—it awakened new senses, and he was never the same again. "Led Zeppelin changed my life," Blanks recalled. "I was a screwed-up-tight schoolboy when I saw them in Auckland, New Zealand, on a midsummer night in 1972, shortly after the release of their epochal fourth album. The stage was a distant blur." Luckily, Blanks was able to share some binoculars from a couple beside him. He watched an unbelievable sight during "Dazed and Confused"—and it had a profound effect on him. Blanks explained what happened: "Jimmy Page began to ravage his guitar with a violin bow and my synapses involuntarily combusted. The sound was so alien, so *witchy*—coming from a man rumored to be in touch with dark forces—that I was whisked out of my seat, compelled to dance in the pagan style popular among mutant hippies of the day. The binocular duo shrank in terror, but I didn't care—in fact, I never really cared again for what people thought of me. A therapist would have called that a breakthrough—but who needs therapy when you have Zeppelin's Jimmy Page, Robert Plant, John Paul Jones, and John 'Bonzo' Bonham?" Right on, Tim Blanks.

Afterwards the band flew back to Sydney and played to a crowd of 26,000 on February 27th. On the way home from Australia, the band stopped off in Bombay, India, to do some experimental recordings with the Bombay Symphony Orchestra. Plant and Page, always interested in other music forms, found new inspiration for their own upcoming compositions. Around April, there was something else new—this time an addition for Plant's family—a baby boy, named Karac. By the time May rolled around, the band was back in Olympic Studios, at work on their as yet untitled fifth album. The music was to be different from *Zeppelin IV*. In 1970, the Welsh countryside had served as Plant and Page's inspiration for songs on the third Zeppelin album. But travels to more exotic parts of the world, the Far East on their way home from Japan, no doubt influenced their most recent recording efforts. There was also something different in Page's appearance—his hair was now cut shorter and his beard was gone.

Around the spring of '72 there were some changes in my life, too. I decided to have a change of environment and moved from San Clemente to the small, sleepy coastal town of Dana Point. My roommates and I, Mike Buirge and Geoffrey Ooley, got this little apartment at the top of Granada Street where we had a partial ocean view at the bargain price of $200 a month. We all had long hair—mine was this stringy mass of what looked like a buffalo mane down to my shoulders. Another change for me was a new car—I traded my tired VW bug and $200 to a guy down the street for his 1964 Volkswagen van. There was plenty of room for my surfboards, and it was just the thing I wanted for surfing trips to Ensenada in Baja or camping trips to Northern California. I got it repainted to a forest green, had a new 8-track player installed and was ready to roll.

But I still needed a way to make money. How could some long-haired surfer guy pull in enough bucks for the rent? I'd seen these other hippie types in San Clemente driving little old ladies to the store in these Plymouth Furys and older Checker cabs to Albertson's during the day and also taking Marines back to Camp Pendleton at night. So I became a driver for San Clemente Yellow Cab. What a way to get to meet people! In fact, there were times when we had some pretty interesting customers.

Sometimes when President Nixon was at what the press called the "Western White House," we'd take reporters and Nixon's entourage there, a large gated area above Cotton's Point surfing

area, near San Onofre. We were the only cab company around, so
here was this freaky little band of hippie cabbies driving these government guys in black suits around. We'd take them and these
young, call-girl types in tight, slinky dresses down to Oceanside
Harbor Inn, where there were private parties. Since the cabbies
never got invited, we had our own parties back at the Dana Point
pad that we became pretty well known for. Each party had different events going on, and sometimes it got pretty crazy. It usually
revolved around music we liked, and we'd invite our girlfriends—
good looking dispatchers that we'd gotten to know over the cab
radio or these wild hippie waitresses from a local café called
the Halfway House. My girlfriend from there whom I nicknamed
"Glitta" helped me redecorate my Volkswagen van into what
looked like an Arabian sultan's tent with tapestries hanging down,
a bed, large pillows and incense holders.

My roommates and I were on a big blues kick then—we'd play
lots of records all night like Bo Diddley, Muddy Waters or Albert
King. We'd also just blast albums like *James Gang Rides Again* and
Zeppelin's latest—we liked "Rock and Roll" and "When the Levee
Breaks" a lot. Then we started contests where we'd compete to see
who could play the best updated blues tunes like the Doors doing
"Who Do You Love" or "Build Me a Woman" off *Absolutely Live*,
the Stones' "Little Red Rooster" and "Mona," Eric Clapton's "Key
to the Highway," or Zeppelin's "I Can't Quit You Baby," "You
Shook Me" or "Since I've Been Loving You." It got too loud sometimes and we didn't want the parties to be all the same, so we had
to figure out something else that could entertain everyone.

Then some of the hippie waitresses found out that I had all
these old 8 mm science fiction and monster type flicks and wanted
to see them, so I started putting on these movie shows. We'd have
popcorn and lots of beer and watch special effects–laden flicks like
Jason and the Argonauts, *The Seventh Voyage of Sinbad*, *The Lost World*,
and *I Was a Teenage Werewolf*. Since the movies were silent, we'd
play background music, long rock songs like Pink Floyd's "Atom

Heart Mother Suite" or "Meddle." We took turns humorously nar-
rating key parts in the movies, sort of like an early version of *Mystery Science Theatre 3000*. People got transported to other worlds
from all the weirdness. Word spread around San Clemente and
Dana Point about these nutty parties, and the crowd grew to where
our little pad couldn't handle it. So we ended up having poker
parties by special invite only that sometimes ended with a short
movie.

During April and May, recording sessions for the fifth Zeppelin
album began. Page called ace engineer Eddie Kramer to work on
Houses of the Holy. Kramer had previously worked on *Led Zeppelin
II* and Page knew of his mixing capabilities from his work with
Jimi Hendrix. Page and Kramer had mutual admiration. Kramer
said, "Headley Grange wasn't available to me so we rented Mick
Jagger's mansion, Stargroves. I had a blast being in the English
countryside with a band that I really liked . . . The sessions themselves were intense and productive, as Pagey likes to crack the
whip."

The guitar amps that Page used were either put in the fireplace
going up the chimney or in his own room. More than ever before
keyboard instruments were prominently displayed in the band's
sound during the album sessions, which of course was due to John
Paul Jones. His contributions to Led Zeppelin were enormous,
yet relatively unsung. Jones is a highly underrated musician and
arranger.

One of the band's happiest tours was the '72 summer U.S. tour.
Auditoriums and halls were being sold out without any advertising. The entire band was in top form and the performances
showed how each musician had continued to fine-tune his contribution to the show. Along with Page and Plant getting the excitement going so well from the crowd, the other two members kept
the intense rhythm section churning away with an energy that
enveloped everyone. John Bonham was said to be able "to turn a
set of drums into a brigade of depth charges." But even with his

heavy playing, he really knew how to handle his drums and hadn't broken a snare for quite a while. Bonham himself commented, "I like our act to be like a thunderstorm. But I haven't broken a skin in three tours. You can hit a drum hard if you take a short stab at it and the skin will break easily. But if you let the stick just come down, it looks as though you're hitting it much harder than you really are. I only let it drop with the force of my arm coming down."

John Paul Jones demonstrated his ability with an organ solo that had elements of Bach as well as his own creative keyboard work. He would continue to get more involved onstage with piano, organ and mellotron. But he also stepped back and provided a strong anchor for the rest of the music. Jones said, "I don't mind being in the background. I wouldn't like to be out front playing like Jimmy . . . I believe you should do what you have to do, and if I'm bass, rather than try and lead on bass and push myself, I prefer to put down a good solid bass line." His role was still crucial, for he was always there to solidify the groove with a sense of order in the midst of the musical thunder that went on.

But Led Zeppelin was only half of the concert. The kids—thousands and thousands and thousands of kids—were the other half. Of all the concert variables, they were the most important. Nothing could have happened without them. But with them, when they started to smile and shake, to stand and shout, to forget why they came, how they got there and what they planned to do the next day, to forget everything but being right there—then everything happened. It was no longer just a concert, but a wild high-time happiness that everyone shared.

There are a million theories about rock and roll, what it is and what it means, but what's most obvious is most overlooked: the music. Plain old music: rhythm, melody and harmony; mathematical relationships of frequencies and time intervals; those pleasing combinations of vibrations which some philosophers declare to be the ultimate mystery and reality of the universe. And these kids, ordinary American kids we all knew and recognized, were true music lovers. They just loved it, that's all—spent vast sums on it, listened to hours of it, thought about it incessantly, found their heroes among its makers, dated their lives by it and in geometrically increasing numbers, made music themselves.

Zep was in prime swagger, fresh off their masterpiece, *Led Zeppelin IV*, with *Houses of the Holy* just around the corner. As the band landed at one of its favorite haunts, Los Angeles, they demonstrated on June 25 why they were known for their no-holds-barred concerts. Zep always seemed to go the extra mile in Los Angeles. Their performance was staggering and magical. They'd lost none of their energy—in fact their energy had matured into confidence. The sexuality just oozed right out of Page and Plant. Plant could sing like never before—he used his voice like a sledgehammer, a saxophone and an air raid siren. John Bonham was the band's loaded gun. He wasn't showing off. It wasn't done just to make himself look good; it was done to make the rest of the band and the fans feel good. Bonham pointed out there was a great atmosphere in the group: "We seemed very close, and you could feel it in the playing."

The L.A. and Long Beach performances have been legendary with Zep scholars and bootleggers. You can hear why from the 3-CD release of 2003, *How the West Was Won*. These shows were originally recorded nine months before *Houses of the Holy* was released. There are some songs from that album like "Over the Hills and Far Away," "Dancing Days" and "The Ocean." And the acoustic set was there—Page knew the value of this material, in the studio or onstage—a balance was created that gave the harder songs a lot more impact. There were also the old favorites too— a twenty-three-minute version of "Whole Lotta Love" that had a wild rock oldies medley, a twenty-five-minute "Dazed and Confused" and a nineteen-minute "Moby Dick." These shows just come zooming out of the speakers—the band was on top of it. Bonham was totally into it: "I like to yell out when I'm playing. I yell like a bear to give it a boost." If there ever was a wild, bear-man drummer who was still somehow in control, Bonham was it.

Engineer Kevin "the Caveman" Shirley worked with Page on both the Led Zeppelin DVD and *How the West Was Won* CDs. He has his particular reasons as to why the L.A. Forum show was so special. Although Miss Pamela was history, Page was still attached to Charlotte Martin back in England. But now Page connected with Lori Maddox, a 14 year old model. She looked like a young Bianca Jagger—tall, extremely attractive with long, dark hair, luscious lips and big brown eyes. And she was a virgin! Page was smitten. For Lori, it was a rock and roll fantasy. Shirley commented that "Jimmy was showing off for a girl that he was infatuated with. She was seeing the band for the first time and standing on his side of the stage. Also, all the tempos at the Long Beach show two nights later were a little quicker than the ones at the Forum, because the band wanted to finish up the show so they could get back to L.A. to party. You know, the alcohol stopped at 2 A.M.!"

But in spite of the intensity of the shows and the incredible crowd reaction, Zeppelin was overshadowed by another band that was back on the road—the Rolling Stones. It had been a three-year wait since their infamous '69 tour had ended tragically at Alta-mont. In the movie *Easy Rider* Peter Fonda and Dennis Hopper went looking for America. The Rolling Stones found it.

The Stones were the darlings of the press and mass media, with their social escapades during their thirty-city summer tour making headlines. Mick Jagger even got on the front covers of *Rolling Stone* and *Life* magazine. But Zeppelin's shows were vastly more rewarding than ones put on in America by the Stones. The Stones played an hour and a half, preceded by an hour of Stevie Wonder. Zep fans went to see Zeppelin and only Zeppelin for over three and a half hours. There was a no-nonsense approach to play-ing—Led Zep showed how good rock and roll could sound, much in the same way Elvis did in 1956, with a sound that was almost a feeling. Also, the Stones stuck mostly to material from their last three albums, while Zeppelin did nearly every song they knew. There were more oldies tributes than ever—"Heartbreak Hotel," "Party," "Hello Mary Lou," "Slow Down," and in the second encore, "Louie, Louie." The crowds went wild. And as far as musicianship goes—even a Stones fan might have to admit that Jimmy Page proved that he was a better overall guitarist than Keith Richards and Mick Taylor combined!

In August and September the band took a holiday break. Then in October, Zep paid a return visit to Japan. In contrast to the energetic and frantic performances of the '71 Japanese tour, the 1972 shows were much more relaxed and laid back affairs. Unfortunately, this would be the band's last visit to the Land of the Rising Sun. The opportunity just never presented itself again in planning for future tours. By November the new album was ready, but problems with the cover's artwork delayed its release. This time it wasn't due to Atlantic liking the art, but with the way the colors didn't come out right.

Zeppelin had ascended to their artistic and commercial prime. They ended the year with their biggest British tour, taking in eighteen cities, which ran through December and continued in to January 1973. There were twenty-four dates, with 110,000 tickets getting sold out in four hours. Fans slept out in the streets in freezing conditions for a chance to buy tickets. Afterward, Peter Grant earnestly planned the 1973 summer tour of the United States. In that year, Zeppelin was to become bigger than the Beatles with the release of their fifth LP and a mammoth, sold-out tour that would smash concert attendance records in America.

CHAPTER 5

Houses of the Holy

E arly in April 1973, a series of press releases appeared, LED ZEP-
PELIN TO MAKE BIGGEST ROCK TOUR IN U.S.A. HISTORY. Another
release boasted, LED ZEPPELIN IS THE MOST POPULAR GROUP SINCE
THE BEATLES. And still another, LED ZEPPELIN'S HOUSES OF THE HOLY SHIPS
GOLD.

Peter Grant hired PR consultant Danny Goldberg to get the
word out. Goldberg recalled: "It wasn't so much that they were
demanding, it was that the job was demanding. Because there was
such a swirl of activity around Led Zeppelin . . . They were the
biggest thing in the music business."

Few kids in the United States would not have heard of Led
Zeppelin by tour's end, and the claims made that spring no longer
seemed outlandish. Grant estimated that their 1973 earnings would
amount to $30 million. Earnings from the tour alone grossed nearly
$5 million. Zeppelin trampled underfoot stadium attendance
records from Atlanta to San Francisco previously set by the Beatles.
Peter Grant had escalated travel from a mere twelve-seater private
plane to a full-size Boeing. Their mode of travel this time was their
own plane that they named the Starship One. It had been con-

verted to a forty-seat luxury liner complete with a bedroom, shower, bar, video machine, and even an electric organ for John Paul Jones. Page had first choice of the bedroom and he really liked the idea of a horizontal takeoff. And the group's name was emblazoned in gold letters across the side of the plane. Even the Beatles never had their own plane.

Houses of the Holy was released in early March, sixteen months after the fourth album. It marked the first time that Zeppelin gave a name to an album. A wrap-around strip of paper printed with the lettering was the only outward clue. The cover depicted naked little children ascending multi-tinted rocks. Naughty overtones on the sleeve? Child pornography? Page saw it as "Children are houses of the holy; we're all houses of the holy."

I remember the first time that I laid eyes on *Houses of the Holy*. My friend Mike Buirge and I often went to Sound Spectrum to buy blues albums—we'd get anything from John Mayall and Canned Heat to John Lee Hooker and Albert King. When *Houses of the Holy* came out, we were down there looking for new albums for our parties. The album's cover jumped out at me from the record rack. It was completely different from any other cover. I wondered if the orange sky was a volcanic Pompeiian landscape and if the girls were cosmic tinkerbells, worshipping on pagan ruins. This was too much; I bought the alien-looking thing! Back at our Dana Point apartment, I tore off the outer wrapper and checked out the inside artwork. I wondered what was up with the guy holding up the naked girl . . . was this some sort of sacrifice? And what was the mysterious light beam that came down from the castle wall? Was it the moon or some sort of supernatural being?

The concept of the climbing children was not the only one considered for the cover. The other idea was to have Page's Zoso symbol laid out in rocks like the ancient Nazca art in Peru. But Page and Hipgnosis, the British graphics company, chose to use the children instead. They found their inspiration from the famous science fiction author, Arthur C. Clarke. In his book *Childhood's End*, the final scene has all of the children that remain on Earth climb a mountain to be taken into space. The children of *Houses of the Holy* were mirroring this purpose: ascension towards an enigmatic salvation.

One of the models was Samantha Gates. Samantha didn't think it was strange to be running around naked, but she just complained that the modeling shoot was too cold. But at six years old, she didn't think that she was being exploited. She recalled, "I remember giggling a lot when I was lifted over the guy's head and thinking it was all good fun." The shoot took place at Giant's Causeway in Northern Ireland and the castle was located near the rocks there. The location looked mysterious and added to the mystique because of the mythology associated with the area. Legend says that Giant's Causeway was created by giants to serve as a bridge between Ireland and Scotland, possibly to aid in their war mongering.

It was at night when Mike and I first played the record. I wanted some atmosphere of mystery, so before I threw the record on the turntable we lit candles and fired up some incense. The opener hit me with a wallop. Page's overdubbed rhythm and lead intro was solid and intense. And Plant's opening words, "I had a dream, crazy dream . . ." spoke to me about what my life was like in Dana Point with the nutty parties. I thought Zep would never top their ballad "Going to California" but when I heard the lyrics to "The Rain Song," I thought these lyrics were utterly amazing, Page's chording elegant, Jones's synthesizer melancholy—the perfect mixture.

As "Over the Hills and Far Away" began with Page's acoustic picking, I first thought this was a new folk tune—until the electric part broke loose, spinning the song into a whole new dimension. The title sounded like it came from the hills in "Misty Mountain Hop" or maybe the hills of J.R.R. Tolkien's Shire where the hobbits lived. With "The Crunge," Robert Plant was on a soul trip—he wanted to show James Brown where it was at. His strange wording actually grew out of when he and Bonzo had been mimicking accents from their Black Country, an English mining area. "Dancing Days" replaced "Rock and Roll" as my favorite party song. Page's and Bonham's playing reached a zenith of energy that wove itself right into Plant's lyrics of flower power, summer evenings, music and dancing. "D'yer Maker" is British slang from a joke: "My wife just left on vacation." "D'yer mak'er?" (Did you make her?) "No, she wanted to go." This song took some getting used to since I'd never heard anything before like this from Zeppelin—like a reggae meets do-wop sort of thing. Now I knew that this record was really stretching the limits on what Zeppelin were, a heavy blues band.

Then came "No Quarter"—the album's highlight for Jerry. He put it this way: "For me, 'No Quarter' is the album. It gave the music an eerie, foreboding feel. It was a different direction, and gave John Paul Jones a chance to really shine." Thanks to Jones' synthesizers, one can imagine Viking long ships adorned with sea serpents, sailing through the mist. No quarter—no one gets taken prisoner. Adding to the sound were Page's frightening riffs that rose and fell in spell-binding, hypnotic peaks. As I listened, the incense smoke lazily drifted upwards in the candlelight like heaven bound snakes. This was atmosphere to the max. I was entranced and amazed. Zeppelin had created something new and incredible.

"The Ocean" was a great ending—back to a steady rock feel and a wonderful love song Plant wrote for his daughter, Carmen. The whole song had an unusual tempo, with an extra beat taken away after every four bars. I really liked how Plant asked, "Has the ocean lost its way?" and how after three minutes the whole style changed into something like a jam session, Page's riffs leading the way for Bonham's churning, crashing drums. It was a celebration, a climax, and an electrically-charged ending.

The combination of funk, folk, reggae, rock and roll and even psychedelic were somehow all blended together. Page called his influences "C.I.A.—Celtic, Indian and Arabic influences. I guess my Celtic roots come out in that 'Over the Hills and Far Away' type of thing." One can feel the fun the band had recording the songs as well as the dedication and commitment that went into them. Each album was different from the last—in about four years, the band had covered all sorts of ground. *Houses of the Holy* became a No. 1 album in many countries including European ones. The album was okay for Jerry, but it was too much of a mix. It was the most offbeat LP, and the biggest departures were "The Crunge" and "D'Yer Maker." He knew that the one after *Zeppelin IV* would be a tough act to follow. But this LP would pave the way for *Physical Graffiti*. The press didn't particularly like it—*Rolling Stone* called the band a "limp blimp." What was Plant's response to the critics? He said it was, "a very crisp thing, to the point—there it is, take it or leave it."

Ledhead Jerry decided to leave it, and for him the album of 1973 was the Stooges' *Raw Power*. The vocals are bitchin.' The playing is powerful. The recording VU meter was buried in the red. Iggy and the band returned with a vengeance, screaming the anguish and ecstasy of America at the beginning of a desperate decade. Put it on your speakers. It'll knock you down!

At the start of 1973, Clyde Johnson and I finished our final journey into the realm of the fantastic—a new collection of eighteen songs that we called *About Monsters and Things*. The most far-out sounding tunes had to be an outer space mini-opera of three Pink Floyd-type tunes telling the stories of "Rocket Ship 45," "Cosmic Tear" and "Comet Queen." "Atomic Reptile" was a short synthesizer instrumental that had the notes swirling back and forth from one channel to another. But the most electrified freak out had to be "Wizard's Lizard," a tale about a dragon that lived in the lake of an ancient castle. This wasn't for those who liked quiet music—it sounded like Frank Zappa, Alice Cooper and Cream thrown into an electronic mixer with fuzz tones, smashing drums and my

Muddy Waters-style vocal in reverb. Another strange one was "Dinosaurs Reincarnate" that had an organ intro taken from Johann Sebastian Bach mixed with Yardbirds-style fuzz tone leads. The lyrics asked what would happen if ancient creatures ever returned.

There were also mellower, pensive moments about strange places—"Griffin Groves" sounded like a slow Doors song with classical piano, guitar and drums. Acoustic guitars strummed on a changing earth song, "Volcanic Vibrations." The mind trip "Brain Trains" likened our thoughts to a train, traveling by tracks of our brains. And "Sea of Spirits" took a look at what was in the minds of those in the afterlife.

I didn't design a cover this time—I asked my dad to do it. In between his oil and watercolor painting projects and his work at Disney's, he created a fold-out cover that showed a prehistoric panorama of exploding volcanoes, fin-backed dinosaurs crawling in a swamp, and ptranodons cruising overhead. The whole affair looked pretty cool on the outside—an entire reptilian fantasy land. But the finished recordings sounded way too gimmicky in spots with Clyde's remastered echo effects—too much electricity!

I bravely played the new demo at some of our parties. Some people, like the Halfway House hippie chicks, were intrigued with all the griffins, dinosaurs and strange sounds that jumped out. In fact, my waitress girlfriend Glitta loved the creature songs and began writing her own illustrated poems in the same vein.

But some other waitresses from Denny's were horrified and told me to "quit all the weirdness and write more commercial stuff" about emotions, love and relationships. Throughout 1973, I'd actually been experimenting with writing more realistic songs about problems people face, and some got recorded, although none fit theme wise on the *Monsters and Things* demo. The hardships of dealing with crazy customers while driving a taxi were documented in "Grab That Cab," played to an acoustic surf beat sound. The stress of city life, pollution, and crime were dealt with in "L.A.

Heat Wave." More sonically-charged and off the wall was "Electric Cyclops," which described the hypnotic power that demon television, living off an electric socket, has over people. This sounded like a cross between Zeppelin's "Immigrant Song" and Black Sabbath's "Paranoid," with Clyde's wildly distorted guitar, drums and my rough Howlin' Wolf vocals. It was hard-edged and frightening.

My personal favorite was "Cigarette City," a hot, slow smokin' blues recorded in one take with a blues band Clyde had. The lyrics warned about lung cancer and said, "at Cigarette City, your lungs will burn to the nitty gritty." I also tried my hand at writing some depressing love songs, but none ever made it on tape. Thank goodness. As 1973 wore on, Clyde and I drifted apart in our interests, and I quit recording with him. But I kept writing poetry and also a mix of short stories, mostly about cab driving and also science fiction adventures about some galaxy gremlins.

Led Zeppelin were still tight, and April found the band rehearsing for its upcoming two-part spring/summer American tour. Grant had tremendous insight and a gut feeling for what would and what wouldn't work. This tour brought the band before more American kids than ever before. It would span over thirty dates. There would be no gimmicks, no intermissions, no mandatory opening act, no platform shoes, no dancing girls, no bullshit. Just four men and three hours of music. Once I heard that Zep had its own plane, I knew this tour would be big.

It all kicked off in May at Atlanta Braves Stadium. The second show was Tampa, where the Beatles had an all-time American attendance record of 55,000 in 1965. Zeppelin eclipsed it with an audience of 58,000. Plant must have thought, "Take THAT, you critics!" Zep had drawn an audience thirteen times the population of Woodstock and caused a two-hour traffic jam. During the show there was a unique touch with the release of 700 doves, and the crowd responded by lighting matches. Page remarked the scene looked "like a galaxy." Peter Grant instructed press agent Danny Goldberg to state, "The 49,000 people at the Atlanta Led Zeppelin

show was the biggest thing since *Gone With the Wind"* and to attrib-
ute the quote to the mayor of Atlanta. In both Atlanta and Tampa,
the band got front page billing with the Watergate hearings.

Starting in '73, a persistent stretch of bad luck and timing
started that would dog the group for years to come. On tour in
California at the end of the month, Page injured his hand and
wrist. With the help of codeine tablets and Jack Daniel's to deaden
the pain, Page carried on through the band's demanding three
hour set. Dates were shuffled around. When Zep arrived in Los
Angeles, the band created a whole new era of rock and roll excess.
An entire floor of the Continental Hyatt House on Sunset Blvd.
was taken over by the band. Led Zeppelin were party animals
beyond party animals. The whole place was turned into a sex and
drugs funhouse. There were stories of nude swimming parties at
the rooftop pool. The lobby was filled with nubile young girls in
hot pants and platform shoes. The word was out—Led Zeppelin
was back in town.

After the L.A. show on May 31st, the band celebrated Bonzo's
birthday in grand Zeppelin style. Hosted by the owner of KROQ,
the party's guests included former Beatle George Harrison. Among
the ruckus of the party, which included the showing of the X-rated
adult film *Deep Throat*, Harrison decided that it would be fun to
throw the top tier of the birthday cake at Bonzo's face. Naturally,
he retaliated by chucking the second tier at Harrison, who ran out
of range. So Bonzo caught up with Harrison and threw him in the
swimming pool. It was par for the course for a Zep party.

Despite all the fun it appeared that the group had, there were
downsides too. Robert Plant explained, "You see, my little boy's
just started to walk, and I haven't seen him bloomin' walk yet.
Those are the things that upset you about being on the road: the
very fact that you miss fantastic occasions like that."

The band moved on to San Francisco, where fans had slept out
on the sidewalks in order to get tickets for the June 2nd Kezar Stadium show. Fan loyalty was now at an all-time high. After this,

there was a mid-tour holiday in Hawaii, which gave Page's wrist time to mend.

The second leg of the tour resumed in Chicago for two sold out shows on July 6 and 7. The Zep plane plane flew on to Indianapolis, St. Paul, Milwaukee, Detroit, Buffalo, and landed in Seattle on July 17. Robert Knight was there. "I had not seen the band for about a year and got the invite to come over and shoot the Seattle and Vancouver shows as Peter Grant had used one of my photos on a Zepp album without photo credit and Peter thought this would be good payment! We all set off for the arena for the sound check. The drive up was a scene out of the movie *Bullitt*, driving up one way streets and otherwise terrorizing the people of Seattle. When I walked into the area I grabbed a shot of the stage set up and was straight away tackled from behind by Peter Grant who mistook my pager as some sort of recording device. Having now figured out who I was, all was in order."

Just before the concert there was another problem that came up, having to do with a guitar. Knight recalled: "Another highlight of the day was my young friend Harry had gifted a beautiful vintage Les Paul to Jimmy Page; what he had failed to mention was he had stolen it from his music teacher. Just before the Zepp took the stage the Seattle police were there to greet Jimmy and retrieve the guitar." During the show, the music could be felt just as much as it could be heard. Three-story banks of lights and speakers surrounded the four performers. "Moby Dick" lasted for a staggering 30 minutes. All hell nearly broke loose during the show and Knight got rescued from one of the band members. "It was one of the wilder shows with Robert Plant having to pull me out of the pit as a near riot was unfolding. The band placed me next to John Bonham and I was able to get some amazing shots of his playing live very close up from a vantage point most photographers never got."

Everyone got safely away from the concert. But the craziness continued after everyone got back to the hotel. Knight went on: "After the show we returned back to the Edgewater for a nice evening of destruction with certain band members. Bonham was able to procure a fireman's ax and soon was chopping everything in the room and tossing it out the window into the Puget Sound."

Jerry had heard over the FM dial of the upcoming Led Zeppelin show in Pittsburgh on July 24th. Jerry remembered, "FM radio was my tribal drum and a doorway to the music world. It was exciting and magical." But he couldn't find anyone to go along with him on the 90 mile drive down the road from Struthers. So he passed on it. But there was a show in Pittsburgh that he did go to by himself back on May 2, 1970—the Doors. The highlight of the show for him was Morrison's between song rap in which he made fun of himself and the police with reference to the infamous Miami incident by saying, "the last time it happened, grown men were weeping. Policemen were turning in their badges . . ."

When Zeppelin hit Pittsburgh, Cadillac limos waited to take the band to Three Rivers Stadium. Since they were a little late, the Caddies zoomed to the stadium, a police guided motorcade led the way behind a wall of sirens. It was a hot, tight performance by the boys, and 40,000 fans boogied their brains out.

Not many groups in '73 ever played a show that big. Performances had some wild, spectacular effects—a light show, cannons, and fog. The lighting effects included two mirrored balls that spun in all directions and a revolving disk that was covered with broken glass with a mirror wheel inside. Spotlights hit it and threw light everywhere, with the effect being like you were in the middle of a diamond. Fog from dry ice poured across the stage as John Paul Jones worked out during "No Quarter," enveloping the performers.

Back at the hotel, the band was sitting around and someone suggested that it would be interesting to do a Led Zeppelin film. Grant explained, "So in order to give ourselves as much control as possible, the four members of the band and I put in money . . . What we wanted to avoid was making just another rock and roll movie. We jokingly felt that even if it flopped, we'd get a video cassette copy each—making it the most expensive home movie in history!"

A film crew was hired to capture the excitement of three concerts at Madison Square Garden on July 27-29th. Eddie Kramer,
who was recording the shows, recalled the wild audience response:
"I rented the Bearsville studio mobile truck to record the show. The
fans were cheering and stomping throughout the entire concert—
so much that I thought someone was actually trying to tip our
sound truck over, which we had parked backstage. The floor was
shaking so much that I actually had to step out of the truck. It was
incredible."

By now, the band really had the confidence to not only play,
but also to project onstage. The music was more diversified now,
and sets were enhanced by an improved repertoire of new songs
like "The Song Remains the Same," "Over the Hills and Far Away,"
and "The Rain Song." Page had his guitar theatrics down more
than ever and was sporting his infamous black-and-white stage
outfits at Madison Square Garden, which had occult symbols
embroidered on them. And Plant perfected the bare-chested
bravado frontman pose for thousands of others to imitate.

It looked like the tour would end in triumph, but there was
one flawed moment—the notorious safe deposit heist at the Drake
Hotel in New York City. At the time, it was the biggest heist of a
hotel's safe deposit box in the city's history. It made the front page
of New York's *Daily News*. Headlines read: LED ZEPPELIN ROBBED OF
203G. The receipts from the Madison Square Garden shows had disappeared. The reason there was so much cash on hand was that it
was the day for the band to leave and Zeppelin had to pay for
their airplane, the film crew, and the hotel rooms. The hotel was
crawling with cops and F.B.I. agents. The band's roadies had to get
into the rooms fast and get rid of the drugs, which they did. The
press accused the band of faking the robbery. Zeppelin's position
was that someone who worked at the hotel stole the money. It
became an unsolved crime. But Zeppelin got the press.

After America, the band returned to England for a well-earned break. Plant took a vacation in Morocco, and in September he was voted the Top Male Singer in the world by *Melody Maker* readers. By October new filming started on individual "fantasy" sequences at homes of the members and Grant. The film's title was drawn from a current Zeppelin song that made a musical statement—*The Song Remains the Same*. As opposed to typical concert films that were straightforward documentaries, the Zeppelin movie tried to have symbolic representations of the individual band members. So they filmed scenes that tried to portray who they were as individuals.

John Paul Jones' sequence showed him at the head of a band of masked riders, threatening a village. Then he returned home to the bosom of his family, removing his mask as he crosses the threshold. This was presumably an analogy of his split role as band member and family man. Jones confessed, "Touring makes you a different person, I think. You always realize it when you come home after a tour. It usually takes weeks to recover after living like an animal for so long."

Robert Plant chose a role that portrayed him as a medieval hero, part Viking, part chivalrous knight, roaming the country on a quest. He battled evil, crossed mountains, all in search of a mysterious woman. Plant said, "Mine wasn't just a role that I was playing, it had some relation to what I consider my role in life. I really do think that life is a journey, and it has its pitfalls and pleasures . . . the princess in my sequence, which is the sort of ultimate, disappears. She just vanishes. It would have been too easy for me to have . . . well, gotten it."

Jimmy Page climbed a steep rock face near Boleskine House for his bit. Once he reached the summit, he faced a strange, hooded figure. When his face is visible, you can see it is Page himself, but greatly aged. Then, the face regresses to babyhood then back to elderly man again. The portrayal could be seen as presenting Page as a seeker of truth, or of the Holy Grail.

John Bonham's piece started off with him and his wife Pat

strolling down a road. Then he was filmed tearing about country roads in a hot rod. He's seen as one of the locals when he gets out and shoots some pool at a pub. After that, he tore down a quarter-mile racetrack in a long, thin dragster, flames flying out the back. The entire segment was an exercise in speed and power that coincided with "Moby Dick." This could also stand for Zeppelin's fast-paced touring life. But the most touching scene to me as a father showed Bonham at home with his son, Jason. Jason's playing on a drum set, and his dad is joining in with him on a conga drum. More than anything else, this shows Bonham's value in the father-son relationship.

Peter Grant, the band's manager, also got a bit in the film. Two different versions were filmed for his section. The first showed Grant as an antique collector, which he enjoyed doing on tours, and driving around with his wife in a vintage car. He was seen as a family man, playing with his children and a cat on a bed at home. The second scene showed a whole different guy—an Al Capone-like figure decked out in 1920s clothes who drives around town in a Pierce Arrow 1928 gangster car. Grant pulls up to a house and fires a machine gun into the place. Being a manager, he may have metaphorically been conveying his attitude about manipulation of talent in the music world.

By year's end all the basic footage for the film was in the can. But a further three years would elapse before it finally reached the screen. Jimmy Page was finishing his own pet project: creating the soundtrack for the film, *Lucifer Rising*, by the renowned underground filmmaker and author of *Hollywood Babylon*, Kenneth Anger. Page recalled, "I've always got on very well with Anger. He's a good friend, really. He's never been as awe-inspiring and unapproachable to me as some would probably tell you . . . One day he asked me to toss some ideas around for a soundtrack and I went away feeling something but never being able to really express it, until one day when it all sort of poured out and I got down immediately to recording it," said Page. The filmmaker/actor/author that created the film shared Page's fascination with the occult and was also a follower of Aleister Crowley.

1974 would be a quiet year for Zeppelin. In January, Peter Grant announced at a press conference that all future Zeppelin recordings would appear on the band's own label, Swan Song. Zeppelin was looking forward to signing their favorite groups on Swan Song, so as to help them gain greater recognition. But first, before they could concentrate on Swan Song's protégés, like The Pretty Things, Maggie Bell, and Bad Company, Led Zeppelin needed to work on their next album. In February and March tracks were laid down for the next album at Headley Grange. Hot off the road, excited about their new record label, and at their artistic and commercial best, songs came quickly to the musicians. There was a lot of momentum and also a stockpile of good material from the past, so there was enough for a double album. They returned to straightforward hard rock, something they seemed to have lost on *Houses of the Holy*.

At this time the American audience was undergoing the strains of a political upheaval, and was ripe for the counter-culture, hypnotic tunes of Zeppelin. It would be in the middle of 1974 that the transcripts of Nixon's pleas to cover-up the Watergate break-in would be released to the public. In July, the *Los Angeles Times* printed parts of the presidential transcripts. They showed a president who planned to avoid facing the music at all costs. Nixon was recorded as saying " . . . I don't give a shit what happens, I want you all to stonewall it, let them plead the Fifth Amendment, cover up or anything else, if it'll save it—save the plan. That's the whole point . . ." This was the final nail in President Nixon's coffin, the last piece of evidence needed to force Nixon to resign.

A month later, it was official: Nixon had quit. His resignation was a result of his attempt to thwart the FBI investigation of the break-in at the Watergate. This governmental conspiracy really destroyed many young people's trust in law and authority. It made many turn to music and spirituality so they could find something they could trust and believe in—something real, something bigger than they were.

I had a type of awakening like this in early 1974. One evening, a lot of Marines needed rides back to Camp Pendleton, and we only had four cabs running. We were totally swamped for hours with cab fares, and I drove back and forth without a coffee break. At 3 A.M. while coming back to San Clemente on the 405 Freeway, I fell asleep while going around 70 mph. My Plymouth Fury went about half a mile and started to head at a 45 degree angle for the center divider. Then a miracle happened. Just before my left front fender hit it, something woke me up, I saw the divider and spun the wheel to the right. The back and front fenders got banged up pretty good, along with the rear tire losing its tread from scraping the bent fender.

Sparks flew wildly off the overpass onto El Camino Real, where my buddies Geoffrey, Mike, and Charlie Dailey were sitting on the cab line. Mike said, "That must be Ralph coming back from his last run." They both laughed as my smashed up cab crawled into the driveway. But I wasn't laughing. I was in shock because I knew what woke me up. It was a guardian angel! I'd been totally out and there was no way that I could have woken up by myself. And I was totally awake within a second. I'd ran from God and instead lived for surfing, partying and working twelve-plus hours five days a week to get more and more money. I had pushed myself to the limit, and now it had nearly killed me. But God reminded me that He was real, cared about me and had a purpose for me. Now I knew that I had to thank Him and get away from my present lifestyle before I self-destructed. I decided to leave the cab business in a few months and go back to finish my English bachelor's degree at San Diego State.

Shortly after my near-fatal accident, my friends Mike, Geoffrey, and I went to a rock concert to see one of music's songwriting legends. Bob Dylan and the Band played some shows at the L.A.

Forum, and we got tickets through mail order for the February 13th show. The show kicked into high gear right off when things started off with a driving "You Go Your Way and I'll Go Mine." An energized Dylan sang and shouted out the chorus. For me, it felt like hitting a home run when I was twelve—total elation!

The energy that night was contagious and overpowering. The musicians were all extremely talented—with many songs different members of the Band went from one instrument to another—bass, organ, piano, and drums. The entire event was a spectacle, well documented on the Asylum double album *Before the Flood*.

During his passionate acoustic set, Dylan even held his harmonica holder out to the crowd in tribute to everyone. And some lyrics really hit home in a huge way, too. During "It's Alright, Ma" when he sang "even the President of the United States must sometimes have to stand naked"—the crowd cheered wildly. No one in the place missed the obvious reference to Nixon, whose days as President looked numbered. The establishment couldn't be trusted—we were really on our own in the 1970s. When the words "How does it feel, to be on your own, like a complete unknown, like a rolling stone?" flew out at the crowd, everyone jumped up and sang along as the stage lights swirled around the audience. The music united us in a way that our national leaders never could. This wasn't magic or fantasy—this was real. There was energy and enthusiasm like I hadn't sensed since the first time I'd seen Led Zeppelin in 1969. It was the catalyst that gave us strength to face the day-to-day rigors of life. Zeppelin also gave an outlet to the teens and young adults to vent their feelings of powerlessness in regard to the political atmosphere. But before Zeppelin could perform again in America, they needed to complete the promotion of their new label.

As part of marketing Swan Song, Plant, Page, and Bonham attended a Valentine's Day concert for Swan Song's newest addition, Roy Harper. The concert was held to promote Harper's LP, *Valentine*, and was held at the Rainbow Theatre in London.

Accompanying the Zeppelin trio were Ronnie Lane, Max Middleton, and Keith Moon. While Jimmy played guitar with the act, Plant and Bonham wandered around being rock stars: Bonham was sporting a lovely pair of ballet tights and Plant was decked out in heiny-hugging leopard print pants. Roy Harper dedicated the *Valentine* album to all four Zeppelin members as thanks for the support from the Swan Song label.

The name of Zeppelin's label came about unexpectedly. Swan Song was initially considered for the title of the sixth Zeppelin LP. During a session where Page was creating a semi-classical twenty-minute acoustic solo to go along with a six-minute vocal section, someone asked him what it was going to be called. Page shouted out: "Swan Song!" A swan song is the euphemism for the sound a swan makes as it dies, a purportedly beautiful noise. Everyone began to say what a great title it was for the new album. The name had beat out other such classy options like Slut Records, Slag Records, De Luxe, Stairway Records, and Zeppelin Records.

Now that the label had an imaginative name, it needed an equally intriguing logo. The band found their inspiration from a painting by William Rimner. The painting, *Evening, Fall of Day*, describes the image of an angel with outstretched arms and back-wards-craning neck. This winged man became the Swan Song logo, showing, perhaps, a half-man, half-swan creature in the final throes of death. It can also be seen as the mythical Icarus, about to fall after his wings melted off during a fatal flight toward the sun.

The record label was finally complete with title, logo, and headliners. Now it was time for the launch parties. Two were held in the United States: one in New York and one in Los Angeles. The New York event was hosted at the Four Seasons Hotel and cost the band over $10,000. An official hired a flock of geese instead of swans and thought that nobody would notice. But Plant noticed and was outraged. He shouted that since he lived on a farm, he knew the difference between a goose and a swan. A few days later, on May 10, the band came to L.A. to host the biggest record industry party of the year, with 150 guests. This was truly a Holly-wood event. And this time there were actual swans and not geese in the pond. Photographer Neil Zlozower documented the entire affair. "The record industry was quite a bit different in those days," he noted. "I mean, all the bands had parties every week, whether it was the Bel Air Hotel, the Beverly Wilshire or the Beverly Hills Hotel . . . there was free booze and amazing food, they were all catered back then." Zlozower went on to point out that when Zep-pelin had parties, it was anything but laid-back or boring. "Any Led Zeppelin party wasn't a mellow party . . . there were a lot of drunk people, a lot of drugs going around, a lot of hot chicks, so they were always a little bit more wild than your typical, standard everyday party from the rest of the rock bands."

All the rock press attended the Bel Air event, along with Atlantic Records executives. And a variety of music stars also showed up—Bill Wyman of the Rolling Stones, Dr. John, Billy Preston, and Bryan Ferry. Also there was ex-Free vocalist Paul Rodgers, now fronting Bad Company. Robert Plant greatly admired Rodgers' singing style. Bad Company would soon end up getting the new label off to a great start, when its first album topped the U.S. charts in October. There were a few film stars—Lloyd Bridges and even Groucho Marx. Zlozower noted that although people were happy to meet this legendary film figure, Marx didn't partake much in the festivities. "Groucho was pretty much a zombie by that day and age—he didn't really say much or do much, he just sort of sat there . . . he was with his girlfriend or his keeper . . . that sort of oversaw him and made sure that nothing happened to him."

Speaking of companions, Lori Maddox had given herself exclu-sively to Page for two years, but now she was yesterday's paper. Bebe Buell, a 19 year old New York model was now the new girl on the block that had caught Page's eye. Page brought her along to the L.A. launch party. The party was scheduled for cocktails at 7:00 P.M. and dinner at 8:30 P.M. The guests were disappointed at the level of sobriety and soon turned the party around. What began as a tame, civilized affair, eventually degenerated into a childish food-fight, after which the hotel manager requested that the partygoers leave the premises.

The L.A. launch event might have been crazy—but the third party was a lot more wild, provocative and imaginative. To celebrate the first Swan Song release in the U.K. by the Pretty Things, Zeppelin threw a Halloween party at England's Chislehurst Caves. These caves are twenty miles of an underground labyrinth that were built by the Druids, Saxons, and Romans. It was used as a bomb shelter during WWII, before it became a tourist attraction. According to local legend, the caves have been the scene of many murders and are now haunted. At the party, old movies and ancient paintings were projected onto the cave's walls. Naked or half-naked women lined the various dark recesses of the caves or reclined before sacrificial altars. And there was enough booze to last a month, which was all nearly consumed. Peter Grant was dressed as a sailor while the security staff was in monk's outfits. Ditching the bird life, Led Zeppelin aides played it safe, hiring strippers dressed as nuns to pleasure any willing guest.

Even with all the projects, parties, and craziness, there was something missing for Plant. More than anything, he loved being onstage, being part of this creation called Led Zeppelin. He sensed that the band members needed each other more than ever, that the whole was so much more superior to the individuals. Everyone had been apart doing different things. He said, "When we had that party in Chistlehurst Caves . . . that I really missed the unity of the four of us, the side of the whole thing that I really dig. I realized that above everything else, above record companies, above films, above all of that—we were Led Zeppelin. And the place I dug most was standing just a little bit to the right of Bonzo's drum kit."

There were no Zeppelin appearances or new product during the year. The band rested during the summer. Then rehearsals started for the upcoming North American tour, set to begin after the New Year. Bonham had been taking his time in practicing and, pleased with his playing, was looking forward to the coming tour. He noted, "I find that not playing for a couple of weeks here and there I actually play better. If I was practicing every day of my life . . . I think that would get on top of you . . . If you've got so much to do you have to leave it alone for a while. You're really keen to play when you do go back to it—like the next tour we do. I'll be really keyed up to play, rather than thinking 'Oh, no. Not another gig.'"

On the contrary, Page knew that he had to be ready physically and emotionally, since the last tour had taken so much out of him. He pointed out, "At the moment I've got to start building up my stamina, because every time I've toured the States, I've returned a physical . . . and mental wreck. I mean, after the last tour they tried to get me put in a mental hospital. It was either that or going to a monastery! Ultimately, I just went to sleep for a month."

Zeppelin didn't exactly know what was going to happen in the coming tour. Fans' expectations were building more than ever in America. They knew that this band put out all it had for audiences. Ultimately the upcoming tour would be greeted with mass hysteria.

CHAPTER 6

Physical Graffiti

For the high school generation, attendance at a Led Zeppelin concert was as mandatory as freshman English. To take in a Zeppelin concert was to undergo an astonishing, mind-blowing experience. The sound was hurled at you through 24,000 watts of amplification. The band represented an entire code of behavior: cool, fast, young and cocksure. Once more, Zeppelin mania swept America. Fans had waited nearly 18 months to see the band set foot on an American stage. It caused panic in any city where mere whispers of a Zeppelin concert were heard. To get Zeppelin tickets, fans had slept out in the open in zero-degree January temperatures in New York City, had lined up for three days due to a communication breakdown and had even rioted in Boston when rowdy fans wrecked the box office.

The tour had just begun in January 1975, and somehow Zeppelin had already managed to make all the other rock news/concerts/groups pale by comparison. It was backstage at the Chicago Stadium, on the tour's second night, when Robert Plant turned to now Swan Song President Danny Goldberg and remarked, "It's not only that we think we're the best group in the world, it's just that in our minds we're so much better than whoever is number two."

On yet another record breaking US tour, the band added some new effects—a 300,000 watt lighting rig plus use of lasers. Jimmy Page caught a finger in a train door back in England, broke the tip and was forced to play with only three fingers on his fretting hand. His guitar wizardry on "Dazed and Confused" had to be omitted on the earlier dates. Plant caught a touch of the flu in freezing Chicago. And Bonzo had stomach ailments due to nerves and homesickness, since his wife was pregnant. Even with the problems, the band never went onstage and just messed about, but roared their way across the country playing some of the finest moments heard onstage in years. "Rock and Roll" was high powered. The new material was superb—"Kashmir," "Trampled Underfoot," and "In My Time of Dying," off the forthcoming album. "Moby Dick" always got standing ovations.

On the heels of its tour came Zeppelin's debut album on their Swan Song label, the double album *Physical Graffiti*. The cover art represented a façade of a New York apartment building, located at 97 St. Mark's Place. There were windows cut out to show people within the dust jacket, suggesting a voyeuristic, teasing experience. There was an eclectic variety of people in those windows—the cast from *Wizard of Oz*, Flash Gordon, Charles Atlas, the Queen of England, King Kong, the Virgin Mary, Peter Grant, and the band in drag.

Jimmy Page, once again the band's thematic creator, came up with the name of the new album. He recalled, "It came out in the usual panic of trying to find a title for an album. I came up with that title because of the whole thing of graffiti on the album cover and it being a physical statement rather than a written one, because I feel that an awful lot of physical energy is used in producing an album."

Recorded at Headley Grange, the music itself was a garage-type of street band thing. *Physical Graffiti* was the longest album in the making, taking nearly two years, with its fifteen songs stretching to eighty-two minutes. It seemed a good idea to use some songs that had been left off previous LPs. "Bron-Yr-Aur" was left over from *Led Zeppelin III*, while "Down by the Seaside," "Night Flight" and "Boogie with Stu" were from the fourth LP. "Black Country Woman" and "The Rover" were originally for *Houses of the Holy*. The new music was a bit of a return to the more raw approach and looser production of the first two albums. "In My Time of Dying" was a good example. The way Page put it was: "It was just being put together when we recorded it. It's jammed at the end, so we didn't even have a proper way to stop the thing ... I liked it because we really sounded like a working group. We could've tightened it up, but I enjoyed its edge."

On the other hand, "In the Light," "Ten Years Gone," and "Kashmir" were more ambitious and refined. "Kashmir" had a sort of magnetism within itself, which grew in intensity as more instruments were added. Page said, "It was just Bonzo and myself at the start of that one—he started the drums and I did the riff and the overdubs, which in fact got duplicated by an orchestra at the end, which brought it even more to life. It seemed sort of ominous and had a particular quality to it: it's nice to go for an actual mood and know that you've pulled it off."

The wax was finally here after two years of silence—unrelenting, steaming wax. The music was exciting and exotic. It showed all the different roads the band had taken and the breathtaking extent of their versatile repertoire. Zeppelin whipped up a wall of intense total sound, a fearsome barrage of crazed, scorching density that let up only when it wanted to. It put you in sensory overload and you wondered if your ears were going to bleed. There was only one word to describe it. Awesome. Even the critics considered *Physical Graffiti* worth the wait.

When I first heard the album, I was visiting my mom's beach house in Laguna. I'd just come back from surfing at Oak Street and found no one home. I flopped on the couch and saw my young sister's copy of *Grafitti* leaning against the wall in the corner by my mom's stereo. Since I hadn't heard the new album yet, I decided it was a great time to kick back and hear some music, so I threw *Graffiti* on the turntable. There was a lot to take in, but some songs really jumped out at me.

"Custard Pie" was a manic, hypnotic rifferema. With "In My Time of Dying" Page's slide completely redefined Blind Willy Johnson's blues; Bonham propelled it forward as he traded notes with Page. Then "Trampled Underfoot" really put the pedal to the metal. Jones pounded the keys, Plant ripped out the lyrics and Bonham brought down the hammer. And Page's solo threatened to overload the Marshalls! As "Kashmir" faded out on side two, I knew Zep had broken new ground. Jones' mellotron work put me right in the middle of a Sahara sandstorm. Plant's lyrics were seductive, and Page's guitar burned hotter than the desert sun. Bonzo's stomping beat sounded like the last dinosaur on earth coming up the path. For me, this song would have been good enough to end the album.

Jones' extraordinary synthesizer work on "In the Light" seemed to build to the threat of a blockbusting riff about to burst forth. It was only heavy rock . . . but you had to love it. As a contrast to heavy riffs, the acoustic "Bron-Yr-Aur" segued beautifully into "Down by the Seaside" to give a little balance between heavy and light sounds. And speaking of riffs—"Ten Years Gone" sounded like Page had assembled an entire guitar army, an overpowering chorus that became like one huge instrument. "Sick Again," had the same frantic chording to kiss the two platters off. Of course, I felt far from sick. The album finished, and I was more than impressed—Page's playing had left me speechless.

Not that it was all due to Jimmy Page, though. Throughout the sides Plant's frenzied vocals and harmonica send the VU meters hurtling into the red and the John Paul Jones–John Bonham rhythm section rolls on regardless, reaching new levels of bump and grind white funk. *Physical Graffiti* was a total team effort. It always headed in the same direction, blitzing the same collective skull. Zep was still delivering the goods, in devastating style. For millions of kids, teenage depression was easily aided by a good pair of headphones and a copy of *Physical Graffiti*.

When the album topped the charts in March, Led Zeppelin became the first group to have six albums simultaneously in the *Billboard* Top 200. The band was now at the height of its fame, outselling even the Rolling Stones. Led Zeppelin owned the music world. Even *Rolling Stone*, which had knocked them in the past, had surrendered to the mighty music power of the Zeppelin and said that *Graffiti* was the band's *Sgt. Pepper, Beggar's Banquet*, and *Tommy* all rolled into one. Zeppelin was featured for the first time on the cover of the March 13, 1975 issue. Cameron Crowe, still a teenager, was on assignment for *Rolling Stone* to interview Jimmy Page and Robert Plant. What a lucky dog! I would've given almost anything to be in his shoes. The interview took place over a period of two weeks while he traveled with the band. Subjects discussed ranged from the Yardbirds to the first Zep tour to Swan Song. It ended with Crowe asking for any final comments. To which Page replied, "Just say that I'm still searching for an angel with a broken wing."

Things got better the second half of the tour as the band shifted into second gear. Page's finger had healed to the point that "Dazed and Confused" was introduced into the set. The lighting around Page during the violin-bow solo was spectacular—all green and purple in a demonic triangle shape, with green lasers beaming into the crowd. Each night the band took chances and improvised, which meant that there would be occasional mistakes. But Page pointed out that, "The sheer fact that you're trying to fly necessitates that. Otherwise, it's note-for-note perfect every night, and that gets boring."

The volume may have been overpowering at times, but it was controlled. Page's philosophy about this was: "I turn up pretty high, but I vary my pick attack—I don't play hard all the time. I find that this approach helps me get more tonal and dynamic variation, especially when I'm playing close to the bridge or close to the neck. Then you have the power if you really want to hit it hard."

This American tour was a little different because Peter Grant had invited members of the press to accompany the band on the *Starship*. Then he pointedly ignored them as he sauntered around on the plane in his Davy Crocket hat, tweed jacket, and silk scarf. The atmosphere of *Starship One* was much calmer than it had been in 1973, possibly because of the watchful eye of the press. Bonzo sat around quietly drinking and fiddling with his new bowler hat. Jones passed the time playing chess and backgammon with the reporters. Jimmy and Robert spent most of the flights back in the bedrooms, relaxing after the exhausting concerts.

The concerts were glorious spectacles that left the audiences awestruck. The amount of equipment the band toted around with them was massive. There were 184 loudspeakers, 172 lights, laser apparatus, mirror-balls, and an essential dry-ice smoke-machine. The tour also used the biggest sound and light system up to this time. The $250,000 speakers had 24,000 watts of power and provided up to 120 decibels of sound. The light-systems, worth $300,000, were perched on a horseshoe-shape ring of 28 light-towers around the stage. This equipment had to be set up every day of the tour by the roadies. In addition to the colored lights, the spotlights, the glitter, and the pyrotechnics, Led Zeppelin had a new toy. They were the first band to take a digital delay echo and repeat device with them on the road. It created the haunting tones on Plant's vocals and the eerie feel to Page's guitar magic. On the first few gigs, Bonham had gotten to the concert halls earlier than the others, not satisfied until he got his drum sound perfect. For him, precision was the key that made the difference.

Audiences were immediately drawn in with "Rock and Roll," the usual starter, a straight-ahead, no-nonsense song that celebrated the rock spirit. One longtime fan, Tony Gold, remembered the shows as "marathon excursions of drama." The lights, the lasers, the effects, the colored wheel in Bonzo's drum podium, all combined to create an entire production, not just a show. "It wasn't just going to a concert . . . you knew you were in for something but you didn't know what . . . no two nights were the same," Gold added. In comparison to other bands like The Who, Pink Floyd, Kiss, and The Beach Boys, Zeppelin delivered much more bang for the buck. Gold noted that on the final show of their tour, The Who performed for ninety minutes with no encores. Led Zeppelin routinely played for three and a half-hours straight. Zeppelin held nothing back and with this tour became the hardest working band in rock history.

Cameron Crowe described the band in action: ". . . Jimmy, his gold Gibson Les Paul hung at crotch level, jumps across the raised platform, raises one arm skywards and sends a heavy hundred-decibel wave of metallic sound surging through a bank of amplifiers. Robert Plant's screaming vocals filter through an echo unit and blend with the high-pitched barrage. Behind them, right out of *Clockwork Orange* in a . . . bowler hat and white boiler suit, sits drummer John Bonham . . . The sounds come from twenty-five mikes on stage, twelve on Bonham's drums alone. John Paul Jones, wearing a gold-embroidered waistcoat, black pants and shirt, and smiling a lot, played a twenty-minute keyboard solo during 'No Quarter.'" At the New York shows, Krypton laser beams were used to highlight band members and send swirling rainbow light effects through the crowd. There was both power and drama at nearly every show.

In Dallas on March 4, the band opened with "Rock and Roll" then transitioned into a song from the new album, "Sick Again." As Page played his solo on "Over the Hills and Far Away," Robert shouted out to him, "Acapulco Gold!" The band genuinely had fun at this show. At the start of "No Quarter," Plant introduced John Paul Jones as the man "with the impeccably clean fingernails," another great moment of the band celebrating with its audience through dry humor. During "Kashmir," the light effects really stole the show. The silver mirror-balls rotated throughout the song, throwing lights all around the audience. When the show ended, explosions went off atop four light-towers and bright lights spelled out the name "Led Zeppelin."

A later concert scheduled for West Palm Beach on March 8th had to be canceled because the police were worried about the troublemakers in the audience—kids would leap out of their seats, run around, and sometimes throw firecrackers. Zeppelin was very upset at this date being canceled, since they had enjoyed great success there on the 1973 tour. Despite this disappointment, the band went on to play their other concerts with furious abandon. It wasn't a manic fury that flew out at audiences, or merely overpowering volume—but more like an exploding volcano of controlled music.

The Seattle show in March was Zeppelin's first use of lasers. Hugh Jones, who had seen Zeppelin's inspired 1969 Fillmore East show, was at Seattle. He recalled: "Midway through the bow solo a trio of laser beams suddenly appeared from behind the drum set, vividly piercing the dark arena from stage to rear ceiling, an absolutely amazing sight." Page wore pants with the moon and stars. Even though Bonham was hidden from view behind his drum set, the power of his drums was right in everyone's face! Robert Plant was resplendent as always in his abdomen-flashing attire. He confided in, encouraged, and joked with the audience throughout the concert. "As you can imagine, it's more than our pleasure to be back in this coastal town . . . a town of great fishermen, including our drummer," he said, referring to the incident in 1969 with a shark and a groupie.

It was time to switch off the amps for a while. For the tour's final ten days Zeppelin used an entire floor at the Continental Hyatt House in L.A. as its base. Locals began calling it the "Riot House" because of all the zaniness that went on. Only Jones seemed to avoid the tour antics. Reports claim that he always insisted on his hotel suite being at least two floors away from the rest of the band. Having an entire floor was like having one big playground taken from the script of *Animal House*. It was crazy, it was mad. There were wheelchair races in the hallway. TVs were thrown out the window. Groupies were tied to the beds. "Coke Lady," an aide employed solely for the purpose of passing out white powder to band members and crew, was kept busy. Bonham played his records very, very loud at three or four in the morning and somebody would go downstairs and complain. The hotel ended up moving the person who complained. It was just the idea that, "We can get away with anything because we're Led Zeppelin."

At their Los Angeles concerts, rock and roll's elite came from Hollywood to experience Zeppelin's newest offerings. Rod Stewart, Ron Wood, Mick Jagger, John Lennon, Keith Moon, and David Bowie all came to see the spectacle. Page's finger had healed since the New York shows, and he was now doing his workouts with his bow on "Dazed and Confused." Audiences were in awe of Jimmy's showmanship: he would "command" the lasers to fly through the audience with the power of his bow. Jimmy himself was pretty proud of his new "magical" skills, and strutted the stage in his mystical black outfit, walking past the Marshall amps with Zoso across them. At times, he would strike a power chord and in a flash jump skyward, raising his arm and doing splits.

Neil Zlozower was watching it all, right up against the stage taking photos during the L.A. Forum concert. As in 1970, Page's guitar bowing was spellbinding to him. Zlozower pointed out: "As soon as he'd do that I'd always shoot tons and tons of film because I thought that was the coolest thing in the world. Some of my favorite Led Zeppelin shots are the ones where he's playing the bow. If you look through my photos there really isn't much John Paul Jones and there really isn't too much John Bonham because basically to me, Page and Plant were the whole band."

Zlozower wasn't real interested in watching all the members play the whole time. In fact, since the shows were three hours long, photographers looked for a chance to take a break. The cue was five minutes into "Moby Dick." And where did they go? To the band's dressing room? That's right. This was because in 1975 there was only one type of backstage pass, and if you had one, you could go anywhere you wanted. The dressing room was where all the really nice free goodies to eat and drink were. But someone surprised them all. Zlozower explained, "So I remember there's about ten of us back there, and all of a sudden Robert Plant walks in the room and he looks around and he sees all the photographers backstage, and he sorta got this look on his face. And then he said, 'Whatsa matter? Don't you like the drum solo?' And then he had this big smile on his face. So he basically knew that it was a little on the boring side hearing any drummer play for twenty-five minutes. He sorta was asking us, 'What's the problem?' but he knew in his mind in reality that we were all pretty bored. And that was the perfect chance to drink all the band's beer and eat all the band's food."

Despite Plant's joke about Bonham's twenty-plus minutes onstage drum forays, this particular tour was the most successful in terms of music quality, stage effects—and especially fan response. Rock music appeals to a mass audience, and demand for tickets was overwhelming. Music, like all the arts, is magical and ceremonial in its origin—and rock has hypnotic power. Page commented, "The important thing is to maintain a balance. The kids come to get far out with the music. It's our job to see they have a good time and no trouble." Those who were lucky enough to see the shows went away more than satisfied.

In two months of sold out concerts, the band had conquered America again. The tour ended in late March, and estimates were that it had earned more than $5 million. There were other successes, too—*Graffiti* had gone straight to number one in the *Billboard* charts and earned nearly $12 million. Reporter Lisa Robinson was given total access on the tour. She remarked that, "The Beatles and the Stones battled it out in the parking lot and Led Zeppelin won." She just may have been right.

In May, Peter Grant presented the group's first English concerts in two years at London's 17,000 seat Earl's Court Arena. Many consider these four-hour marathons to be the greatest series of concerts that Zeppelin ever performed. Bonham even said, "I thought they were the best shows that we've ever put out in England." Opening night was on the 17th, and fan Robert Godwin was there. For him, there was a definite feeling that something more than just a concert was about to happen. To put it mildly, Godwin was amazed and transfixed during the performance. Godwin said, "The band played with tremendous fire, possessed by almost a demonic power. Page, in full black dragon suit, flailed his violin bow against his guitar strings, producing eerie, gothic howls. My hearing did not return to normal until three days later."

Over the course of the five shows, 85,000 people came to see Led Zeppelin perform. A new visual enhancement was introduced in these shows: two 24 × 30 video screens. These screens relayed live video pictures of the group so the entire audience could see everything close up. As in America, the show opened with "Rock and Roll." Robert Plant showed off his torso bared to the navel, tossed his hair during powerful songs, and stroked his locks during the acoustic numbers. Meanwhile, Jimmy Page was all over the stage with his guitar slung low, feeling the music with his strings. John Bonham was raised on a platform above the other members so he could be seen by everyone. John Paul Jones in black trousers and a classy dinner jacket continued to contribute his rock-steady bass patterns that formed a foundation for Page's flying riffs and Plant's powerful voice.

The effects during "Kashmir" were stunning and filled the audience with an incredible sense of awe. The five silver mirror-balls threw light across the arena. Bonham's bare-handed gong pounding electrified the spectators. The dry ice poured eerily across stage during "No Quarter," highlighting the song's mystic overtones. To top it off, John Paul Jones improvised a twenty-minute solo on his keyboards. Throughout the shows, Robert Plant kept up a dialogue with the crowd, telling of their journey, the good and bad times, explaining the meaning to some songs, and sipping tea and honey for his throat. Before "Bron-Y-Aur Stomp," Plant dedicated the song to his dog, Strider. And because of the band's hassles caused by English tax law, Plant sarcastically dedicated "In My Time of Dying" to the man responsible for them. Also included in these shows were "Trampled Underfoot," "Dazed and Confused," "Stairway to Heaven," "Whole Lotta Love," and "Black Dog." The band always included the fans' favorites along with the songs from their new album. They played to the crowd, not for themselves—and everyone knew it!

The band had decided to film some of the shows so they could have a record for themselves. All of the close-ups and playing scenes from the video screens were transferred to film, and this is what Page used on the 2003 DVD set. Plant later called the decision to keep a film record a lucky one—the results are spectacular. The brilliant sound jumps right out at you, and Page shows why he's the guitar master. "Going To California" and "That's The Way" have an intimacy that makes it seem like Zeppelin are performing right there in your living room. John Paul Jones' mandolin rings out beautifully around Page's playing. The newer *Graffiti* material shows a newly energized band that had moved forward. "Trampled Underfoot" demonstrates Jones' prowess as a keyboardist. And Page's doubleneck classic "Stairway" is perhaps final proof that Earl's Court was a milestone series of shows—complete mind-blowing experiences to those lucky enough to see them.

Stuart Whitehead, a fan that attended the Earl's Court shows remembered them as the best live concerts ever. "After the initial rush of the rockier songs came the acoustic set which just oozed with a warm mellow maturity. This was heaven, they had never sounded or looked better. The highlight for me was 'Trampled

Underfoot'—not my favorite Zep song on *Graffiti* but here in the flesh it felt like a hurricane blasting in your face. I left Earl's Court absolutely drained of emotion, after having my senses assaulted and this was only the first night, there were still four more to go!"

Another spectator, Dave Lewis, the premier Zeppelin authority and future editor of the Zeppelin magazine *Tight But Loose*, also was amazed by the awesome music and visual display at the Earl's Court shows. He remembered each show for its own unique atmosphere and highlights. He was understandably enthralled on the May 24 show because, "I was lucky to be in the second row, near Jimmy. I have a vivid memory of Robert swirling past Jimmy during 'Black Dog' and looking down at the front rows with a beaming smile. I saw Led Zeppelin a total of fourteen times but they never took me higher than that legendary Saturday night in Earl's Court."

There was more in store for Lewis, then just an eighteen-year-old fan. He and four friends missed the train home to Bedford. (They ended up sleeping in the station next to some disgruntled Scotsmen who were returning from the England versus Scotland soccer match. England had won, 5-1.) Missing the train wasn't so lucky, but Lewis, a fervent follower, had been lucky to have tickets for the final Earl's Court show too, where he experienced more than he bargained for— another story of a fan's dream come true. The show had just ended with a final encore of a stunning "Heartbreaker" and "Communication Breakdown." Lewis and a few friends hung around and sneaked into the backstage area, hoping to get a glimpse of the band. They were astounded at what happened next!

"There was Robert sitting on the limo," Lewis recalled. Plant wore a blue jacket with sparkles all over it and a white scarf, with his wrists draped in bracelets. There was a small party going on for Swan Song, and it was like Plant was being grand master over the ceremonies. He looked "like some Greek god, which at the time was exactly what he was. An unforgettable image. He then walked with his wife Maureen over to the party entrance and told us about his jewelry. I asked him when we'd see the band play in the UK again, and he replied, 'Well, there's a lot of traveling to do first.'"

Lewis hung around the party until early morning. Then he went on a small pilgrimage, sort of a short visit to a Mecca for the band. Lewis said, "Around 3 A.M. I strolled onto the Earl's Court stage—now deserted except for some PA gear and Jonesy's grand piano. It was an incredible feeling to be up there where all the action had taken place. We saw them all leave the party around 4 A.M.—Jimmy looking very frail in a white suit and matching scarf. Then it was home on the early morning Bedford train, back to reality."

The party that Lewis visited had a variety of stars from the music industry, including Chris Squire, Marianne Faithful, Denny Lane, Jeff Beck, and Jon Anderson. Music for the party was provided by one of Robert Plant's favorites, Dr. Feelgood, and Gonzalez. The party was intended to last a while. (Jeff Beck stayed until 4 o'clock in the morning.) A turnout like this from the celebrities who had seen Zeppelin in American concerts illustrates how admired the band was by those in the industry. Led Zeppelin was more than a rock and roll band—they were now a phenomenon. The band had accomplished all they'd ever dreamed of.

As the summer began, I was now involved in a new pastime—photographing rock concerts. I'd gotten some pictures at Dylan's Forum concert the year before with my dad's 35 mm Pentax and decided to check out what was happening in the concert scene in San Diego. In August, Eric Clapton and Santana played at the San Diego Arena. I picked up a tenth row seat at San Diego State's ticket office and was able to bring my tripod, camera and telephoto into the show. I got a few pictures of each band's set from my seat. I even walked up to the front of the stage to get some close-ups. There were these huge, Jamaican-type security guards in yellow shirts and straw hats in front of me, who waved me back after I took a few pictures. Then the last ten minutes of the show, Clapton's band left the stage—but the amps stayed on. Then he came out and Carlos Santana jammed for a while, which blew me away. I had some film left and was able to capture some intense moments of Santana hitting some high notes and throwing his head back, with Clapton smiling at him. This was something that wouldn't happen again! I was definitely getting excited about rock concerts now.

After this, I went to a "Summer Spectacular" at Balboa Stadium, site of many historic shows—the Beatles, the Stones, and Crosby, Stills, Nash, and Young had all played there. Tickets for this extravaganza went for $10 and featured Lynyrd Skynyrd, Fleetwood Mac, Loggins and Messina, and Rod Stewart and the Faces. You could cruise right up on the grass and get next to the stage, which is just what I did. I was able to bring in my camera and an old ice chest to stand on. That was a good idea because everyone stood the whole time and I had to be able to take pictures over everyone's heads. It was like a Dionysian festival, with people sharing bottles of wine and smoking pot. As the day went on, the huge stadium filled up with rock fans ready to party.

All the bands were incredible, but the first two rocked out the most. Skynyrd guitarists Gary Rossington and Allen Collins had the longest hair that I'd ever seen, way past their shoulders. And this Southern band jammed like nobody's business! The dual lead guitars on "Free Bird" were an electric intensity that I never knew was possible. The second act, Fleetwood Mac, started out mellow but gradually built up to some soaring rock with some unique vocalists in the forms of two skinny, good looking girls. Christie McVie played beautiful piano and wore purple knee high boots and the shortest cutoffs possible. The other, newer girl, clad in blue jeans and white silk blouse, Stevie Nicks, spun, danced, and shrieked her brains out to a new song called "Rhiannon." She was intense. And her boyfriend who had a cool-looking Afro, guitarist Lindsey Buckingham made his white Les Paul howl and scream, all done with finger picking.

After this came the best musicianship that day—some beautiful acoustic songs by Loggins and Messina, followed by their electrified country rock. Messina, an alumnus of Buffalo Springfield and a vastly underrated guitarist, played amazing country rock leads, and Kenny Loggins smiled and jumped all over the stage. Rod Stewart and the Faces ended the festivities with a wild dose of British rock. Ron Wood, about to leave permanently for a spot in the Stones, played at scorching volume from his Gibson Firebird, Stratocaster and Les Paul, also sharing vocals on the same mike with Stewart for nearly the last time. Stewart leaped and whirled his mike stand around like a madman. It was very loud, crazy, and exciting—the crowd was thrown into a complete frenzy. There was a swirling mass of people around me all day, but no one knocked me off my chest, which was nothing short of a miracle. Being so close I was able to take some pictures that caught some of the action. It seemed like this photo-taking gig worked, at least for now.

I repeated the same plan a little later when Jackson Browne, Linda Ronstadt, and the Eagles played there. Since the early 1970s, country rock had grown hugely popular in America. The Eagles now epitomized both the laidback and acoustic and the electrified, hard rocking California music scene with their current album *On the Border*. Jackson Browne had collaborated with the Eagles and was now a hot item as a prolific songwriter with his apocalyptic album *Late for the Sky*. And Ronstadt's strong voice filled the entire place as she danced and kicked up her heels in a red and white ankle-length country dress. California talent was cooking up a menu of unbelievably high-powered music on the West Coast.

Shortly after the Eagles show, I had an unbelievable music experience—I got to meet blues giant Willie Dixon after taking pictures of his show at San Diego State. When he invited me backstage to have pizza with his band and talk music, I blew my mind and said yes. This was the guy who'd written some of the greatest blues songs ever, many being covered by bands like the Stones—

"Little Red Rooster," the Doors—"Back Door Man," Cream—
"Spoonful," and Led Zeppelin—"You Shook Me," "I Can't Quit
You Baby," and "Bring It On Home." Dixon had also worked with
a who's who of blues legends like Muddy Waters, Howlin' Wolf,
Little Walter, Chuck Berry, and Sonny Boy Williamson. Dixon had
a unique music philosophy—successful artists should assist other
musicians become better and gain some degree of success, instead
of trying to just make more money or stay the most popular. He
told me, "Those guys on top shouldn't worry about that because
no one stays on top forever anyway. The guy who gets to level
one's sometime gonna slide back to level two, so why worry about
it? He just oughta enjoy being on top while he's there . . . and be
able to help others."

For Led Zeppelin, it now looked like they had indeed reached
their pinnacle for albums and live performances. After the fantastic Earl's Court shows, the band's members organized some much
needed individual holidays for themselves. In June, Bonham's
second child, a daughter named Zoe, was born. The reality of
having three lives in his hands awakened him more than ever to
the importance of being there for his family. It was also for the purpose of tax exile time, too. The excessive 95% publishing royalty
tax that England imposed on its successful musicians was simply
too much. Plant remarked, "It's a very sad situation, you know, to
have to leave one's own country for the sake of money . . . Not
only did I want to preserve some of the reward for what I've
worked like hell for . . . but it was almost the principle of the
thing!"

Robert Plant and his family went on vacation with Jimmy
Page in Greece to pass the time of their tax exile. After Page left
Rhodes in Greece for Italy, Plant, his wife and two children stayed
behind. August 4th started off as a day of sightseeing but turned
out to be a terrible day for them. Amid screams of terror and the
buckling of metal, their rented car plunged off a narrow highway
on the Greek island of Rhodes and slammed into a tree! It was a

near-fatal car accident. Maureen was in a terrible state from facial lacerations, a concussion, and four fractures of the pelvis. She spent several weeks in the hospital. Plant's daughter, seven year old Carmen, had a broken wrist and cuts and bruises. His four year old son, Karac, suffered a fractured leg and also had multiple cuts and bruises. Plant came out of it with multiple fractures of the ankle, bones supporting the foot and elbow. Doctors told him that he wouldn't be able to walk for at least six months.

Peter Grant announced that the August-September American stadium mini-tour was postponed, as was the October tour scheduled for the Far East. How would Plant come out of this—would his leg allow him to perform again? Or would he even want to? When there's a near-death situation, people often change in many different ways. My car wreck changed me—and Plant's accident changed him, too. He admitted afterwards, "I find that time is very precious to me now. I am much more appreciative of my family."

Plant, Page, Jones, and Bonham were all caught up in a crisis. The pain and doubt were there. This was much more than cancelled dates on the line—it was the future of the band. Would they split up or face it head on?

CHAPTER 7

Presence

Led Zeppelin had their backs against the wall. Nearly eight years of accumulated battle fatigue had worn them down. And now with Plant's serious car accident, it was time to rethink the future, but Zeppelin would come back fighting. They turned an accident into an album and had to marshal every last bit of energy to record this testament of reaffirmation. And it was Zeppelin's triumph over forces not directly under their control.

Due to tax problems, Plant could not recuperate at his own home, so as soon as he was mobile, he was sent to Malibu, a sunny coastal community north of Los Angeles, to mend. Jimmy Page flew out to join him. The two started from scratch to get some rough ideas for a new album, as *Physical Graffiti* had taken most of their leftovers. The call then went out to Jones and Bonham that their services were now needed, and the whole group convened in Los Angeles. It was an odd sight—Led Zeppelin with Robert Plant in a wheelchair.

Fortunately, the injuries had no effect on his voice. Plant recalled: "In L.A. we just rehearsed and rehearsed . . . I found me wiggling inside my cast. The whole band really wanted to play and had wanted to do that tour . . . It was a unique situation where we rehearsed for three weeks—on and off in true Zeppelin style because we're not the greatest band for rehearsing. We've always felt that too much rehearsing on a song can spoil it for us . . . sort of take the edge off the excitement, but this time it worked in the opposite way, because the enthusiasm was contained in such a small space of time."

When rehearsals concluded in November 1975 and this time to flee American tax laws, the band split to Munich, Germany, to record. "*Presence* was recorded while the group was on the move, technological gypsies. No base, no home. All you could relate to was a new horizon and a suitcase. So there's a lot of movement and aggression . . ." remembered Jimmy Page.

The plan was to push the limits. Every waking hour was spent in the recording studio. Page firmly took control, came up with all the riffs, and lived the record uninterrupted from beginning to end. Seven tracks were whipped out of the studio in the fastest time—in eighteen scorching days (*Physical Graffiti* had taken over 18 months)! It was a totally electric guitar-oriented album that packed a considerable punch—their most spontaneous sounding album to date. Also, lyrically gone were "girls with flowers in their hair," replaced with their endless touring cycle: tales of drugs, groupies, transvestites, and loneliness.

"Achilles Last Stand" could be the Yardbirds twelve years down the road. Incredibly, it just doesn't let up. "For Your Life" was a seething indictment of poseurs and phony hangers-on of all stripes, when cocaine was the drug of choice of '70s L.A. "Royal Orleans" painted a picture of misadventure in the French Quarter. "Nobody's Fault But Mine" was a hellish tune of life wasted in debauchery. Plant seemed to be admitting all his past sins and begging for redemption. "Candy Store Rock" was most definitely a hard rocker, evoking images of L.A. "Hots On for Nowhere" captured one of Page's greatest guitar solos. The final track, "Tea for One," winds the record slowly down with some compelling soul searching. Plant related how he felt laying on the hospital bed after the car crash, without Maureen—the heartbreak, the loneliness—"A minute seems like a lifetime, baby, when I feel this way."

By this time, Plant was more than a little spooked by his family's misfortunes. The near fatal car accident had a sobering effect on him. Plant remarked, "A guy takes to the road at sixteen, and plays every dive and truck stop for whatever he can get—my intention has always been and still is to carry on and on. But what can I say? Is it growing up? I have seen the true colors of my family and how much it really means to me. But you never see that when you're moving about. Only at the moment when you might not see it anymore."

Presence was a snapshot of a time when the band was stripped of its legendary power. Page agreed: "The whole testament of that Munich album is that it proved to us once and for all there was no reason for the group to split up . . . the LP showed us what we have as a group . . . We're gonna go on forever."

A British blues-rock group that split up in 1971, then reformed in 1972, only to call it quits, was Free. Hailed as being the next Rolling Stones, they were Paul Kossoff, Paul Rodgers, Andy Fraser, and Simon Kirke. The band almost made it. In their too short career, they produced only six studio albums, but never stopped developing. Free's *Tons of Sobs* remains one of rock's most stunning debut albums and still sounds great today. On the record the band displayed an earthy, youthful swagger. Like Zeppelin, Free was the sum of four equal parts, but it was Paul Kossoff and his Les Paul that was the heart and soul of the band. He had a unique style that became an instantly recognizable trademark of the Free sound: "a thick, round tone, snaky notes coiling around themselves at varying speeds, and most remarkable were the long, deliberate note-bending wails which quivered with impeccable vibrato." He moved a lot of people, including Jerry. To Jerry's ears, the "Koss" was one of the greatest guitarists who ever lived. Sadly, Paul Kossoff died on March 19, 1976, at age 25. To die young is a waste. Period.

Was Led Zeppelin showing signs of an imminent death too? The band had been off the road for a long period of time—Plant was still recuperating. Meanwhile in the rock music world, new Zeppelin imitators like Aerosmith and Lynyrd Skynyrd were finding a strong foothold in the American market. And a new movement called punk had turned the music world upside down. Most of the press began to dismiss Zeppelin as a "dinosaur" band. Zep's long hair and rock star posing seemed out of date. *Rolling Stone* sounded particularly biting: "Give an Englishman 50,000 watts, a chartered jet, a little cocaine and some groupies and he thinks he's a god. It's getting to be an old story." The music press turned against the idea of stadium rock and mega albums. Every fast thrashing, simplistically political group belittled Zeppelin. But not one among them could hold a candle to the ferocious frenzy of "Nobody's Fault But Mine" or the biting social commentary of "For Your Life."

Presence was released at the end of March 1976, went platinum before it hit the stores, and would remain one of the best-selling albums of the year, even without the benefit of a tour, a single, or even a photo of the band. Critics' reactions to the new album were mixed—*Melody Maker* praised it, while *Creem* said that, "For a Zeppelin junkie pumping the last drops out of *Physical Graffiti*, *Presence* was a brutal dose of methadone."

To strike wonder in the masses, decorating the album cover, inner fold, and back cover was a mysterious, slightly twisted black obelisk-like item, which appeared in each of the photos (all 1950s Middle America scenarios). It was out of place wherever it stood. This alien black monolith figure was referred to only as "The Object." Jimmy Page commented about the cover: "The way the cover came about was that after we'd returned from the recording, we realized that the only feasible thing to do was to take a picture of the studio and its chaos, but we needed something better than that, so we contacted Hipgnosis and explained to the chaps what had been going on. He returned and said that the thing that had always struck him about Led Zeppelin was a power, a force, an alchemical quality that was indefinable . . . a presence. He came up with the idea of interpreting this through an object which could be related to any object in a community that everybody was perfectly at home with."

Street rumors described it as everything from the new Zeppelin logo to a black arts worship piece. Others have said that the Object covers all aspects of life: family, sports, leisure, education, work. Radio stations and record stores had even started guessing contests. Nobody at the New York office of Zeppelin's Swan Song Records had any idea what The Object symbolized. Robert Plant threw in his two cents: "Whatever you want it to say, it says. The Object can be taken in many ways."

There was a promotional statue of The Object marketed by Atlantic Records and limited to 1,000 pieces. Each black, 12" tall, three pound statue was individually numbered and came with a promo sticker from Swan Song on the box. Years later an exact museum replica surfaced. Like the real thing, each replica was individually numbered and differed only slightly in appearance. The replica was finished in semi-gloss black instead of flat black. Other than that, it was the same in style, weight and appearance as the original. Back then, Jerry had ordered one at $20 through Rick Barrett's Led Zeppelin memorabilia catalog. Even today, his replica object (No. 225/1000) stands proudly on a shelf and has made an excellent conversation piece over the years.

Late May found Jimmy Page and Robert Plant hanging out again in L.A. But this time they were there to check out a show instead of giving one. Bad Company were playing at the L.A. Forum and during the show both Page and Plant came onstage and played with Bad Company for some cover tunes. The two returned to London, then a few days later on May 27, John Paul Jones jammed in London at the Marquee with the Pretty Things. Zep was part of the music scene but not yet ready to go on tour.

Fans awaiting Led Zep's next U.S. blitz prepared for the real

thing by watching the film of their Madison Square Garden concerts of 1973 in *The Song Remains the Same*. It premiered in October,
first in New York as a charity for Save the Children Fund, and then
in L.A. at the Fox Theatre with all members and Peter Grant in
attendance. When it hit theaters across the country, headlines
accompanying movie listings proclaimed, "You Haven't Seen Led
Zeppelin Until You've Seen Them on the Screen."

I first heard about the movie from some friends who saw it in
L.A. and raved about the concert parts as well as some pretty wild-
looking effects during many of the music scenes. I also heard about
how each band member was shown in different sequences and
grew curious about that. When it arrived at the Balboa Cinema in
Mission Beach, I decided to check it out after a day of surfing.
After getting some waves at Sunset Cliffs I headed for the theater.
I made sure my old Hansen surfboard was locked up inside my
van, walked to the theater and got in line. A lot of people I talked
to outside hadn't seen the movie and didn't know what to expect.
But like me, they were really interested in anything about Zep and
were excited about seeing the film.

As the movie unfolded, the audience was pretty quiet at first.
Then after the scenes of the band members at home, the pacing got
faster and started to suck all of us in. Then it happened. "Rock and
Roll" came on and cheers and howls bounced off the walls everywhere. This was great—it was like having a front-row seat to the
power and force of a typically manic Zeppelin show. Multiple track
play backs sent the music soaring from every direction around
the theater. The backstage stuff was pretty neat, too. And with the
sounds came the fantasy sequences of each member, which intrigued
me. The music was the power that drove the film's imagery. We
were lifted out of the arena and into a home movie of the band.
Even the black-and-white footage of the Drake Hotel robbery
seemed honest.

For me, Jimmy Page was the star of the movie. He was the
model guitar hero—cool, flowing mane of hair, with his Les Paul

hanging low, a torrent of notes or a landslide of powerful chords reverberating from the amps. I left the theater feeling like this had been a wild, unbelievable experience brought to me by four English musicians who knew how to rock, create, and have fun.

The movie may seem dated by today's video and music standards. But don't forget this was the 70s, before video, before MTV. Nowadays, video has become a crucial medium for music artists. Zep was a forerunner of things to come—using jump cuts, split screens and freeze frames. For Zep historians the movie is cinematic proof of the band's performing ability in 1973. It had been started that year on a low budget, was shelved, then started again, then stopped—three times in all. It was a miracle that the film even came out at all. Even so, reviews of the film were negative.

From the enthusiasm in the theatre during the live sequences, it seemed obvious that fans appreciated Zeppelin's film. The media response, on the other hand, was another story. *Melody Maker* had one of the only positive reviews and called the film "classy" and "surely enormously successful." Most other critics were less than pleased. *Rolling Stone* went even further and bashed the members themselves by ridiculing the individual fantasy scenes: "While Led Zeppelin's music remains worthy of respect . . . their sense of themselves merits only contempt."

Page was defensive about the film and explained that, "The music for the footage mainly came from the first night [of the filmed New York concerts]. It was the best vocal performance and wasn't like they had drop-ins and that sort of thing, but they just didn't have complete footage, so we had to come up with the fantasy sequences to fill it up. Had we been a band that's the same every night, it would have been very easy for them to link one performance with another. As far as live albums go, most groups will record over half a dozen nights and take the best of that, but we just couldn't do that."

The live soundtrack of the film, a double LP set with the same title, followed soon afterwards in October. Depicted on the cover is a rundown movie house. "Rock and Roll" starts the album, the standard concert kick-off number at that time. As I played the album at my little apartment, the energy powered through the speakers of my record player. Then there is everything in between—from "Celebration Day," to "The Rain Song," and "No Quarter." The twenty-six-minute version of "Dazed and Confused" showcased just how brilliant a musician Jimmy Page is. The track featured some of the most demonic sounding guitar/violin bow effects ever to appear on record. "No Quarter" shows the versatility of John Paul Jones on organ. Perhaps the highlight is "Stairway to Heaven"—a song of hope, fantasy and love. The version of "Moby Dick" demonstrated how the song had progressed from the original. The ending rock anthem, "Whole Lotta Love," is everything in vocal gymnastics and dynamics that we know Robert Plant can produce.

Like most things Zeppelin, the live album that coincided with the film was received with lots of trepidation. The reviewers were dissatisfied; they had waited for an unreal, blockbuster album that rivaled the excitement of Zep bootlegs. But for them *The Song Remains the Same* didn't deliver—the quality of the songs was disappointing. *Crawdaddy* magazine complained that the music was "unadorned versions" of some of Zep's more well-known material. Another reviewer called the album a "strange and sterile introduction" to the movie. Page was apologetic that the album wasn't up to par. "When it came to the live shows, we were always trying to move them forward . . . The songs were always in a state of change. On *The Song Remains the Same*, you can hear the urgency and not much else . . . There's no editing, really. There is loads of howling guitar mistakes on it. Normally one would be inclined to cut them out, but you can't when it's a soundtrack. It's an honest album in its own way."

My own memories of 1976 were built upon many of the concerts I attended and photographed. I had settled into college life at San Diego State by taking creative writing and literature classes, tutoring expository writing at the Study Skills Center, and writing

and photographing entertainment articles for the university newspaper, the *Daily Aztec*. Long gone were the twelve-hour-plus
stretches driving a cab to Camp Pendleton. The change was
refreshing and exhilarating. My new goal was now to go into
teaching English and become a writer. I met other aspiring writers
and photographers, many of whom were really into the entertainment scene.

Another reason for my newfound excitement was I had also
totally immersed myself in the concert scene. Although San Diego
didn't have L.A.'s reputation, there were still many venues, including the San Diego State Amp, the Sports Arena, the Golden Hall,
and Civic Center downtown, and a couple of movie theaters that
provided plenty of assorted shows. I'd have to wait another year
for Led Zeppelin to return. But there were still a variety of artists
that I was able to photograph. I became a regular fixture at the
Sports Arena and made sure that I'd get close to most of the acts
that played there. Always feeling that this opportunity wouldn't
last forever, I took plenty of pictures from the first ten rows. And I
kept my eyes open for when I could get up to the very front to get
real close pictures. And there were some spectacular shows coming
to the States. The one that everyone was talking about was a new
one by one of the former Beatles.

Jerry's sister Stephanie was a big Paul McCartney fan. His post-
Beatles band, Wings, was touring America for the first time in 1976.
This would become the tour of the year—Wings Over America.
Like Led Zeppelin, the band commuted to and from concerts by
private jet. McCartney also got a lot of help from Showco, the
Dallas based sound and light company. He had discovered Showco
at Led Zeppelin's Earl's Court shows and was impressed how they
managed to fill the arena with such a crisp sound.

Jerry had a friend in Chicago who got his sister tickets for all
three Wings shows in June at Chicago Stadium. Jerry also provided
the wheels from Ohio to Chicago. Stephanie fondly recalled,

"Three nights of Paul McCartney and Wings! All the shows were fabulous, but especially the second night, when I had a front row seat. During the acoustic set as Paul sat and sang his ballads, I threw a bouquet of red roses at his feet. He picked them up and laid them on his piano as he sang my favorite song, 'Maybe I'm Amazed.'"

After the show Stephanie heard a rumor that the band would be attending a party at a hotel named the White House, so she decided to track it down. She and Jerry had a tough time finding the place but finally did and parked a block away. What happened next was a complete surprise. Stephanie remembered: "As we were walking up to the hotel, I noticed a limousine pulling up to the entranceway. Getting out of the back seat was a guy with shiny long black hair and a jacket with the Wings 'W' logo on the back. Clutching to his arm was a lady with straight blond hair. Could it be Paul and Linda McCartney? My heart and pace quickened and suddenly I was right behind them."

There was a crowd gathered out front, and it parted to let the couple inside. Stephanie knew then who it was, and walked along as if she were with them. She got inside and followed. "As Paul and Linda awaited the elevator, I approached—in shock—and just stood there," she said. "Paul waved his hand at me, as if to awaken me from a trance. I just stood there—and finally spoke—'I just love you.' Paul answered, 'We love our fans.' And then said, 'Gotta go—there's a party going on upstairs.' Paul and Linda went into the elevator, and Linda smiled and said, 'Ta-ta.' When I finally recovered, I walked out and was bombarded with questions from everyone still waiting outside the hotel. I felt like a celebrity. What a night. Even today, I'm still amazed."

I missed seeing McCartney's tour because in June I was on a road trip to Massachusetts. Glitta and I had gone our separate ways back in Dana Point. My new girlfriend that I had met at San Diego State had family in Leominster, so I hit the local concert scene in nearby Boston for a week. There were blues, folk and rock artists playing all over. It was hard to pick and choose what shows to check out.

In mid-June at Paul's Mall, a tiny downtown club, I took some pictures for a few nights and afterwards met and interviewed one of my blues heroes, Muddy Waters. After the show I approached his dressing room, which was nothing more than a small room with some folding chairs, an old couch and peeling paint on the walls. The bluesman was very approachable, down to earth and outspoken. He enjoyed sharing memories about singing at a Baptist church when he was young and then later creating electric blues in Chicago clubs, and watching the Rolling Stones record at Chess Studios in 1964. Waters recalled, "They were good, played really fine, and enjoyed working there. They were real interested in what we were doing there. . . . I enjoyed meeting them." When I asked Waters what he thought of Willie Dixon's idea of $500,000 limits musicians should have in earnings, he exclaimed, "Willie's living in a dream if he thinks that could happen. The music industry's not set up like that and nothing's gonna change it." When Jimi Hendrix's name came up, Waters let me know that Hendrix once had worked for him. Then when I asked what he thought of songs like "Purple Haze," Waters frowned and retorted, "I'm not into that shit; didn't dig it. That stuff's not my bag."

Then on June 26, Stephen Stills and Neil Young hit the Boston Gardens arena with their new band. I headed down there and found a tenth row seat the night of the show. The music was eclectic, with the opening number being a Latin-rock flavored version of "Love the One You're With," followed by Young's "The Loner" and his new song, "Long May You Run." Young glanced incredulously at Stills as the two launched into "For What It's Worth," a bow to their musical bonds from Buffalo Springfield. There was a fiery intensity between the two guitarists all evening, with Stills blazing away on his white Firebird on "Black Queen" and Young churning out explosive solos during "Southern Man." To mix it all up, there was even an acoustic set that showcased many beautiful songs, including Young's "On the Way Home" and Stills's "Change Partners."

There was no doubt about it—Boston had a very happening music scene. I was able to take photos the entire night, and the security was very mellow at the Gardens—I walked around in order to get different angles and clicked away with no problem. At the San Diego Arena, I was known as the crazy photographer who often walked up to the stage, camera in hand, took a few pictures and then got chased away by security guards. I returned to San Diego and got in more trouble there in August, this time at a concert at Jack Murphy Baseball Stadium.

"If you don't put that camera away, I'll put it away for you!" snarled the huge, six-foot-plus-tall roadie at me. He had waded into the crowd about twenty feet from the stage where I had my tripod set up. By his voice, it sounded like he meant business. I decided to find out if he really did, so I asked him who said so. "The Blue Oyster Cult does," the roadie yelled back. "They won't come out and play unless you get that thing out of their sight. Do it now!" I still refused and told the roadie that the stadium rules allowed still cameras. We argued a few more minutes back and forth and got nowhere. So he escorted me to the head stage manager, an even bigger, fatter guy with a Blue Oyster Cult T-shirt and a baseball cap. He was a lot less easy to talk to than the first roadie—he stopped setting up equipment long enough to yell at me to put the camera away or he would personally smash it. That ended the conversation really fast.

I went back to my tripod, feeling defeated and angry. But an attractive blonde had set up her beach towel next to my photo equipment. She saw that I was mad, shared her beer with me and said not to worry—just take the tripod down to make it look like I gave up. Then just hold the camera and take pictures later during the act. She gave good advice. It worked through the Cult's set, although lead guitarist Buck Dharma seemed to glance over at me a few times and frown, as if he didn't want to see a guy taking his picture as he wailed away on his white Gibson SG. During the well-known hit, "Don't Fear the Reaper," some fans excitedly waved purple flags emblazoned with the Oyster Cult symbol, a sort of weird fish hook design with a horizontal line through it. Others were passed out on the grass from smoking too much hashish. Although this band specialized in an overpowering, metallic sound, I didn't think this band was a commercial, derivative version of Zeppelin that did songs for over ten minutes, like Deep Purple. They had some variation on vocals from Plant, with some harmonies. But nevertheless the next year the Cult would include a wild laser light show during their *Godzilla* tour, reminiscent of Zeppelin's 1975 blockbuster shows.

The rest of this concert included a really lively set of blues-rock Texas style by Johnny and Edgar Winter and an even louder ZZ Top after that. The Winter Brothers, who came on before the Blue Oyster Cult, were the best act of the entire day, due to Johnny's biting guitar style and Edgar's unbelievable sax playing. The set climaxed with a versatile medley that paid tribute to rock and roll's roots, including "Slippin' and Slidin,'" "Jailhouse Rock," "Tutti Frutti," "Reelin' and Rockin',", and "Good Golly Miss Molly." In the same way, ZZ Top paid tribute to their roots with their raucous version of Willie Dixon's "Mellow Down Easy" as well as John Lee Hooker with their monstrous hit, "La Grange." Bands were paying tribute to their roots more than ever, just as Zeppelin had done in their shows in the early 1970s, particularly the 1971 Japan tour. Zeppelin was known as a band that was setting trends and in a class all their own. The only other band that came close to them was a British band older than Zeppelin that hit the San Diego Arena in early October—the Who.

Back in my old haunt, I managed to sneak down to the floor seating area of the arena shortly before the Who came onstage. I did not have a floor ticket, so I confidently walked along down sections B and C like I knew exactly where I was going. But I found nothing. Then the house lights flashed out. Throngs of

Dazed but not confused fans.

"It is more interesting to talk about sex and music than drugs and music."

Living Loving Zep in Japan.

We're Gonna Groove in Rochester, 1971.

Let's have a party!

"I only wanted to have some fun . . ."

Whole Lotta Volume, Seattle, 1973.

The greatest
rhythm
section in
rock history.

This one's for our critics.

Celebration Day—Swan Song launch party in L.A., 1974.

In The Light.

Zoso summons
the spirits with the
violin bow.

"Let me take you to the movies."

Jamming on "The Song Remains The Same," from San Diego.

The last performance in America, Oakland, July 24, 1977.

Jimmy Page's guitar arsenal.

Led Zeppelin Over Europe, 1980.

people yelled and jumped out of their seats. A line of yellow-jacketed security guards by the stage moved toward everyone. I had to do something fast or I'd be thrown off the floor.

Townsend and the rest of the band came out and blasted into the first number. The swarming mass of people was slowly forced back, and soon I was the only one left in the aisle. My time was up—but miraculous help came from—a chicken! KGB radio's mascot was this huge guy in a chicken outfit, who often danced around in the aisles during rock shows. He ran past me, grabbed a chair out of the second row, and hopped away with it, waving it in the air next to the stage. Here was my chance! I sped into the open spot and crouched down. "Summertime Blues" thundered out into the arena as I snapped away with my camera. What sights— Townsend whirled his arm in windmills, danced around and got his cord tangled around his legs. Roger Daltry flung his mike skyward, then back again. John Entwistle's bass rumbled throughout. Keith Moon attacked his drums in fury. Irrepressible as ever, he stood atop his drums and drank a toast to the cheering crowd.

But my good luck didn't last. As "Baba O'Riley" started a red-jacketed usher shined his flashlight in my face and kicked me off the floor. I took more pictures from the loge. The band made full use of laser lights during the medley from "Tommy" and the climax, "Won't Get Fooled Again." Like Zeppelin, the Who had reached new heights in their live act. The audience was completely captured by the show's loud, untamed music, Townsend flailing away on his Les Paul, Daltry's theatrics and the dazzling lasers.

Townsend's emphasis on this tour, *The Who by Numbers*, was his disillusionments with the trappings of success. How important was rock's creativity and excitement? Whether performer or spectator, rock music offered a spontaneous energy that was addicting. Being part of shows by taking pictures was like going to a nonstop party. The Who's spectacular 1976 tour would be one that many fans would talk about for a long time. But in spite of the Who's worldwide success, Townsend questioned rock's craziness and so-called values. A behavioral law called the Law of Balance states that too much of a good thing ruins it. Pursuit of pleasure taken to an extreme can be destructive. For the Who, this became all too apparent in light of future events.

Unfortunately, the Who lost Keith Moon in 1978. He was found dead of heart failure, and alcohol abuse would be a contributing factor. Throughout the 1970s, rock's reigning monarchs would continue to fall from their thrones of royalty. The party was still on, but it would decidedly wind down as the decade ended, and rock music would never be the same.

The year 1976 was no picnic for Jimmy Page. He'd lent Kenneth Anger editing machinery used for the Zeppelin movie so Anger could finish editing on his *Lucifer Rising* project. Then, in a British rock newspaper, Anger claimed that he was stiffed on the *Lucifer Rising* soundtrack by Page. Anger made all sorts of wild accusations and implied that Page was possibly having drug problems, among other things. Page maintained the charges were untrue: "I gave him everything in plenty of time. Okay—I had a lot of respect for him. As an occultist he was definitely in the vanguard. I just don't know what he's playing at . . . In fact, if you read between the lines, it'll be apparent that maybe the creditors were on his back to deliver the finished film, and because he hadn't gotten it, he used me as a scapegoat and an excuse."

On a more positive side, the past twelve months had seen Page return to Charlotte, his old lady of long standing and the mother of his daughter. And the band was back in rehearsals. The first number the band ran down was "Achilles Last Stand." Robert Plant's foot was supposed to be pretty much healed. Zeppelin was itching to be back on the road in the States. Page seemed incredibly enthusiastic. He said: "When we did that first rehearsal something just clicked again . . . Something epic is going to happen musically. That's what I feel. This next tour . . . you'll see."

CHAPTER 8

"Achilles Last Stand"

E ight years after and as many albums later as their maiden flight, Led Zeppelin continued to soar. While other bands of Zeppelin's stature packed up their amps and faded away, Zeppelin maintained its altitude. This was largely because of each member's loyalty and respect for one another. The bond between them really showed; they were like four brothers. As a result, Zeppelin seemed to be the only group whose members had not veered off course to produce a solo album. Robert Plant remembered, "If you can't bring out everything that comes to mind musically with the group you are working with, then to go away and do a solo album and then come back is an admission that what you really want to do is not playing with your band. . . . I know I couldn't find anybody as musically imaginative as Jimmy, anybody who could play as hard as Bonzo, and anybody who could play as steadily as Jonesy."

Finally, Plant's foot and the band's chops were to be put to the test by their eleventh American tour, starting in early spring. Not having played the States in two years, the group wasn't nervous but was anxious. A Led Zeppelin show was more than just a concert—

it was an event. The task in 1977 was not merely for the band to live up to the Zeppelin image. By now, both group and fans demanded that the reality be better than the image. Their reputation was on the line. Otherwise, Led Zeppelin would be seen as just another nostalgia band. Manager Peter Grant knew this tour had the potential to become the biggest grossing event in entertainment history. It could be the tour to end all tours. This grueling tour would consist of forty-nine dates staged over five months from April to August. A team of fifty-five roadies ensured that the tour would progress with the precision of a military exercise. This became the blueprint for the Rolling Stones and U2 with their mega-dollar-grossing touring campaigns of the 80s and 90s. Over 1 million fans would see them perform.

Excitement for a major rock show begins building long before the day of the concert. The first surge is when the tour is announced. Then there's the scramble for tickets. Radio stations add to the fervor by stressing the band's records. Newspapers carry advance articles.

A Led Zeppelin concert was almost like a ritual—a coming of age for many, for others a reassurance of the rebelliousness of youth. Fans knew Zeppelin were the real story in rock. The press never really mattered. That's why the band didn't court them. There was no junket to Dallas for the start of the tour, like the Who in 1976. There also weren't backstage receptions after each show, the way Paul McCartney did it the same year. Grant explained, "The main thing to remember is the people in the street. Their belief in the group is what is important. It doesn't matter what anybody says about a group, it's what the group does on stage or on record that counts. Zeppelin has always delivered. That's how we can have kids camping outside the Forum in the parking lot for days without taking out an ad or sell 20,000 tickets in Detroit just because one disc jockey says tickets are going on sale."

For this tour, the band would be spontaneous and get down.

Jimmy Page remarked, "I think that if you've got a set so cut and dried, so well-rehearsed that you've got no other option but to play it note-for-note each night, then it's bound to get stagnant. We've always structured things so that there's an element in which we can suddenly shoot off on something entirely different and see what's happening. Personally speaking, for me, that's where the element of change and surprise comes in—the possibilities of having that kind of freedom, should you suddenly require it in the middle of a number."

With an average performance time of three hours with no intermission, their set featured numbers from most of their albums. This time around, "Achilles Last Stand" and "Nobody's Fault but Mine" were the highlights.

The opening date was April 1 in Dallas. After two years of uncertainty, it was an emotional return for Led Zeppelin, especially Robert Plant: "It was a chapter in my life that I really never knew if I'd be able to see. I tried to keep a positive attitude in the months after the accident, but even after I was able to walk again, I didn't know how the foot would hold up onstage. Even rehearsals didn't prove it to me . . . The whole show possessed an element of emotion that I've never known before. I could just as easily knelt on the stage and cried. I was so happy."

But it was not all smooth sailing. During the early part of the tour, the band turned in some shaky and uneven performances. They seemed to struggle through certain songs to reach the climatic high. Part of the problem could have been that Plant had to rely on pain-killers for his ailing foot. It wasn't just the state of Robert's health that was of concern. His voice seemed to be working at reduced volume and range. Neil Zlozower noticed the difference in Plant during the '77 tour: "By then I didn't think Plant's voice was very good. It seemed like he was, you know, *talking* the songs than really *singing* the songs. It lost a lot of the dynamics to me." On top of this, Jimmy Page was not believed to be in a good state, an assumption fueled by the news that the band had taken along for the ride a resident rock and roll doctor to care for the guitar hero. Page looked as wasted and frail as anything this side of Keith Richard. And Bonzo's extreme weight must have slowed him down. On the off nights, the ever reliable John Paul Jones, who seemed genuinely fit, picked up the slack and carried the band. In addition, Peter Grant was said to be severely depressed following a divorce. Plus there was reported rampant drug use by the crew.

Jimmy Page remained defiantly upbeat, stating that, "Led Zeppelin is a stag party that never ends." The demand for tickets was so intense in some cities that mini-riots occurred. At Cincinnati's Riverfront Coliseum, over a thousand crazed Zep fans tried to gate crash the show. At Cleveland, tickets were being scalped for over $100. The first leg of the tour ended at the giant Silverdome in Pontiac, Michigan, on April 30th. In attracting 76,000, the band broke its own record set in Tampa in 1973 of drawing the largest-ever audience for a single rock band.

The first two weeks in May were a break from the tour, as Page headed for Cairo and the rest of the band returned to London. On May 17th, the members met up at Heathrow airport to fly back to the U.S. for the second leg of the '77 U.S. tour. Dates would include Birmingham, Baton Rouge, Houston, Fort Worth, and Landover. On June 3rd, it was anything but sunny in the Sunshine State. Over 70,000 fans packed Tampa Stadium, and a big rain cloud loomed as the members took to the open-air stage. The band had gotten through the opening segments of "The Song Remains The Same/ Sick Again" and "Nobody's Fault But Mine." Then it started pouring—rain was sheeting into the stage mouth, threatening the band with electrocution. Grant summoned Plant to wind it up and get the hell off the stage.

The crowd was asked to leave peacefully. But bottles and rocks immediately began to pelt the stage and the crowd erupted into a chant of "We want Led Zeppelin!" Riot equipped police with billy clubs waded into the crowd and a major riot began. Up to 125 fans were hurt in the melee, with at least fifty people requiring hospital treatment, suffering broken arms and split scalps.

Then it was time for Zeppelin and entourage to get out of Tampa's rain soaked skies. On this tour, there was no *Starship One* since it was out of service. So the band leased from Caesar's Palace a plane named *Caesar's Chariot* that was just as luxurious as the *Starship*. One of the stewardesses aboard explained how she made a lot of extra money: "When people on the plane used to sniff cocaine, they'd roll up $100 bills to use as straws. Then after they were high or pass out, they'd forget about the money. I'd go around and grab all the money that was laying around."

The mood of New York's Madison Square Garden shows seemed fresher and less hostile than that of Tampa. It was the fastest sellout in the Garden's history—six shows in front of 120,000 fans. This proved to be a triumphant reassertion—not only in terms of sales but also with some first class Zeppelin performances. The band's first date on the West Coast was in San Diego on June 19, sort of a set-up for the Los Angeles shows. On break from classes at San Diego State, I made sure that I bought a ticket from the University ticket sales office.

Guards paced atop the arena's high concrete walls and scanned the crowd below with binoculars. Streams of rock fans wound their way across the parking lot like an excited, slightly dazed snake. Scalpers secretly sold floor seats in the parking lot. My seat was in the upper level, commonly called the "nosebleed section." I had bought it for insurance the day tickets had gone on sale months ago in case the show sold out, which it did. For $30 and some photos of Jethro Tull I had taken, I got a floor seat from a scalper. Then I sold my seat to an ecstatic teenager in a red Zeppelin 1975 tour shirt for $30. I was starting to get ecstatic myself—I'd broken even and would be about twenty rows back. I'd shied away from seats in the first ten rows because they were going for anywhere from $100 to $500. The arena doors were open. I went in.

The emotion in the crowd was contagious. It swirled around at a fever pitch. People talked about the last show in San Diego two years earlier. Some college girls were worried that they would get trampled by a rush of people near the end. The floor used to be a swirling mob of fans who would jump the loge railing and crush together near the stage. But it didn't look like that would happen, since there were rows of seats on the floor instead of the festival seating used last time. Numerous yellow-jacketed security guards stood at all strategic areas, including a barricade of seats across the tenth row. Sometimes a pretty groupie type in bell-bottoms or dolphin shorts would come up to a guard and talk, gesturing toward the stage. But the answer was usually a shake of the head. There were some wild rumors of a few guards that "helped" some women get close to the front, with a price attached. It wasn't money—the guards were alleged to have had their sexual flings before the arena doors were opened. Anywhere was the rule: vans in the parking lot, backstage areas before the entourage arrived, and even under the stage. I knew that I would have to use strategies that had worked when I was photographing various shows for the San Diego State *Aztec* newspaper: don't do anything hasty, watch all the security people, and wait. Then, if an opportunity presents itself, *move fast*.

Suddenly the lights flashed out, and the crowd leaped to their feet. Screams and cheers echoed off the metallic risers above everyone. The aisles were filled with people, so I left my seat and moved toward the barricade to see if the front area had the same insanity building up. People around me began to run to the front, and I followed. The band blasted into "The Song Remains the Same" and yellow lights flashed on Page. He churned out power chords and screeching notes from his Gibson double neck, a bent knee holding up the guitar. I reached the barricade and looked around. A small crowd pushed against the right side by the loge wall, and some chairs clattered down. People fell as others pushed from behind. There were cries and yells, and the guards by the barricade rushed over to the little struggling throng. I saw my chance and leaped over the chairs. Now there was no turning back. I ran toward the stage, and saw Page in front of John Bonham's raised drum set, knees slightly bent and head down, concentrating as he wailed away on guitar. I paused in the aisle and shot off a few pictures of Bonham and Page. I noticed how Bonham was striking his drums along with Page's notes. One of the elements that made Led Zeppelin so exciting was the tension generated by the juxtaposition of Page's sense of time with Bonham's—the big ringing chord right on the heels of the snare hit.

Bonham didn't follow the bass player like many other drummers—as his son, Jason, pointed out, he followed the guitarist instead. "In Led Zeppelin, my dad's approach was that he'd watch Jimmy, and he'd play with Jimmy," Jason said. "John Paul Jones would have to watch my dad and play with my dad. Jimmy'd be watching Robert. Usually people say, 'Oh, the bass player and drummer want to stick together.' Not if you want to be fiery. If you can go with the guitar, and then the bass player will go with you, you've got an awesome setup there."

"The Song Remains the Same" thundered on. I lowered my camera, looked around, and saw that there were no empty seats so far. The middle section was completely packed, with some people sharing seats. I'd soon be spotted by the guards and thrown off the floor since I was the only one sneaking around in the aisle. I decided to walk calmly ahead with confidence. Plant had begun slowly walking up to the edge of the stage. I took a quick picture of him with Page behind him. He wore gold pants, a necklace with a lightning bolt, and a black jacket. To complete the effect, a rustic-looking, plaid scarf hung around his neck.

I reached the tenth row and saw nothing in the middle B section. On my right, though, fate had saved me an aisle seat, right at the start of the tenth row in section C. I grabbed it, breathed a sigh of relief, and shot the rest of the first roll of film. The owner could come back anytime and get me kicked out, so I figured I had better shoot while I had the chance. But no one ever claimed the seat—maybe he'd found a better one or had been thrown out. Next, during the blues-rock "Sick Again," the crowd really started screaming. Then the fireworks went off, one after the other, as Zeppelin started "Nobody's Fault but Mine." And this time, Plant didn't scold the audience for the firecrackers . . . everyone was having too much fun.

Afterward, Plant moved into a more metaphorical mood for his intro to "In My Time of Dying." He said, "This is something out of a teapot. It's a blues thing. It comes, I guess, from what you'd call the American Negro blues trip." And before anyone could start to think too deeply on the business about that teapot, Page slid into the song. After the song ended, Plant chatted up the audience again. After he made several innuendos about John Paul Jones's social life, he added, "It's about time somebody in the press noted it down that John Paul Jones doesn't just play backgammon!" Up next was "Since I've Been Loving You." Then Plant lay on the piano during Jones's solo for "No Quarter," stared at the ceiling, and had a smoke.

Plant joked with the audience, "John is wearing a light sailor's uniform. A little bit of political unrest I'm afraid. I hurt my foot in a soccer match yesterday, Jonesy hurt his foot playing backgammon, Jimmy hurt his when a firecracker hit it in New York, BUT we're still here!" The band went to the chairs for the acoustic set, and Plant announced, "It's our version of Crosby, Stills, Nash and *Bonham*!" The songs mesmerized the crowd, thanks to Jones's mandolin, Page's picking, Plant's lyrics and eerie purple lighting. Plant introduced "Goin' To California" by saying: "This is a song that's got very little to do with Wales, England, Scotland . . . in fact, it's got a lot more to do with you than it has to do with us." Then a highlight came as the group improvised and played bits of Elvis's "Mystery Train." Plant started the lyrics and Page jumped right in on guitar. It was wild, loose and spontaneous. "Black Country Woman" and "Bron-Y-Aur Stomp" finished up the acoustic part. Now it was time for Page to show off.

As "White Summer/Black Mountain Side" began, Page stood in front of his humming amp stacks and threw his arms out, as if to put a magic spell on them. He triumphantly held his violin bow high. As the song went on, the laser pyramid slowly rose over the crouching guitarist, enveloping him in a series of red, yellow, green and blue beams of light. Then the arena's walls shook with "Kashmir." Plant held his mike upwards and the band was thrown into a white light and smoke. A frisbee landed near me, and I grabbed it and flung it toward the stage. It sailed toward Plant, and he glanced over it as it veered to the right and landed on the stage. Page played an extended solo, and next "Achilles Last Stand" soared out to the audience. By now the music was at a fever pitch. Then Page picked out the first notes to "Stairway to Heaven" and the fans cheered wildly. Near the end, with one of my last exposures, I zoomed in with my lens and caught Page as he held his double neck upwards in a victory salute.

The audience was ecstatic—what else could happen? Page grabbed his sunburst Les Paul and slammed out the opening chords to "Whole Lotta Love." Everyone jumped up, clapping and yelling. Page and Plant danced across the stage, Page singing along with Plant into the mike. They both smiled at each other. Then at the point where the drum solo would start, the band stopped and two huge firework explosions shook each side of the stage. Blinding colored sparks flew upward, and as the white shower of sparks cascaded onto the stage Bonham took over. He smashed his cymbals, Page held his arm upwards, then flung it down and churned out the first chords to "Rock and Roll." Everyone went wild. Girls stood on their seats and danced, arms waved everywhere, and there were cries and cheers all over the Arena. Plant, master of ceremonies, sang out the first line and everyone joined in. It was like New Year's or the opening of the Olympics and World Series rolled into one. A tour de force that left everyone exhausted but more than pleased, the show had the feel of a simple, good old rock and roll party. I wondered how Zeppelin could top this show the next time. I didn't know it then, but with this tour the band would leave its mark on the '77 music scene.

Frank Zappa left his mark on me when I had a beer with him, then had a relaxed talk with him and photographed for the *Daily Aztec* newspaper after a show at San Diego State's Amphitheater. I admired him because just like Zeppelin, he never believed in selling out and pretty much played by his own rules. He learned what he was up against when he began playing music in the early 1960s around Torrance and Pomona. Zappa said: "Club managers there felt that musicians were a piece of furniture or a jukebox—you were there to serve them. I didn't want to do that, so I got fired. The music that was making it then was cute, personality music, while the Mothers were ugly and a real mess. I figured, though, that if there was a market for Creature from the Black Lagoon dolls, there was one for us."

Zappa's fortunes changed after record producer Tom Wilson caught the Mothers' act at the Whisky A Go Go. "Wilson saw us doing a song about the Watts riots, and said we were a great white blues band," Zappa recalled. "He got us a contract, and our first album, *Freak Out*, cost $20,000 to produce, which was astronomical in those days. It was also the first double rock album, which was also unheard of, and MGM didn't know how to sell it." Zappa clashed with MGM over how the Mothers were marketed and later sued the company over sales records for his albums. "We finally settled with MGM. I never learned how many Mothers albums they sold, since they told me a freak fire and flood at MGM totally wiped out their sales records. They gave me back the Mothers master tapes, and that settled it." Zappa also had strong opinions on types of music and claimed that popular 60s artists like Cream or Jimi Hendrix had legitimacy, while other more modern 70s art-rock groups like Genesis did not. Zappa claimed: "In the 60s, so-called art-rock was played by groups like Renaissance, who would pop up on the East Coast, wear tunics and play classical licks on the guitar. A group today like Genesis could have stolen its act from a band who never got a contract and is still lurking around out there in the bushes." For Zappa, there was nothing new about another current music form—punk rock. "I liked 60s punk rock like Sky Saxon and the Seeds," Zappa said. "But I saw the Sex Pistols on TV and I didn't think they were too suave."

I'd seen and photographed more variety and talent than ever at the San Diego Sports Arena in 1977. There was the wildly crazy and aggressive Aerosmith that cranked out one hit after another, with an ending tribute to the Yardbirds with "Train Kept A-Rollin'." On the mellower rock side was Fleetwood Mac, with three talented songwriters and performers in Lindsey Buckingham, Stevie Nicks, and Christie McVie, at their peak with their hugely successful *Rumours* album. Torch queen Linda Ronstadt, her skinny frame clad in a cub scout uniform, showed her powerful range in both loud rockers like "That'll Be the Day" and soft ballads like "Love Me Tender." Blue Oyster Cult tried to outdo the Who and Zeppelin with their own wild laser light show for their "Godzilla" extravaganza. Flute-playing rock minstrel Ian Anderson led Jethro Tull into a brilliant acoustic-electric foray with the *Songs from the Wood* tour. Crosby, Stills, and Nash put on a milestone celebratory show, showcasing each member's musical talent with both mellow acoustic tunes and more upbeat electric material. Lastly, the complete opposite of Crosby, Stills, and Nash had to be two outrageous rock extravaganzas: Alice Cooper and KISS. Cooper's show was modeled after a circus act and included him being surrounded by huge machine gun–wielding machine chickens, being carried off by a twelve-foot Cyclops and getting guillotined. KISS's insanely wild pyrotechnic show featured a gigantic stage set with stairways, hoists that took band members skyward, and blinding flames, flashing lights, and exploding fireworks. But Zeppelin had topped them all in San Diego with a fantastic three-and-a-half-hour-plus marathon of their very best music. Many hardcore music fans probably also thought this after the Forum shows.

Led Zeppelin were gods in L.A. The newspaper ad stated: "The Only Rock Group In History To Sell Out Six [6] Shows At The Fabulous Forum!" The combination of Led Zeppelin and the L.A. Forum produced unforgettable results. It was a high energy assault in an age of smooth and easy listening pop. Even though tickets for all six nights at the Forum were sold out, I decided to go there a few days after opening night to see if I could get into one of the shows. The crowd scene I found in L.A. was in complete contrast to the one outside of the San Diego shows. The Forum scene was scary and crazy.

Los Angeles police patrolled the streets around the Forum constantly, and other police drove around the parking lot in little electric golf carts, looking for ticket scalpers and anyone selling anything. There were also Forum security guards in bright blue jackets walking around on foot. They were giving citations for selling on private property and the fine was $200. But the lot was still swarming with fans selling tickets, food or homemade Zeppelin shirts. I went out there to sell some of my San Diego Zeppelin photos.

I walked into the lot toward a large group of fans. There was a skinny, longhaired fellow with a beard and sunglasses, sort of a thin version of John Bonham, going to and fro with a bunch of black bootleg Zeppelin T-shirts draped over his arm. They had a white outline of the Swan Song logo stage picture with the four symbols around it, sort of a cheap copy of the back cover of the tour book program. A little crowd gathered around him, but suddenly some police in an electric cart pulled up behind him. The shirt sale ended as he zigzagged off into the crowd, dropping some of the shirts. People scrambled to pick them up and it became a wild free-for-all. The police backed up, darted around the mob, and went after the T-shirt guy. I quickly turned away and headed for the edge of the parking lot, where there were fewer large crowds and no cops. Now maybe I could make some bucks.

There was a row of cars parked in the lot, about 20 feet from the sidewalk. "What could possibly happen here?" I thought. There were some girls in a red Camaro, so I went up to them, started talking and showed some photos to them. Then I glanced around, and to my horror, saw four huge, blue jacketed security guards surrounding the car. "Well, I guess I'd better take off," I told the girls, who were trying to hang on to a few of the Plant shots. "Go ahead and keep the pictures. See ya!" I grabbed the box and began to sprint to the sidewalk. The goons would leave me alone since I wasn't like those scalpers trying to get $500 for a floor seat. Right? Wrong!

"Hold it! Don't move or you're dead meat!" a deep voice boomed close behind me. I wondered if I was about to get tackled. The concrete didn't look very inviting, so I stopped, turned around and looked at my pursuers. It looked like the Forum had recruited a few linebackers from the Oakland Raiders for some security work. All four guys were at least six-and-a-half feet tall and had huge, broad shoulders. "What's in the box?" one of them asked, pointing at me.

"Just some Zeppelin photos," I replied, thinking fast. "But I didn't sell any. I was just showing them to those girls back there. That's all." I was such a rebellious rock and roll fan—and a bad liar.

"Come on, bud—you're going with us," the other burly guard announced. He waved a huge arm and walked toward some L.A. policemen further inside the lot, near the Forum. The others got on each side of me and followed along. It didn't look good. As we neared the Forum I figured that I'd better find a way to get out of this mess—fast.

"What's the hassle? Where're we going?" I asked, knowing full well where I was being escorted. A few more cops in carts sped by us. They were undoubtedly looking for more lawbreakers like me.

"You know where," muttered a guard behind me. "You've been selling without a permit. Now shut up and keep moving!"

More police in carts sped by, heading for a little huddle of fans. They all bolted when they saw the cops coming. There was no doubt about it—things were nuts here today. We stopped at a police officer next to a cart who was busy writing a ticket to some guy who'd been selling candy apples out of a grocery bag. Two of my escorts left and I turned to the two who remained. My mind was racing—time had run out. It was now or never to do something. I thought, *This is all so stupid and dumb. People getting busted just for candy apples and Zeppelin pictures.* Then suddenly I got an idea.

"Look, you guys—take all these photos," I said quickly. "Otherwise, that cop'll confiscate 'em, you'll leave, and the only person who gets anything is me—a ticket. You could make money on these—there's a lot of 'em here!" I concluded. I handed the box to the guards, and they opened it and looked at the forty or so eight-by-ten photos inside. It was a long shot, but the only one I had. They moved a few feet away from me and had a brief conference. One guy was shaking his head; the other started thumbing through the pictures.

The guy with the candy apples was handed his ticket and he left, frowning. Just then, the security guard with the photos quickly closed up the box and came up to me. "All right, longhair—get your ass outta here," he barked. "And we don't want to see you around this parking lot again! Now git!"

I left my photos and the guards behind and crossed the street. My Volkswagen van was parked around the corner. I opened it up and got out another box of photos, for I never believed in putting all my eggs in one basket. But the rest of the evening I walked along the sidewalk and stayed close to a little row of other illegal vendors who hawked their wares to fans on their way to the Forum. Some sold from little display boards—Zeppelin patches and other regalia—while others circulated, like one tall fellow I'll never forget. He wore a huge trench coat that he opened as people approached, and the inside was plastered with Zeppelin pins and photo buttons. The whole area was like a small carnival, run by longhaired entrepreneurs, and the customers were partying concertgoers. Groups of fans came and went—guys in Levis and Zeppelin T-shirts, girls in short blouses and bell-bottoms or granny dresses. Many looked as if they'd been zapped from the late 60s or early 70s by a time machine into 1977.

I went back the next evening on June 24 to hang out and try and get a ticket. The parking had a lot of security guards, so I went to the Forum press cancellation window. Sometimes some good floor seats filtered in through there. But there were no extra tickets, and floor seats were being sold by scalpers for hundreds of dollars in the parking lot. I left and walked on over to the little sidewalk selling area I'd hung out in last night. But it was completely deserted, except for a few straggling concertgoers. I asked them where everyone had gone. The story went that some police vans had pulled up to the area, and everyone selling had been rounded up and taken to jail. I may not have gotten into the show, but I still felt lucky that night. Besides, I thought, Zeppelin will be back here real soon. They always came back, especially to the Forum.

Despite what anyone said, the tour would be an incredible success with a projected gross income of around $10 million! In spite of the negative press coverage, concerts everywhere were sold out, and the enthusiasm from audiences was still as alive as it had been in 1969. But there was a strange undercurrent of growing foreboding on this tour as well. It wasn't only the violence at concerts that was a problem, but rumors persisted of rampant drug use.

It was well known that Bonham was a heavy drinker, but now reports were surfacing that heroin was fast becoming Page's nemesis. At times, his playing still sparkled on the blues workout "Since I've Been Loving You" and the frantic "Nobody's Fault But Mine." And he also still had the familiar classic stage moves to keep the excitement at peak levels, like holding his double neck skyward. But he appeared distant as he played his low-slung Gibson Les

Paul, his eyes hidden behind aviator shades and scraggly hair covering his pale face. There were a number of "off" nights when it seemed that Page could barely finger the guitar, much less produce the speedy runs of "The Song Remains the Same" or "Achilles Last Stand." During the acoustic set, Page chilled out along with Plant. Many fans that I talked to after the San Diego show thought that although the show had been good, Page had definitely slowed down. In between shows he would stay in his hotel room that was hung with black curtains, lighted candles and FM radios. To keep Page going, the band's rock and roll doctor was always there with a medicine bag full of various legal drugs. And when something was in short supply, the doctor just wrote out prescriptions.

Page admitted that while on tours, drugs were an important part of his life—and they even drove him to the point where he did crazy, suicidal things. He recalled: "I can't speak for the others, but for me drugs were an integral part of the whole thing, right from the beginning, right to the end. And part of the condition of drug taking is that you start thinking that you're invincible. I'll tell you something that is absolutely crazy. I remember one night climbing out of a nine-story window in New York and just sitting on one of those air-conditioning units, and just looking out over the city. I was just out on my own and thought it might be an interesting thing to do. It was totally reckless behavior. I mean it's great that I'm still here to have a laugh about it, but it was totally irresponsible. I could've died and left a lot of people I love. I've seen so many casualties."

A law of life had come into play—the law of diminishing returns. This law says that once one has bought into addictive behavior, it needs to be repeated more and more often in order to get that same "high" or "buzz." The desire to please ourselves and choosing to do whatever we want comes about by free will—but is there also a larger, more sinister force behind that drives one toward insanity or death? What causes people, even nations and empires, to do themselves or others in? How does one explain not only war, but genocide, corporate greed, prostitution, and pornography—is there something that pushes mankind toward catastrophe? Robert Johnson portrayed the Devil as a being whom he'd met and struggled with during his short life. Johnson's poor choices at the ill-fated crossroads and at his final performance epitomize mankind's dilemma—people want to do their own thing way too often, which can get them into big trouble.

If I'd been saved from crashing on the 405 freeway from a protective angel, then couldn't there also be evil ones that want to do us in? But many rock stars probably don't give much thought to an ongoing struggle between good and evil if they are intoxicated with popularity, wealth, or having any drug or sexual pleasure met anytime. Led Zeppelin was larger-than-life to their fans—they would follow the band no matter what. The band was truly a rock and roll icon—but Zeppelin was something else, too—mortal. Everyone has their faults, areas where they will ultimately fall. But like the mythical Achilles, who believed that no one could hurt him, we may not know where our weakness is—until it is too late.

After Zeppelin played the final Forum show on June 26, the group returned to the U.K. for an eighteen-day break. On July 17, the third and final leg of the tour opened at the Seattle Kingdome in front of 65,000 fans. A week later, on July 23 and 24, the shadow of doom that had followed the tour came to a head at Oakland Stadium. Unfortunately, what should have been an affirmation of their greatness ended in violence and tragedy. Looking back on it, it almost seems like the stage had been literally set for just that type of occasion. Put on by legendary promoter Bill Graham, the Oakland dates were part of his Day on the Green shows. Led Zeppelin drew a sellout crowd of 115,000. The gates opened at 9 A.M. and the show began two hours later. Rick Derringer and Judas Priest opened for Zeppelin.

The massive stage set depicted England's Stonehenge, the most enigmatic prehistoric stone circle in the world. Huge spotlights illuminated the interior of the stage, which was covered by a canopy. To top it off, an enormous mock dirigible was suspended from behind the stage. There was also something else—a coincidental symbolism of death and the end of an era shown with Page's choice of stage outfits. At many shows he had worn white. But at Oakland he wore black on both cool, windy days. At the first show he wore his costume embroidered with the Chinese dragon with black T-shirt underneath. On the 23rd show Plant wore something a little more humorous and light—a blue T-shirt that said NURSES DO IT BETTER.

Rolling Stone magazine's original photographer, Baron Wolman, looked out at the crowd from the stage. Wolman would be able to photograph the immense stage as well as be right next to the band to get pictures. "When the great rock and roll impresario Bill Graham was alive I had an understanding with him," Wolman recalled. "I could shoot any concert he produced if I gave him a few select images for the Bill Graham Production files. I had long been gone from *Rolling Stone* by then but still loved the music, the musicians and the scene—both the actual concerts as well as the backstage scene with the gorgeous groupies and the delicious catered food. Plus, being onstage with the 'best of the best' gave me a photo high as well as a natural head and heart high. I had no idea how privileged I was to be onstage . . . to record them, to watch the kids in those huge crowds react, each with his or her own personal ecstasy."

Wolman walked onto the stage before the show. It was the calm before the storm. He saw Page's guitars lined up at the side of the stage and decided that this would be something very unique and interesting to catch on film. They were all there—Page's acoustic guitars, the Les Pauls, the Danelectro, and the red Gibson double-neck. So he went up to the instruments and clicked away with his camera. Wolman remembered, "The shot of the guitars just appealed to me as a great little visual—it had never occurred to me the guitarist used so many guitars during a performance. One of two or three maybe, but this was a major collection . . . I count my blessings that I was alive and well with my camera during those halcyon days of music and was able to record at least some of what I experienced."

Zeppelin played some twenty numbers over three hours, including "The Song Remains the Same," "Nobody's Fault But Mine," "Achilles Last Stand," "Black Country Woman," "Kashmir," "No Quarter," "Stairway to Heaven," "Going to California," and "Whole Lotta Love." Following their set, the band received a ten-minute ovation. But the vastness of an outdoor stadium had a detrimental effect on the element of closeness and intimacy with the band. The *San Francisco Chronicle* reviewer hated the locale, and pointed out, "From 300 feet away, center-rear, the sound is adequate and the view is terrible. The view is non-existent, for that matter, unless you specialize in studying ant colonies." The review even ridiculed the audience, for "they're not interested in a proper, civilized musical concert but rather with being in the same geographic location as Led Zeppelin and 'sharing the vibes,' or whatever it is that youths do today when at a loss for some crime to perpetrate." It was almost as if no one but hoodlums went to rock concerts. The assumption was one-sided, but easy to make in light of all the violence by fans in 1977. There was indeed violence at Oakland—but not from fans.

At the end of the first show around 6 P.M. came an incident that would again darken the band's reputation. Backstage where the various dressing room trailers were parked, a young boy tried to remove a Led Zeppelin sign from one of the trailers. It turned out that the youth was Peter Grant's eleven-year-old son. According to Graham, one of his stagehands, Jim Matzorkis, nicely told the child that he couldn't have the souvenir. According to Bonham, who saw what happened from the stage, the stagehand hit the kid. A violent scene followed. Graham's employee was lured into a trailer and cornered. Then Bonham, Grant, and John Bindon, a thug who'd been hired for extra security, beat the shit out of him.

Graham's staffer was rushed bleeding to the hospital. Zeppelin refused to play the next day's show unless Graham signed a paper that absolved the band of all guilt. Fearing a riot if the show was cancelled, Graham signed the agreement.

The band took the stage ninety minutes late for the second show. Page was decked out in high riding boots and baggy white pants. A *Rolling Stone* account of the show stated that Page sat through most of the show "in protest" to Bill Graham's threats. There were bad vibes all around. Though no one knew it at the time, this would be the last concert Led Zeppelin would ever perform in America. It was a disappointing coda.

After the show an outraged Bill Graham filed charges against Led Zeppelin. On July 25, Grant, Bonham, and Bindon were arrested and taken to jail by the Oakland police department. Though immediately freed on bail, there were lawsuits and vows from Graham to "never in good conscience book this band again." Grant had to get a local lawyer to handle the case, and their dealings together were not very friendly. According to the lawyer, Grant called him at all hours to settle the case quickly. When it wasn't moving fast enough, Grant threatened to make sure that he wouldn't practice law again if he didn't get Zeppelin out of their jam. Evidently, Grant wanted to end the case right away before Bill Graham found out how much money was in Led Zeppelin's bank accounts. But the lawyer was unfazed and noted, "Grant was pretty paranoid about the money thing even after I assured him that the case was not that big a deal."

In court, the lawyer supported the contention that the Oakland incident was not the first of its type on the 1977 tour. "They basically raped and pillaged their way across the country," he stated, telling several stories of drug deals gone bad, underage girls hanging with the band's entourage, and more physical violence. He even verified a violent incident at a San Francisco pharmacy that involved the band's entourage. A Zeppelin bodyguard roughed up a pharmacist because he wouldn't fill a prescription from the band's resident English doctor. The druggist relented, and the Zep guys threw ten $100 bills on the ground as they left. Despite what Grant wanted, the band's whole legal affair didn't end soon. It dragged on for about a year before finally being settled out of court for something like $50,000.

There were also others who weren't impressed with how the Zeppelin entourage behaved. Brian Cunningham, one of Rick Derringer's roadies, noted that Page was really screwed up from drugs and said that "He basically had to be led around." Cunningham added that Zep's road crew was not like those of other bands he'd known. He stated that "They weren't too friendly like brother roadies are supposed to be" and that they were totally drugged out—"maybe even more than Page."

Shamed by the press, the band left California, intending to complete the final dates of the tour. The next date was to have been at the Superdome in New Orleans. After checking into the hotel, Robert Plant received a transcontinental phone call from his wife, Maureen. She gave him the shattering news that Karac, their five-year-old son, had died from a mysterious respiratory infection! He had collapsed from stomach pains and was rushed to the hospital, but was dead on arrival. The remainder of the tour was abandoned. A devastated, grief-stricken Plant, supported by Bonham, immediately flew back to England to be with his family. Maureen was under sedation, and Plant went into seclusion.

Plant's father talked to reporters: "All this success and fame, what is it all worth? It doesn't mean very much when you compare it to the love of a family. They are heartbroken. Karac was the apple of my son's eye. He was a strong child, mischievous and bright and full of life. He had never been ill before. His death seems so unreal and unnecessary."

CHAPTER 9

"In My Time of Dying"

Led Zeppelin was grounded in 1978. The band virtually vanished from the spotlight. Rumors of a break up ran rampant and no new material had been released in over three years. Due to the tragic death of his son, Robert Plant felt the need to reflect and soul search with his family. His family was his light. He was given breathing space by the group to decide his next move. Would the song remain the same?

The press wrote about Page's bad karma and of a Zeppelin curse. Were the misfortunes due to his dabbling in the black arts? Page emphatically denied the reports by stating: "All I or we have attempted to do is to go out and really have a good time and please people at the same time . . . I can't think of anything better than doing what you really want to do and seeing just a mass of smiles. That's utopia . . . I just don't see how there could be a bad karma or whatever." About Led Zeppelin's future, Page said "that there was no question of splitting up."

Despite their inactivity, Zeppelin, as well as the group members, achieved an almost complete sweep of the awards in *Creem* magazine's annual readers poll. If the band were to split up, I thought Van Halen would become the next Led Zeppelin. Emerging from the West Coast, their self-titled debut album put the swagger back into rock and also gave the world a new guitar hero in Eddie Van Halen.

When Robert Plant walked off the Oakland stage in 1977, life would not be the same. After losing his son, he reportedly considered a career change in teaching kindergarten and was accepted as a student teacher. Plant explained: "One day everything had been fantastic, and the next everything was as devastatingly wrong as you could possibly imagine. As a family unit on the way out of all that—or in the way around it—I thought going away on tour and being the other guy just ain't worth it. I'd realized that kids were infinitely more important than the footlights and dry ice and dodgy cocaine with someone you don't know."

Jerry Prochnicky also considered a change—a change of location. He was trying to forget about someone, and not doing a good job at it. Was this love or was this confusion? He made up his mind to make a new start. The West has always been the hope of continental America. If you can't make it where you are at, go to California. So he did, with an aching in his heart. Like Jimmy Page, he's also "still searching for an angel with a broken wing."

Plant had his angels in wife Maureen and daughter Carmen. And he still had his best friend since he was a teenager in John Bonham. Bonham persuaded Plant to face the music again. So in May, Zeppelin started working as a group with rehearsals at Clearwater Castle on the Welsh border. It had been ten months since they last played together. Things looked more hopeful for future recording and live dates. The question was, with past tragedy and present expectations weighing them down, would Zeppelin be able to get their heavy load off the ground?

In July, Plant appeared in public for the first time since his son's death, sitting in with local bands around his home. The following month Plant ventured onstage during a Dr. Feelgood concert in Spain. Slowly, he was easing back into the public life.

I was easing into a new slow paced lifestyle of my own. During my time at San Diego State I'd lived in an apartment off University Avenue. After I graduated in 1977, I decided I'd had enough of city life and moved just south of Oceanside. I bought a condo in the little coastal town of Encinitas. Life was lived at a much slower pace there. I really got into the area's surfing scene—there were many places to find great waves, and at this time it wasn't that crowded. There was the reef at Swamis, near the Self-Realization Temple, and some large beach breaks at Bekins and Grandview. It was a laid back, relaxing change from the city life I'd lived near San Diego State for four years. And when I wanted to get into some excitement, there was always the concert scene in San Diego or Los Angeles.

On June 2, Bob Dylan's *Street Legal* tour arrived at the Universal Amphitheater in Hollywood. I got in there with my camera and took pictures of his new band, which included a horn section, a violinist, a flutist, and female backup singers. Once again Dylan followed his own creative muse, transformed his music, and reinvented himself. Gone were the days of The Band's impeccable yet furious playing, or the multi-talented Rolling Thunder Revue. His new musical format had the jazzy, big band feel of a Las Vegas spectacle. Like his change from acoustic to electric in 1965, fans either embraced the change or hated it. Shortly after this tour Dylan would shock fans again by converting to Christianity. Like Zeppelin, Dylan always broke new musical ground and did whatever he wished, apologized to no one for it, and just kept on going no matter what critics said.

Many artists in '78 explored new music forms, and David Bowie was one who really stood out. In going for a completely different sound from his previous outings with space-rock and soul, Bowie collaborated with Brian Eno from the progressive Roxy Music. The resulting tour for the *Low* album was incredible. Although there was great rock and roll, like "Hang Onto Yourself," other songs like

"Heroes" and "Warzawa" had a huge move toward a synthesized keyboard sound. There was definite change in the air.

Other shows at the San Diego Arena that year showed me how some bands had borrowed from Zeppelin's lessons in light and shade. The best example was Heart during their *Dog and Butterfly* tour. Much of the band's music emanated from Zeppelin's inspiration. "Mistral Wind" had the slow, menacing buildup of "No Quarter"; "Barracuda" attacked with the same driving force as "Song Remains the Same," and "Love Alive" reflected the acoustic Renaissance style of "Going To California." Even lead guitarist Roger Fisher went so far as to imitate Jimmy Page by prancing around the stage in pants that had a dragon design. Sisters Ann and Nancy Wilson were brilliant songwriters and performers, but they paid tribute to Zeppelin by doing their songs like "Battle of Evermore," "The Rover," and "Rock and Roll" onstage. It was evident as the 70s were ending that Zeppelin by now was a major influence for many upcoming rock bands. History would repeat itself, for this trend lives on today with new bands that owe a huge debt to Zeppelin.

By November, 1978, Zeppelin was based in London rehearsing for their ninth album, *In Through the Out Door*. As Page explained the title, "That's the hardest way to get back in." Tax laws meant that the album, like *Presence*, would have to be recorded outside the U.K. So the band lifted off to Sweden for Abba's state of the art Polar Studios. The Swedish nights were long and dark, with the sessions somber compared with what had gone before. With Plant affected by his son's death and Page semi-detached, John Paul Jones took artistic control and was credited with six of the seven songs. Whereas *Presence* was a guitar-oriented album, there would be a dominance of keyboards and synthesizer on the new album.

After the Polar sessions, Plant returned to the bosom of his family, where Maureen was pregnant again. The new year marked a son for Robert Plant, christened Logan Romero. And the best news in 1979 for English fans was that Zeppelin would headline the Knebworth Festival on August 4. It would mark the first time in four years that Zeppelin played live in the U.K. Some other artists on the bill were Todd Rundgren's Utopia and Fairport Convention. The show became a highly anticipated event, and two months before the concert all available tickets sold out. Another date on August 11 was added, with the New Barbarians taking Fairport Convention's place on the bill. The total attendance for both shows was estimated to be over 400,000. What a spectacle of an outdoor show. This was a far cry from the band playing heavy blues in small clubs.

By the same token, Zeppelin owed a huge debt to the early bluesmen, especially the Delta-style players. John Lee Hooker, creator of the boogie sound, was honored by Zeppelin when the band jammed during "Boogie Chillen." Hooker influenced many artists, from John Mayall and Canned Heat to ZZ Top. He was one of my all-time blues heroes and in February I photographed and interviewed him for *The Daily Aztec*. Like Jimmy Page, Hooker believed that blues is a music form that can be drawn from again and again. Being honest music, it moved the listener. Hooker pointed out that even jazz players use it: "Cannonball Adderley once told me that a good jazz player's got to be able to play some blues. Blues is parallel with jazz, structure-wise . . . from inside, like jazz, not out . . . The blues says it like it is. It's the roots."

Hooker told me that he enjoyed visiting England during the '60s Folk-Blues Festivals because audiences really appreciated quality music. And although he'd never changed, he pointed out that today's music scene had. Hooker noted: "I've always played just what I wanted to. It'd seem like there's not a lot happening in music now because everybody's on a big money trip. But blues never went out . . . there's a lot of fly-by-night groups who'll have a hit single overnight. They they'll hit the ground just as fast, like an earthquake hit 'em."

Hooker was right about how making a lot of money had

become a big part of the music scene. By 1979, rock shows in Southern California were making big bucks and had become more intense, wild, and unbelievable than ever. In April, I returned to Los Angeles for what was the hugest music event that year. It was a gigantic two-day rock extravaganza held at the L.A. Coliseum called the World Music Festival. There was a wide assortment of performers that epitomized the widely changing American music scene—Cheap Trick, Toto, Eddie Money, Ted Nugent, Aerosmith and Van Halen. It was totally nuts. I liked the concert scene, but what went on up there was too much for me.

I squeezed my way into the crowd near the stage for two exhausting nights to get pictures. Cheap Trick's vocalist Robin Zander seemed to be an imitation of early Robert Plant. Aerosmith was caught up in the 70s drug craziness—especially vocalist Steven Tyler. The band played a sloppy set at best, with Tyler's slurred words barely audible over Joe Perry's ear-shattering guitar work. During Van Halen's performance, I tried to keep my balance as I nearly got crushed in the swaying, surging mob. This local L.A. band had grown incredibly popular in three years. For many, Van Halen was the next big thing in rock music. Young, half-crazed girls screamed and shoved their way past me as David Lee Roth leaped through the air and did splits. New guitar god Eddie Van Halen held his instrument high and pulverized the strings with his trademark lightning-fast riffs. I thought the excitement was way overblown. But it was also obvious that the popularity of these bands had filled the void left by Zeppelin's touring absence.

Knebworth was to be a new beginning. The music scene in 1979 was filled with punkers and new wave music, and Led Zeppelin was looked upon by some as "dinosaurs" of corporate music. But the group was far from being extinct. Before the show, Bonham watched his eleven-year-old son, Jason, sit in on drums during the sound check. "He can play 'Trampled Underfoot' perfectly," Bonham said. This was the first time that he ever saw Led Zeppelin from the audience. Very few people were allowed in the closed-off backstage enclosure that housed the dressing room trailers. The band seemed nervous. Plant was with his wife, Maureen, and daughter, Carmen. His six-month-old baby boy Logan was at home with his grandparents. Jimmy Page flew in by helicopter to the site, located north of London, a half-hour before the show with his wife, Charlotte.

Knebworth was Britain's largest outdoor venue, sitting in a panorama of parks and stately homes. It had natural amphitheater-like surroundings. In the cold and dark of the evening, the degree of fanaticism from the monstrous crowd seemed unequaled. The atmosphere was thick with anticipation. It was not the same as Earl's Court, but the feeling of an impending event was unmistakable. Fans camped out in tents with "Knebworth '79" painted on the sides. People cooked meals over campfires, watched fire eaters and jugglers, and ran around campgrounds in the dark playing with glow-in-the-dark frisbees. This show was to become Zeppelin's English comeback. The '70s had been their decade, and the band was closing it out in style. Showco had brought across from the States the biggest system they had ever assembled—100,000 watts of sound and 600,000 watts of light. The band appeared dwarfed by huge video screens at the back of the stage which provided giant images of the group in action. There were lasers, dry ice, spotlights—the works.

The band played erratically but forcefully for over three hours. Fires burned eerily in the audience as Zeppelin dived into "The Song Remains the Same," "Celebration Day" and "Black Dog" and "In the Evening." If one watches the Knebworth segment on the Led Zeppelin 2003 DVD release, it's obvious that the band hadn't lost its sheer power. Just turn it up on a good system with box speakers. "Rock and Roll" was overpowering, and the crowd, ecstatic to see Zeppelin again, sang along about it being a lonely time. The sheer majesty of "Kashmir" jumped right out—a torrent of volume that surrounded everyone, then dragged them right in. "Achilles Last Stand" was intense as it gets—Page's riffs never sounded better—he hung his head in concentration, sweat dripping off his hanging hair. Bonham's drum rolls sounded like machine gun bursts, going perfectly with Page's notes. At the end, it's clear that Page really had a blast during "Whole Lotta Love," shuffling his feet and dancing around. There was an energy that went back and forth from the stage to the audience. The sheer size of the crowd meant that the cheering wasn't coordinated but sounded like the swelling of surf on a beach. At the end of "Whole Lotta Love," Plant looked teary-eyed and said, "Thanks for the eleven years!" Fans proclaimed the show a complete triumph. Despite the success of Knebworth, Zeppelin's glory days were now largely behind them. This was because it wasn't the same band that had stepped onstage ten years before. Plant likened Knebworth to a blind date—you didn't know if you would see her again. After Knebworth, there would follow another lengthy period of stage absence. Time, it seemed, was running out for them.

In November 1979 Zeppelin released their last studio LP, *In Through the Out Door*, in the midst of an industry recession that had already caused the commercial deaths of many other "dinosaurs." The album sold a phenomenal four million copies! Whereas John Paul Jones was underused on *Presence*, he was overused on *In Through The Out Door*. Although he was an excellent musician, Jones functioned best behind Page, not in front of him. The record sounded almost frail in comparison to the sonic roar of "Achilles Last Stand." Instead, Zep fans heard pop hits like "Fool In The Rain" and "All My Love." For Jerry, the best number on the album was "In The Evening" because it had the only great guitar riff on the entire album.

For many fans, including Jerry and me, the first two albums *were* what Zeppelin was about. Was it closing time? I was looking forward to the next album, as was Jimmy Page: "John Bonham and I had discussions and we were very serious that the next Led Zeppelin album would be riff-heavy and really smoky. *In Through the Out Door* was us starting to sound a little too polished."

Despite the contrast to the more blues-based sound of earlier albums, the new record continued the growth of Zeppelin and pushed the band into different musical styles. Punk and New Wave music had come to the forefront during Zeppelin's absence from the music scene. The song "Wearing and Tearing" was recorded for the album, but didn't really fit in with the blues feel. Jimmy Page called it the beginning of an "energetic punk type thing." He believed that the new album was the beginning of a transitional stage for Zeppelin. But instead, *In Through the Out Door* would be Zeppelin's actual swan song, the final chapter in the band's odyssey. Like the first album, it was different from anything that had gone before.

The album's cover became an extension of the music's experimental feel. The cover was again designed by Hipgnosis. There were six variations of the basic cover that showed a scene of a bar, each seen through the eyes of the different people in the photo. It looked like the last watering hole. There was a man in a white suit burning a piece of paper—was it a phone number of a love gone wrong? Was he drinking away his sorrows, learning to forget? Whereas *Presence* was plastered with black obelisks, *In Through the Out Door* was plastered with Schlitz bottles. Buyers didn't know which of the six covers they were purchasing, since the new LP was packaged in a brown paper bag with only the band's name and album title on it. Peter Grant said the album could be put in a brown paper bag and it would still top the charts—which it did, and he was right.

When I first bought the record, I anticipated some new, heavy Zeppelin moments to be unveiled. The cover reminded me of some 1940s gangster movie set. Then as I listened to the record back at my condo, I realized that the band had gone in a whole new direction. No time was wasted on setting the album's tone. "In The Evening" opened with a droning, Indian-like, backwards guitar effect bleeding back and forth across the channels. It was a classic Zeppelin orchestrated guitar rumble. Page explained: "That's me, with the bar really super-heavily depressed at the start of the solo. I just held the bar down and let it come up real fast." Page utilized ideas from his ill-fated *Lucifer Rising* soundtrack for the song's intro. For me, after the monumental opener, the rest of the songs went downhill.

"South Bound Suarez" had a honky tonk piano intro and conjured up a New Orleans barroom feel. The lyrics told of having a good old time and dancing your cares away—but Page's guitar didn't shine with intensity. Instead it sounded strained. No heavy riffs here. "Fool in the Rain" was Jones' track, the Brazilian feel being a lurking presence. The congas, whistles and steel drums threw a new spin on Zeppelin's sound. It may have been an effective radio single but it sounded way too commercial. "Hot Dog" seemed like Zeppelin was playing at a country square dance, a sound that came off as idiotic at best. "Carouselambra" conjured up a complex merry-go-round of sound. It was a mix of techno and electric guitars that marked a new step forward for Zeppelin. Fueled by keyboards, the heavily synthesized barrage of sound was a little too long, clocking in at ten minutes. This song sounded interesting to me—there was an intense wall of sound. "All My Love" was Plant's song, a celebration of life, death and rebirth. Page's precision acoustic work here sounded better than most of the other guitar work on the album. It also became a successful single—but it sacrificed the classic heavy blues sound in order to sound like a Beatles pop tune. Page's riffs sounded muddled. "I'm Gonna Crawl" shined from Plant's stormy singing and a haunting melody that dragged me completely in. It was a grand blues that I thought was a great way to end the album. But I thought the new record was really uneven. It was a keyboard marathon and John Paul Jones was awesome. But what happened to the rock and roll? Where were Page's riffs?

This album became Jones' album due to the fact that he was behind many of the musical arrangements. Unlike Zeppelin's other albums, *In Through the Out Door* suffered from less than crystal clear production. On a positive note, Bonham's drumming was more complex and rhythmically varied here than it had ever been. You could hear him loud and clear. But his drumming couldn't make up for the other shortcomings.

There could have been a lot more to the album, but some other songs were ditched. It was later revealed that three hot rockers—"Ozone Baby," "Darlene," and "Wearing and Tearing" were recorded during the Polar Studios sessions. But oddly, they weren't issued until the posthumous *Coda* release three years later. Had they been included, or substituted for the ten minute "Carouselambra," *In Through the Out Door* would have been much more of a Zeppelin album for me. But as it turned out, the album was characterized by a feeling of melancholy that never really lifted. The music was foreboding, as if it proclaimed that the end of Led Zeppelin was not far off.

Though the album wasn't hard-hitting enough for many fans, the reviewers mostly liked it. *Rolling Stone* had positive and negative remarks about the album, using Bonham's drumming as the focal point: "Hearing John Bonham play the drums is the aural equivalent of watching Clint Eastwood club eight bad guys over the head with a two-by-four while driving a derailed locomotive through their hideout. Either you are horrified by all that blood on the floor, or you wish you could do it yourself." *Creem* magazine was more generous and said the new album was "a departure from Zeppelin's standard orientation in favor of different musical styles" with the keyboards, but that Zeppelin's overall style was still there.

While I was living in Encinitas, I got more involved in selling my photography. I began to have pictures of blues and rock artists published in local newspapers, and I also branched out in selling to collectors. There were some swap meets I sold at in San Diego, and then by 1979 I'd gotten really involved in selling once a month outdoors in Hollywood. The place was a parking lot beside the Capitol Records building near Hollywood and Vine. It started out as a small affair but quickly grew into a large underground music event, completely by word of mouth. Sellers started arriving earlier and earlier to get a selling space, and what originally began as a daytime meet turned into an all-nighter.

Hundreds of music freaks from all over Southern California flooded the little lot, and the meet had to move across the street to a larger parking area. The crowd was a cross-section of an entire music subculture—hippie throwbacks, heavy metal fans, and punkers wearing spiked collars and leashes. And there were a lot of record collectors wearing miners' hats with lights on top so records could be examined closely in the dark. Mystery records with mystery origins showed up each month. If a strange vehicle that had new, unseen records pulled up, collectors swarmed over the find like killer bees at an unguarded picnic. There were loads of music items—bootleg records, vintage albums, tapes, buttons, posters, and photos. I had my 70s concert photos on ten particle board displays, everything I'd taken of artists from Aerosmith and Blondie to the Who and Zeppelin.

Anyone could show up and anything could happen. On a few occasions around midnight, I spotted Ray Manzarek walking down one of the selling aisles. I left my stand and was able to talk to him about his touring days with the Doors and what he was doing nowadays with music. Another time, David Lee Roth showed up and tried to pick up Betsy, a New York photographer who was working with me that night. She was selling her pictures of hotshot guitarist Michael Shencker of UFO and lots of other bands. Roth had his arm in a cast and he was drunk. Betsy liked rock stars, but mostly through a camera's lens. She turned Roth down.

It was at this meet that I first ran across Norwood Price, selling his Yardbirds, Jeff Beck, Who, and Zeppelin photos, taped up on cardboard displays. I was amazed at his pictures from so many 60s concerts. We traded photos and shared stories about the Zeppelin Rose Palace show that we'd both seen. I also met Jerry Prochnicky for the first time there, and we talked about the Doors concerts we'd been fortunate enough to attend. A friendship based on our love for music was started, and we decided to keep in touch.

Not everything was so friendly, though. People didn't always come to buy or make friends—they also came to steal. Over the months, I noticed that too many of my Zeppelin photos were disappearing. Sticky fingers indeed. Once after I'd set up to sell, I left some friends at my photo displays to check out what else was around. I ran across a teenager with something I recognized—one of my 8 × 10s of Jimmy Page holding up his double neck.

"Where'd you get the Page photo?" I asked. He pointed in the direction of my picture stand. "Did you get a good deal on it?" I went on. He shrugged. "Well, you stole it! I haven't sold any of those yet!" I yelled. I grabbed at the picture, and he backed away, clutching it next to some Zeppelin bootleg records he also had. That got me really mad, and I shoved him backwards and threw him off balance. Then I snatched everything out of his arms. "You probably ripped these off, too—so here they go." I flung the records across the street. They spun upwards in the air, like bootleg Zeppelin frisbees. One of them smacked into the edge of the Capitol building, where it spun out of control, downwards end over end, and crashed. The thief swore at me and ran off toward where his records landed. I never saw him again.

In January of 1980, Zeppelin was rewarded with a variety of titles from magazine polls. The Knebworth performance was chosen as the best gig of the year in the *Record Mirror*. The next month, Zeppelin received various awards from *Circus* magazine. In *Creem* magazine, the band was chosen by readers as the best in many categories. It was clear that Zeppelin was still winning over hearts and souls in America.

The year 1980 would begin full of hope for the band. This brought the promise of Led Zeppelin's U.S. return. But first the band planned to tour Europe in the summer and play smaller venues in Germany, Holland, Belgium and Austria. This time around, there would be no lasers or video screens, just a stripped-down PA system to try to recapture the spirit of the early 70s tours. Also, Page's dragon suits were retired to the closet. Under the slogan "Tour Over Europe 1980" with a skyward-looking air warden as the logo, the band was set to rock and roll.

Led Zeppelin—the dinosaurs of rock? Not on this tour. It would turn out to be a resounding, sell-out success. Zeppelin still ruled. The warm-up series of concerts produced reports that Page was all over the stage like a madman possessed: duck walking, gyrating, leaping about, and creating crashing open chords that rang as if howling from a long tunnel. And Plant was in fine form, with Jones and Bonham playing with a vengeance. These shows, despite some rocky evenings, were Led Zeppelin rediscovering themselves after an uncertain period. They began their set with the first song they had ever played together, "The Train Kept A-Rollin.'" The other songs were from every stage of their career, including three from the last album.

Nearly all the shows were ecstatically received and the musicians seemed genuinely pleased to be back in action. Bonham seemed fine during his last days on the road. He picked up little dolls that he had collected from every country on the tour for his daughter, Zoe. The image of Bonham the wild man was far from that. He was a family man at heart.

The last date of the tour was in Berlin on July 7, 1980. Jimmy Page even spoke to the crowd, saying, "Nice to see you. Nice to be seen, I can tell you that." But after that, Plant handled most of the introductions: "This tour is still the first one in a long while—sixteen towns in twenty-one days . . . This song is for Showco Sound. A song for Texas—'Hot Dog.'" Another introduction was "something for all the road crew." Then Zep played "Trampled Underfoot." The blues were pounded out with "Since I've Been Loving You," the place shook with "Kashmir," and the last songs included "Rock and Roll," "Stairway to Heaven" and "Whole Lotta Love." Then afterward, Plant said, "We've had a wonderful tour." What no one in the band knew was that it would be the last tour, and the show in Berlin would be the last one ever. Ironically, the Yardbirds played their last show exactly twelve years before, to the day.

After the tour Plant, Jones, and Bonham took separate vacation breaks with their families. Page moved into his newly purchased home in Windsor, north of London. In September, Peter Grant announced a U.S. tour to be named "Led Zeppelin: The Eighties, Part One." Could it really be? The band was coming—initially it was set to play nineteen dates in October and November covering the Northwest and Midwest in America and return to the U.S. for a west coast tour in 1981. By the fall, the band was once again in rehearsals. Jimmy Page was raring to go. But John Bonham felt tentative about going back to America. He appeared to be less than fit. The Oakland incident of '77 was still in the back of his mind and the prospects of leaving his family again for a long tour overseas made him worry. He was drinking to excess and taking Motival, a drug to reduce anxiety.

According to reports, Bonham started drinking at a pub near his home on September 24 and never let up. From there he went to a Windsor studio for a Zeppelin rehearsal, during which he drank more. Bonham proceeded to Page's house and continued to drink for several hours. A roadie put Bonham to bed just after midnight. He would never wake up again. The forty shots of vodka in twelve hours had taken their ultimate toll.

By the morning of the 26th, newspapers around the world were carrying the news of John Bonham's death. The cause of death was said to have been pulmonary edema—waterlogging of the lungs, caused by inhaling vomit. The coroner ruled the death accidental. When I first heard the news, it came over the radio while I was returning home to Encinitas from doing darkroom work. I was terribly saddened—his death reminded me of my dad, a highly creative watercolor artist who also died an accidental alcohol-related death. I'd always admired Bonham's power and precision—how he'd contributed so much to the Zeppelin sound. I thought, "What is going to happen now? How in the world will they ever replace him?"

Jerry also heard the news on the FM dial. One Zeppelin tune after another was played. In good times this exposure would have signaled an upcoming tour or the release of a new album. But this was a bad time. Bonham was dead! Jerry recalled: "I couldn't believe it; wouldn't believe it. I was kind of numb. It was the same kind of sadness when I heard the news of Jim Morrison dying in July of 1971. I also thought about what Page, Plant, Jones, and Bonzo's wife and children were going through. I could only imagine what they felt."

Robert Plant said of John Bonham's death that it "was one of the most flattening, heartbreaking parts of my life. I had a great warm big-hearted friend I haven't got anymore. It was so final."

By the morning of the 26th, newspapers around the world carried the news: "John Bonham, 32, the Drummer of Led Zeppelin, Is Found Dead." If newspapers were reporting it, then Jerry knew it must be true. Although he stopped listening to Zeppelin for a short while to ease the pain, he now hears the music with new appreciation for the world's greatest drummer. Twenty-five years gone, both Jerry and I still have a sense of deep sorrow.

On October 10, John Henry Bonham was laid to rest at St. Michael's Church at Rushock, England. He was survived by his wife and two children. Bonham's final resting place is in a very beautiful setting. It is one that makes a distinct, lasting impression.

Victoria Oliver took the two-hour drive from her home to visit Bonham's gravesite. She recalled the day: "The village is very remote with houses scattered amongst woodland and fields. The roads are just wide enough for one car and due to the remoteness, there are very few signs . . . The church stands in a small church-yard surrounded by a stone wall and an arched gate. I was surprised by the small number of graves there . . . John Bonham's grave is at the back of the church and can easily be spotted by its size. It is a double-width grave and the grass is cut regularly. On our visit there were twenty-four drumsticks, a pair of sunglasses, a toy van, an empty tequila bottle with a rolled up piece of paper inside (I assume it was a message), a guitar pin badge and a piece of wood on the gravestone. The views from the church are wonderful, just miles of woodlands and fields with the occasional house. It is a very open space and is very peaceful. We then went back and had a look inside the church, which is a lovely, quaint village church. We had a look in the visitor's book, which is full of messages to John: 'Rest in peace . . . You will always be in my heart . . . See you in the next world.'"

Everyone wants a life of peace and fulfillment. So what brings these things, anyway—is it extreme riches, sex, or worldwide fame? That's surely what Zeppelin got, but tragedy stepped in. What we value most, what we believe in determines how our lives end up. Plant sang about getting ready to meet Jesus in "In My Time of Dying." This spiritual is about how we enter the afterlife with Christ's help. Jesus said that "I am the way, the truth and the life." This means that if we believe in Christ, and live for him, then He points the direction to God, his claims are real, and His divine life is joined to ours, in this life and the afterlife. If what Christ said is true, then any security and peace—on this earth and in our time of dying—is only as secure as our trust in God.

John Bonham was no saint. He got sucked into the Twilight Zone world of rock and roll, where craziness was the norm. Different people in the entertainment world had their own impressions of him.

Dave Pegg, Fairport Convention's bass player, saw Bonham's drinking as a result of growing up in a drinking society. Pegg noted: "Lots of times when I met up with him in America we'd go out. He was very fond of his glass of ale . . . I think being away from home does it to people. Some of us tend to crack more easily than others."

Vanilla Fudge's drummer Carmen Appice also knew Bonham. He thought that Bonzo was "basically a good guy, until he got drunk. Once Bonzo got drunk, he lost control of what he was doing. He drank all the time. English people drink all the time. That's one of their social habits."

Phil Carson saw a much gentler version. "John was a really nice person: very warm-hearted person . . . a very quick wit. People don't realize he was a very funny man, in a British sense of humor. It doesn't always translate everywhere across the world, but the British do have a certain style of humor and John was right up there with the greatest in his speed of wit. It was a dry humor. He had a very fast mind, which expressed itself in his playing, too. At home, John was very much a family man."

Bonham took his inspiration for his playing from many different sources, including Carmine Appice. Bonham took many of his most famous fills from Appice's playing. Appice recognized the emulation and the similarity between Bonzo's playing on "Good Times Bad Times" and Vanilla Fudge's "That's What Makes a Man."

Bonzo saw himself as an artist, a musician—not just some barbarian who crawled out of the forest with a club and pounded wildly away on animal skins. His drumming was powerful but also very precise, and he worked hard to improve his musical skill. His perfectionism in his music was evident to all who watched him play. He set a standard for aspiring drummers.

Drummer Dave Mattacks knew that Bonham's sound was rare. "What made John unique was that not only did he play properly, but he had the power. And that's what made that drum sound so huge." Bonham loved playing his drums, being the animal in the background that controlled the tempo.

Eddie Kramer, the engineer for some Zeppelin albums, remembered recording sessions with the band and the pure enjoyment Bonham showed for his music. "I'll tell you what comes to mind

about John: determination, a tremendous amount of guts, willing-
ness to please, great personal satisfaction in having mastered a difficult fill or passage . . . In Stargroves I can remember watching his
face during playbacks. When we'd get a great take his face would
light up just like a child's face . . . we had so much fun making
those records."

Page said, "He was the ultimate rock and roll drummer. That's
all there is to it."

Jones said, "He was the best drummer I've ever played with,
bar none. But again, it wasn't done just to make himself look
good, it was done to make us all look good. The band benefited
incalculably."

Plant remarked, "No one could ever have taken over John's
job. Never, ever! Impossible. When he drummed he was right there
with either my voice or whatever Pagey was doing . . . The band
didn't exist the minute Bonzo had gone."

Page, Plant and Jones went away to think things over. Headlines read ZEP TO SPLIT? and WHAT NOW FOR LED ZEPPELIN? In the ensu-
ing weeks, there was much speculation dished out by the press
about the possibility of replacing Bonham. Recording industry
spokesmen and insiders all predicted that Led Zeppelin would
return with a new drummer. But the media and industry moguls
predicted wrongly. The tactics of the Who, the Rolling Stones and
countless other bands would not be followed by the remaining
members of Led Zeppelin.

The remaining members decided that they would not relaunch
Led Zeppelin. They told Peter Grant that there was no desire on
their part to carry on. Grant felt exactly the same way.

On December 4, 1980, Zeppelin released the following statement to the press: "We wish it to be known that the loss of our dear
friend and the deep respect we have for his family, together with
the sense of undivided harmony felt by ourselves and our manager,
have led us to decide that we could not continue as we were."

EPILOGUE

The fifth member of Led Zeppelin was manager Peter Grant. He totally believed in the band from day one. Besides being manager, he was also a friend, confidant, and enforcer. With Grant at the helm, Zeppelin stayed on course and soared high for twelve years. He talked the talk and walked the walk.

On hearing the news of Bonham's death, Grant was shattered. "Somebody told me that I mourned too long for John Bonham. There's no such thing as too long . . ."

Sadly, Peter Grant died of a heart attack in 1995. He was sixty years old. Peter Grant will always remain a part of the band's legend. On Led Zeppelin, he stated: "I'm very proud of Led Zeppelin—I'd say the greatest band of all time, and there'll never be another one like them."

Led Zeppelin was the ultimate rock band. No new Zeppelin has arisen. As for any hopes of seeing the band back on the road, the three have actually shown a commendable sense of respect to John Bonham. They wisely have chosen not to mount a full-scale reunion tour, despite the enormous cash incentives.

As sad as the news of Led Zeppelin's dissolution was in the late fall of 1980, fans should in many ways be grateful to Page, Plant, and Jones for having the sense to know when the show was truly over. Periodic releases of past recording sessions, and CD and DVD issues have perpetuated the legend of Led Zeppelin. The band is the sole province of its former members and their millions of fans.

LED ZEPPELIN DISCOGRAPHY

Led Zeppelin, 1969

Led Zeppelin II, 1969

Led Zeppelin III, 1970

Untitled, 1971

Houses of the Holy, 1973

Physical Graffiti, 1975

Presence, 1976

The Song Remains the Same (sound track and video), 1976

In Through the Out Door, 1979

Coda, 1982

Led Zeppelin, 1990 (4-CD box set)

Remasters, 1990 (2 CDs)

Box Set 2, 1993

The Complete Studio Recordings, 1993 (10-CD box set)

BBC Sessions, 1997

Best of Led Zeppelin, Volumes One & Two, 1999

How the West Was Won, 2003

Led Zeppelin DVD, 2003

BIBLIOGRAPHY

Books, Magazines, Newspapers

Atlantic Records, first press release, 1968.

Atlantic Records, press release for debut album, 1969.

Atlas, Jacoba, "Robert Plant," *Circus*, March 7, 1970.

Bangs, Lester, *"Led Zeppelin III,"* *Rolling Stone*, November 26, 1970.

Barton, Bruce (general editor), *Life Application Bible*, Tyndale House and Zondervan Publishing House, 1991.

Bernardy, Cathy, "Led Zeppelin's first gig as told by the club's teen photographer," *Goldmine*, November 15, 2002.

Blake, Mark, "Let There Be Rock," *Q Magazine*, March 2005.

Blanks, Tim, "A Whole Lotta Led Zeppelin," *Interview*, August 2003.

Bloom, Howard, "Led Zep After the Tour: Bigger Than the Beatles?" *Circus*, October 1973.

Bonham, Mick, *Bonham by Bonham*, Icarus Publications, 2003.

Bosso, Joe, "Glory Days," *Guitar World*, January 1991.

——, "Studio Masters," *Guitar World*, January 1991.

Bronson, Harold, "Yardbirds—We Never Really Made It, Did We?," *Rock*, March 15, 1971.

Burks, John, Jerry Hopkins, and Paul Nelson, "The Groupies and Other Girls," *Rolling Stone*, February 15, 1969.

Burroughs, William, "Rock Magic," *Crawdaddy*, June 1975.

Calta, Louis, "Led Zeppelin Ticket Sales Stir Crowds and Disorder," *New York Times*, June 8, 1975.

Carr, Roy, "We have fulfilled our destiny," *New Musical Express*, February 26, 1977.

Charlesworth, Chris, "Plantations," *Creem*, May 1976.

Chateau, Gilles, and Sam Rapallo, "Led Zeppelin: The Montreux Concerts," *Electric Magic/Led-Zeppelin.com*, ©2001.

Colbert, Ray, "Fear and Led Zep in New Zealand," *Rolling Stone*, April 27, 1972.

Collier, Barnard L., "Pop Festival Lures Youths and Underground Dealers," *New York Times*, July 7, 1969.

Considine, J. D. "Jason Bonham Grows Up," *Musician*, June 1990.

———, "Zeppelin," *Rolling Stone*, September 20, 1990.

Cross, Charles R., and Erik Flannigan, *Led Zeppelin—Heaven and Hell*, Harmony Books, 1991.

Crowe, Cameron, "Secrets of the Object Concealed," *Rolling Stone*, June 3, 1976.

———, "A Conversation with Jimmy Page and Robert Plant," *Rolling Stone*, March 13, 1975.

———, "Led Zep Conquers States, 'Beast' Prowls to the Din of Hordes," *Rolling Stone*, May 22, 1975.

———, "Zeppelin Rising . . . Slowly," *Rolling Stone*, August 12, 1976.

Des Barres, Pamela, "Good Times, Bad Times, The Story of Led Zeppelin," "Heartbreaker," *Masters of Rock*, Spring 1991.

———, *I'm With the Band*, Jove Publications, September 1988.

Di Perna, Alan, "Steady Rolling Man," *Guitar World*, January 1991.

———, "Train Keeps A-Rollin'," *Guitar World*, July 2000.

Egan, Sean, "Yardbirds—A-Rollin' Again," *Goldmine*, May 30, 2003.

Erickson, Bill, "Bill and Richard's Excellent Adventure: Meeting Zep at the Fillmore West," *Proximity*, Oct-Nov-Dec 1999.

Flanagan, Bill, "We Three Kings—The Top Managers Talk," *Musician*, April 1991.

Fortnam, Ian, "Your Time is Gonna Come," *Classic Rock*, June 2003.

Fricke, David, "Robert Plant," *Rolling Stone*, March 24, 1988.

Gaar, Gillian G., "That '70s Music," *Goldmine*, August 6, 2004.

Garner, Jack, "A Good Groove Going," *The Times-Union*, September 13, 1971.

Gett, Steve, "Led Zeppelin—Uber Alles!," *Melody Maker*, July 12, 1980.

———, "Robert Plant's History of Led Zeppelin," *Guitar*, November 1983.

Godwin, Robert, "Led Zeppelin—Alchemists of the '70s," *Goldmine*, August 24, 1990.

———, "Led Zeppelin—The Press Reports," Collectors Guide Publishing (Canada), 1997.

Goldberg, Danny, "Led Zeppelin—Under the Hood: A Backstage Chronicle of the Historic 1975 Tour," *Circus*, May 1975.

Goldstein, Patrick, "Led Zeppelin Says It Is Disbanding," *Los Angeles Times*, December, 1980.

Graustark, Barbara, "Houses of the Holy—A Schizoid Led Zep Roars Out of Hiding," *Circus*, May 1973.

Grossman, D., *"Led Zeppelin I,"* *Los Angeles Free Press*, March 7, 1969.

Gutmann, Peter, "Woodstock and Altamont," *Goldmine*, September 19, 2003.

Halfin, Ross, *The Photographers*, 2.13.61 Publications, 1995.

Heebner, David, *"Led Zeppelin I,"* *Jazz & Pop*, July 1969.

Heineman, *"Led Zeppelin II,"* *Down Beat*, April 2, 1970.

Hendrix, Jimi, Monologue to "Hear My Train A-Comin'" (electric), *Jimi Hendrix: Blues*, CD, MCA 11060, 1994.

Hilburn, Robert, "Led Zeppelin, Cliches and All," *Los Angeles Times*, March 13, 1975.

———, "Led Zeppelin at Inglewood Forum," *Los Angeles Times*, June 23, 1977.

———, "Zeppelin Vies for Rock Legacy," *Los Angeles Times*, June 25, 1977.

———, "The Pilot Who Keeps Led Zeppelin on Course," *Los Angeles Times*, April 17, 1977.

———, "What Now For Led Zeppelin?," *Los Angeles Times*, September 27, 1980.

———, "The Songwriters: Rock's Enigmatic Poet Opens a Long-Private Door," *Los Angeles Times*, April 4, 2004.

Hoskyns, Barney, "Been a long time," *Mojo*, June 2003.

Hotten, Jon, "The Story Behind the Album: *Led Zeppelin IV*," *Classic Rock*, December 2001.

Hulett, Ralph, "Individuality Exemplifies Zappa's Music," *The Daily Aztec*, October 6, 1977.

———, "Hooker Lives the Blues," *The Daily Aztec*, February 15, 1979.

———, "Visions from Festivals: England and America," *Relix*, August 1989.

Johnson, Pete, "Santa Monica Concert Features the Yardbirds," *Los Angeles Times*, July 25, 1967.

———, "Yardbirds Featured at Shrine Exposition," *Los Angeles Times*, June 4, 1968.

Jones, Hugh, "Fillmore East—A Reminiscence," *Proximity*, Oct-Nov-Dec 1999.

———, "Raffaelli—Recollections of a Photographer," *Proximity*, April-May-June 1999.

———, "The First Concert and Zeppelin in Denmark: The recollections of rock photographer Jorgen Angel," *Proximity*, Spring/Summer 2000.

———, and Masanori Ohnishi, "Zeppelin in Japan," *Proximity*, Oct-Nov-Dec 1998.

Kane, Joseph, "Alcohol Blamed in Bonham's Death," *Rolling Stone*, November 13, 1980.

Kellerman, Ron, "My Days with Page: Part I," *Electric Magic*, October 1990.

———, "My Days with Page: Part II," *Electric Magic*, November 1990.

———, "My Days with Page: Part III," *Electric Magic*, December 1990.

Kendall, Paul, *Led Zeppelin—A Visual Documentary*, Perigee Books (Putnam Publishing Group), Omnibus Press, 1982.

Kent, Nick, "Jimmy Page—The Roaring Silence," *New Musical Express*, November 20, 1976.

———, "Bring It On Home," *Q Special Edition* 2003.

Kerby, Bill, "Silent—Rock at SM Civic," *Los Angeles Free Press*, July 28, 1967.

Koch, Rudolf, *The Book of Signs*, Dover Publications, New York, 1955.

Lagano, Dan, "Does Anybody Remember Laughter? A Fan's Final Statement," *Proximity*, July-Aug-Sept 1997.

Lalaina, Joe (as told to), "Eddie Kramer—Jimmy Page's Right Hand Ear," *Guitar World*, July 1986.

"Led Zeppelin Tone Down," *Circus*, July 1970.

"Led Zeppelin—The Complete Story," *Creem Special Edition*, Winter 1980.

"Led Zeppelin," *Q Special Edition*, 2003.

Leimbacher, Ed, "Seattle Gives Peace a Chance," *Rolling Stone*, September 6, 1969.

Lewis, Dave, *Led Zeppelin—A Celebration*, Omnibus Press, 1991.

———, "The Triumph and the Tragedy," *Classic Rock*, June 2000.

———, and Simon Pallett, *Led Zeppelin: The Concert File*, Omnibus Press, 1997.

Ling, Dave, "Communication Breakdown," *Classic Rock*, September/October 1999.

Logan, Nick, "Zeppelin Put the Excitement Back into Pop," *New Musical Express*, January 17, 1970.

———, "Led Zeppelin's Plant Tells Why Group Goes to America," *New Musical Express*, October 11, 1969.

———, "Zeppelin and Fleetwood Take Off with a Roar," *New Musical Express*, July 5, 1969.

Mackie, Rob, "Jimmy Page," *Sounds*, April 21, 1973.

Matre, Lynn Van, "Led Zeppelin Is Up, Up, and Soaring," *Chicago Tribune*, April 3, 1977.

McDermott, John, "The Reel Story," *Guitar World*, December 1993.

Mendelsohn, John, "*Led Zeppelin I*," *Rolling Stone*, March 15, 1969.

———, "*Led Zeppelin II*," *Rolling Stone*, December 13, 1969.

Miller, Jim, "*Physical Graffiti*: Hardest-Core Rock," *Rolling Stone*, March 27, 1975.

Neer, Dan, "Past Perfect," *Guitar*, June, 1991.

Pabic, Christophe La, and Benoit Pascal, *Led Zeppelin: Hexagonal Experiences*, © 1997.

Pallett, Simon, "Radio Dazed," *Guitar World*, January 1998.

Plagens, Peter, "You're Lookin' Swell, Dali . . . Considering," *Newsweek*, February 21, 2005.

"Plant's Son Dies: Zeppelin Tour Off," *San Francisco Chronicle*, July 28, 1977 (From Reuters, 1977).

Pond, Steve, "The 70s," *Rolling Stone*, September 20, 1990.

———, "The Song Remains the Same," *Rolling Stone*, March 24, 1988.

Resnicoff, Matt, "In Through the Out Door: Jimmy Page Goes Back to Led Zeppelin," *Musician*, November 1990.

Rinde, Allan, "Everything You Always Wanted to Know About Jimmy Page (But Were Afraid to Ask)," *Rock*, October 11, 1970.

Robinson, Lisa, "Led Zeppelin On Tour: Once Again Conquering America," *Hit Parader*, July 1975.

———, "Led Zeppelin Dances On Air And It Ain't The Quaalude Shuffle," *Creem*, May 1975.

———, "Stairway to Excess," *Vanity Fair*, November 2003.

———, "Unspeakable Practices, Unnatural Acts," *Creem*, September 1973.

Rockwell, John, "John Bonham, 32, the Drummer of Led Zeppelin, Is Found Dead," *New York Times*, September 26, 1980.

Rosen, Steve, "Led Zeppelin's John Paul Jones," *Record Review*, October 1978.

———, "John Paul Jones," *Keyboard*, December 1977.

———, "John Paul Jones," *Guitar Player*, July 1977.

———, "Jimmy Page," *Guitar Player*, July 1977.

———, "Danny Goldberg's Hideaway," *Guitar World*, July 1986.

———, "Jimmy Page—The Interview," *Guitar World*, July 1986.

———, "Rodney B.'s Endless Party," *Guitar World*, July 1986.

Salewicz, Chris, "Led Zeppelin," *Let It Rock*, May 1975.

Schneider, Jason, "It's Been a Long Time," *The Record*, November 1, 2003.

Schulps, Dave, "Jimmy Page Interview, Part One: Pre-Yardbirds," *Trouser Press*, September 1977.

———, "Paging the Yardbirds," *Trouser Press*, October 1977.

———, "The Final Page," *Trouser Press*, November 1977.

"The Seventies," *Playboy*, January 1989.

Sharp, Ken, "Robert Plant 'The Wild Man of Blues from the Black Country' Comes Home," *Goldmine*, August 6, 1993.

Sherman, Tony, "The Hellhound's Trail—Following Robert Johnson," *Musician*, January 1991.

Snow, Mat, "Apocalypse Then," *Q Magazine*, December 1990.

Sutcliffe, Phil, "Bustle in the Hedgerow," *Mojo*, August 2000.

Swenson, John, "In Search of Jimmy Page," *Guitar World*, July 1986.

Tolinski, Brad, "Heavy Friends," *Guitar World*, October 1999.

———, "High Wire Act," *Guitar World*, July 2003.

———, with Greg Di Benedetto, "Light and Shade," *Guitar World*, January 1998.

———, "Jimmy Page: Inside *Led Zeppelin IV*," *Guitar World*, January 2002.

Tyler, Kieron, "Educating Jimmy," *Mojo*, May 2001.

Wall, Mick, "Been a Long Time," *Classic Rock*, December 2001.

Wasserman, John L., "Led Zeppelin: The Aftermath," *San Francisco Chronicle*, July 27, 1977.

———, "Sharing the Vibes Not Easy," *San Francisco Chronicle*, July 25, 1977.

———, "Zeppelin Violence—A Cause Celebre," *San Francisco Chronicle*, July 29, 1977.

———, "Before and After with Led Zeppelin," *San Francisco Chronicle*, September 15, 1971.

Wittet, T. Bruce, "John Bonham," *Modern Drummer*, July 1984.

Yorke, Ritchie, *Led Zep*, Methuen Inc. (Toronto-New York) 1976.

Young, Charles M., "Jimmy Page's True Will," *Musician*, July 1977.

———, "I'm Not Such an Old Hippie," *Musician*, June 1990.

———, "Sad Zep," *Rolling Stone*, October 18, 1979.

———, "Zeppelin to Zen," *Musician*, March 1988.

"Zep to Split?," *New Musical Express*, October 4, 1980.

"Zeppelin: 'Everybody's Really Pleased,'" *Circus*, December 1970.

Interviews

Muddy Waters interview by Ralph Hulett, Boston, MA, 1976.

Neil Zlozower interview by Ralph Hulett, Hollywood, CA, 2004.

INDEX

ABOUT THE AUTHORS

RALPH HULETT grew up in the Los Angeles area. His parents were both in the arts—his father a Disney artist and renowned California watercolor painter and his mother a music and dance teacher. As Ralph saw bands like the Doors and Led Zeppelin pass through the L.A. area, rock music became a big part of his life. His photographs and articles have appeared in *Relix, Goldmine* and *Vintage Guitar* magazines, and on the television programs *VH 1—Behind the Music* and *ABC News Downtown*. He now teaches in the Orange County area. His website which combines his passions for rock and photography is www.rockretrospect.com.

JERRY PROCHNICKY was born in Germany and came to America at age 3. He is the co-author of *Break on Through: The Life and Death of Jim Morrison* (William Morrow Co., 1991), which the New York Times called "the most objective, thorough, and professional Morrison biography yet." Led Zeppelin and the Doors moved and touched him the most, and thus began his continuous and vivid emotional connection to both groups. Prochnicky has been researching the Led Zeppelin story for over thirty years.

Both authors live in southern California.